Expert Database Systems

The A.P.I.C. SERIES
General Editors: M. J. R. SHAVE and I. C. WAND

1. Some Commercial Autocodes. A Comparative Study*
   E. L. Willey, A. d'Agapeyeff, Marion Tribe, B. J. Gibbens and Michelle Clarke
2. A Primer of ALGOL 60 Programming*
   E. L. Dijkstra
3. Input Language for Automatic Programming*
   A. P. Yershov, G. I. Kozhukhin and U. Voloshin
4. Introduction to System Programming*
   Edited by Peter Wegner
5. ALGOL 60 Implementation. The Translation and Use of ALGOL 60 Programs on a Computer
   B. Randall and L. J. Russell
6. Dictionary for Computer Languages*
   Hans Breuer
7. The Alpha Automatic Programming System*
   Edited by A. P. Yershov
8. Structured Programming†
   O.-J. Dahl, E. W. Dijkstra and C. A. R. Hoare
9. Operating Systems Techniques
   Edited by C. A. R. Hoare and R. H. Perrott
10. ALGOL 60 Compilation and Assessment
    B. A. Wichmann
11. Definition of Programming Languages by Interpreting Automata*
    Alexander Ollongren
12. Principles of Program Design†
    M. A. Jackson
13. Studies in Operating Systems
    R. M. McKeag and R. Wilson
14. Software Engineering
    R. J. Perrott
15. Computer Architecture: A Structured Approach
    R. W. Doran
16. Logic Programming
    Edited by K. L. Clark and S.-A. Tärnlund
17. Fortran Optimization*
    Michael Metcalf
18. Multi-microprocessor Systems
    Y. Paker
19. Introduction to the Graphical Kernel System (GKS)*
    F. R. A. Hopgood, D. A. Duce, J. R. Gallop and D. C. Sutcliffe
20. Distributed Computing
    Edited by Fred B. Chambers, David A. Duce and Gillian P. Jones
21. Introduction to Logic Programming
    Christopher John Hogger
22. Lucid, the Dataflow Programming Language
    William W. Wadge and Edward A. Ashcroft
23. Foundations of Programming
    Jacques Arsac
24. Prolog for Programmers
    Feliks Kluźniak and Stanislaw Szpakowicz
25. Fortran Optimization, Revised Edition
    Michael Metcalf
26. PULSE: An Ada-based Distributed Operating System
    D. Keeffe, G. M. Tomlinson, I. C. Wand and A. J. Wellings
27. Program Evolution: Process of Software Change
    M. Lehman and L. A. Belady
28. Introduction to the Graphical Kernel system (GKS): Second Edition. Revised for the International Standard
    F. R. A. Hopgood, D. A. Duce, J. R. Gallop and D. C. Sutcliffe
29. The Complexity of Boolean Networks
    P. E. Dunne
30. Advanced Programming Methodologies
    Edited by Gianna Cioni and Andrzej Salwicki
31. Logic and Computer Science
    Edited by P. Odifreddi
32. Knowledge Representation: An Approach to Artificial Intelligence
    T. J. M. Bench-Capon
33. Integrated Project Support Environments: The Aspect Project
    Edited by Alan W. Brown
34. Object-oriented Languages
    G. Masini, A. Napoli, D. Colnet, D. Leonard and K. Tombre
35. An Introduction to Programming with Specifications: A Mathematical Approach
    R. Kubiak, R. Rudziński and S. Sokołowski
36. Knowledge-based Systems and Legal Applications
    Edited by T. J. M. Bench-Capon
37. Fundamentals of Spatial Information Systems
    R. Laurini and D. Thompson
38. Inductive Logic Programming
    S. Muggleton

* Out of Print
† Now published in the Computer Science Classic Series

The A.P.I.C. Series
Number 39

Expert Database Systems

edited by

Keith Jeffery
Rutherford Appleton Laboratory

ACADEMIC PRESS
Harcourt Brace Jovanovich, Publishers
London San Diego New York
Boston Sydney Tokyo Toronto

ACADEMIC PRESS LIMITED
24–28 Oval Road
London NW1 7DX

United States Edition published by
ACADEMIC PRESS INC.
San Diego, CA 92101

Ths book is printed on acid-free paper

A catalogue record for this book is available from the British Library
ISBN 0-12-382255-6

Typeset by Mathematical Composition Setters Ltd, Salisbury, UK
and printed in Great Britain by Hartnolls Ltd, Bodmin, Cornwall.

Contents

Contributors

N. Adablah, Department of Computer Science, University of Exeter, Exeter EX4 4PT

Mir Derakhshan, SQL Software Ltd, Latton Bush Centre, Harlow, Essex CM18 7BL

L. Foster, Department of Computer Science, University of Exeter, Exeter EX4 4PT

P. M. D. Gray, Computing Science Department, University of Aberdeen, Aberdeen AB9 1FX

Keith G. Jeffery, Systems Engineering Division, Rutherford Appleton Laboratory, Oxfordshire OX11 0QX

Y. Jin, Deoartment of Computer Science, University of Exeter, Exeter EX4 4PT

B. Lings, Department of Computer Science, University of Exeter, Exeter EX4 4PT

V. A. J. Maller, Department of Computer Studies, Loughborough University of Technology, Loughborough, Leics., LE11 3TU

Alexandra Poulovassilis, Department of Computing, King's College, Strand, London WC2R 2LS

Gunter Schlageter, Department of Computer Science, University of Hagen, P.O. Box 940, D-5800 Hagen 1, Germany

Carol Small, Department of Computer Science, Birkbeck College, Malet Street, London WC1E 7HX

Rainer Unland, University of Münster, Institut für Wirtschaftsinformatik, Grevener Str. 91, 4400 Münster, Germany

Preface

The production of this book has been a lengthy venture – even an adventure! However, collecting together the work of busy people is time-consuming.

The initial idea came from Professor Mike Shave of Liverpool University; the structural framework was defined in cooperation with Andrew Carrick of Academic Press. The objective was to provide a book that is readable; additionally, the aim was to provide the reader with the necessary information on all aspects of the new database technology – extended relational, functional, deductive and object-oriented viewpoints, together with a chapter on database machines. The introductory chapter was, in many ways, the point of departure for the book's concept, and conditioned the book's structure and contents.

The provision of a foreword from Larry Kerschberg of George Mason University is a real bonus; as one of the world leaders in the field his interest and contribution is much appreciated.

The target audience comprises final year undergraduates in Computer Science, postgraduates in Computer Science and in disciplines involving the use of database technology (in the academic field), and database practitioners in the Information Technology departments of commercial organisations.

It is my sincere wish that readers of the book gain as much from it as I did in putting together the work of the talented authors invited to contribute, and without whom the book would not exist.

Keith G. Jeffery
Head, Systems Engineering Division
Rutherford Appleton Laboratory
Oxfordshire, OX11 0QX UK
1991.

Foreword

I am pleased to be able to contribute a foreword to this collection of articles on Expert Database Systems edited by Dr Keith Jeffery. I have been associated with this field of research and practice since 1984, when I organized the First International Workshop on Expert Database Systems held at Kiawah Island, South Carolina. That event, and two subsequent international conferences held in 1986 and 1988, brought together researchers and practitioners from the diverse disciplines of Artificial Intelligence (AI), Database Management (DB), Logic Programming (LP), Information Retrieval (IR), and Programming Languages (PL) to define the major intellectual currents that form the basis for Expert Database Systems.

So what is an Expert Database System? An Expert Database System (EDS) supports applications that require knowledge-directed processing of shared information. This definition allows us to envision a wide spectrum of architectures for such systems. They may be *loosely coupled* as, for example, an expert system which retrieves data from a database. They may be *tightly coupled* in that either the expert system or the database system or both 'understand' how the other functions and can take advantage of this knowledge to improve the performance of the EDS. In its most advanced form a tightly coupled system may embody, in an integrated fashion, characteristics found in both AI and DB systems. By loose coupling we mean that both the AI system and the Database Management System (DBMS) will maintain their own functionality and will communicate through a well-defined interface. The database may be viewed as a *data server* for the AI system. For example, an AI system might send SQL queries to the database system to obtain needed data. Conversely, the database system might send messages to the AI system, placing data onto its blackboard or working memory. In addition the DBMS could pose questions to the AI system in much the same way a user might consult an expert system.

Tightly coupled systems use knowledge associated with both the AI and DB systems to provide enhanced functionality. This may be as simple as using meta-data associated with database file organizations, secondary indices, and query patterns to optimize data retrieval for the AI inference engine. Another approach is to enhance a deductive database with set-oriented primitives and mappings to an extended relational algebra for database processing. Lastly, it may be as sophisticated as endowing a database system with rule-processing capabilities to provide 'active' database functionality.

The first case allows data to be retrieved more efficiently by taking advantage of 'knowledge' contained in the database meta-data. The second approach allows users to pose queries in terms of logic statements and the system compiles these queries into efficient relational algebra expressions. The third approach allows the database application programmer to extract rules and constraints that might normally be found in diverse application programs and to embed them directly in the database schema. Thus, when updates change the database state so that certain rule conditions are satisfied, those rules become 'active' and can be executed to alert users, application programs or AI systems to these new events and states; these rules can also be used to effect changes to the database state.

There are several research prototypes and commercially available systems that support these concepts. For example, the KEE connection from Intellicorp allows the frame-based AI shell KEE to be connected to SQL-databases. The Logic Data Language (LDL) from MCC and SYLLOG from IBM provide logic-based interfaces to relational databases. The POSTGRES prototype and enhanced INGRES support user-defined types and rules embedded in relations.

As the concepts proposed for Expert Database Systems make their way into research prototypes and commercial systems, one may ask whether our work is done? Of course not! We have only scratched the surface in exploiting knowledge/data interrelationships in our system architectures. In addition, there are new applications that impose newer and more exacting requirements on our systems in terms of enhanced modelling capabilities, new modes of reasoning, complex data/knowledge organizations, and new storage structures for vast amounts of data and knowledge.

One such application area I am presently researching is that of Evolutionary Software Engineering Environments. Here we wish to support the complex intellectual processes involved in the engineering of large software systems. In particular, we need to support the entire software life cycle including domain modelling, specification and design. A domain model represents a family of software systems for an application domain, and that family is tailored to generate a specific target instance based on the particular requirements and constraints for that particular instance.

We use an object-oriented modelling paradigm that supports the following: 1) object types and message communication among them, 2) object aggregation hierarchies, 3) object generalization hierarchies, and 4) operations executed by objects in response to message requests. In addition, the formalism supports multiple viewpoints of domain specification such as object communication diagrams, aggregation hierarchies, generalization/specialization hierarchies, and state-transition diagrams.

The environment should support not only the specification and storage of the domain model, but also consistency checking among the multiple viewpoints and knowledge-based tools to tailor the specification of a target system. In addition, such an environment should support the mappings from requirements objects, to specification objects, to design objects, to code objects, and the *evolution* of these object specifications as the domain model is refined.

Recent research suggests a merging of ideas from expert databases, object-oriented databases and object-oriented programming languages. In EDS we have been exploring the interactions between knowledge and data, while object-oriented DB and PL are advancing our knowledge of the specification, compilation and storage of complex, persistent object specifications. It is the confluence of these ideas that will support advanced applications such as software engineering environments and computer-aided design and manufacturing. The concept of an *object repository* is vital to these applications. The repository will store and manage various types of objects, including complex data organizations, rules, constraints, and metadata and meta-knowledge associated with the application domain.

Thus, my personal vision for Expert Database Systems is that they should evolve to incorporate the following capabilities:

1) to support the modelling, representation and storage of complex objects, and to provide object repository services to applications programs and tools,
2) to use domain knowledge and semantic integrity constraints for query optimization, integrity management, and consistency checking,
3) to provide 'active' database support to alert users or application programs when certain critical database states have been reached,
4) to interface with existing expert systems or advanced AI environments,
5) to combine knowledge- and data-driven search techniques in efficient inference schemes for problem solving, and
6) to interact with users to explain the structure of the database and knowledge base, as well as to formulate and re-formulate queries.

In summary, the goal of EDS research and development is to make databases active and knowledgeable agents that can support enhanced modelling and reasoning techniques, and to allow database systems to support applications that access, process and manage large knowledge bases and databases.

I feel that the collection of papers in this book helps to further these goals. They touch upon very important topics such as extensible database systems, the role of functional and logic programming in EDS, the definition of a repository manager to support deductive databases, object-oriented databases and EDS, the relationship between persistent objects in programming languages and object-oriented databases, and hardware support for EDS.

One exciting aspect of this book is that the authors are all European, and this attests to the active research agenda being carried out in the European Community. Several major conferences have been held in Europe recently, and Expert Databases have been a major theme. I hope this will be the first of many such volumes on this exciting and important field of endeavour.

Larry Kerschberg
George Mason University
Fairfax, Virginia, USA
January, 1991

1
The Expert Database Jungle

KEITH G. JEFFERY

Head, Systems Engineering Division, Informatics Department, Rutherford Appleton Laboratory, Chilton, Didcot, Oxon OX11 0QX

INTRODUCTION

The title contains the words 'expert', 'database' and 'jungle'. A word of explanation is necessary before proceeding. The word 'database' is used here in the sense of the area of study named 'database'; not as in the use of that word to mean the store or repository of data. It is used here as a shortened form of 'the area of study concerned with database technology in the widest sense'. 'Expert' is used in the conventional sense – but with a meaning of advanced; this paper – and the rest of the book – explores the frontiers of advancement in each of several directions. 'Jungle' is used to convey the present confused state of 'expert database'; there are great advances being made in each of the different directions but to someone approaching this area of study there appears to be an unmapped, tangled area of exotic and uncontrolled growth.

The purpose of this paper is to provide an overview or framework so that the 'jungle' is mapped and its individual 'thickets' (areas of closely set related information) identified and characterised. As such this paper provides the high-level, introductory guide and the following papers explore different areas (or 'thickets') of expert database in detail.

This paper goes on to discuss the central area of the 'jungle', where the concepts join to promote the concept of 'expert database'. The proposal is that 'expert database' has the virtues of efficiency, flexibility and expressive power – and this paper discusses the contributions to these virtues from various components of the 'jungle' – and proposes a way forward.

THE JUNGLE

Expert database is an area of technology which is multidimensional. Each dimension has interesting aspects, some related to database technology,

Expert Database Systems
ISBN 0-12-382255-6

some to programming, some to logic, some to mathematics. The bringing together of these different disciplines is the catalyst causing the extremely rapid advances in database technology seen in the last few years. The seeds for this explosive evolution were sown in the sixties and seventies; some of the more important events are:

(a) Simula
(b) Persistent programming
(c) CODASYL DBTG
(d) Relational database theory
(e) Smalltalk
(f) Functional programming
(g) Functional database
(h) Logic programming
(i) PROLOG

and the eighties have seen the fusion of concepts from these disciplines into 'expert database'.

The 'jungle' is caused by the continuing rapid growth in each of these disciplines independently, but with some researchers building cross-links between some of the disciplines at different times and using different techniques. These cross-links cause the individual disciplines ('thickets') to be tangled together as they develop, so producing an almost impenetrable mass. If the most dense 'thickets' are separated from each other, it is possible to build a multidimensional view of a set of nodes and links (arcs) between them. If this multidimensional model is then projected onto 2-space (i.e. a page) then a map of the 'jungle' is produced, showing the individual 'thickets' and some of the major links between them.

The map of the 'jungle' (Figure 1) has some interesting features. First, the left-hand side is concerned with repositories or stores of data.The right-hand side is concerned with the expression of operations to be performed on the data. The central zone is populated with concepts or areas of research that integrate the items in the left- and right-hand sides.

Each horizontal zone in the map of the 'jungle' is a field of research in its own right. If there is a corresponding item in both the left- and right-hand zones, then the area of research is concerned with integrating the work on repositories with that on operations. If there is no item in either left- or right-hand zone, then the concept in the central zone draws from the nearest items in the left- and right-hand zones.

Each horizontal zone with corresponding items in the left-hand and right-hand zones is a 'thicket' and will be explored further in this paper. The exploration will include characterisation in such a way that the concepts of importance to the areas of research in the central zone are highlighted.

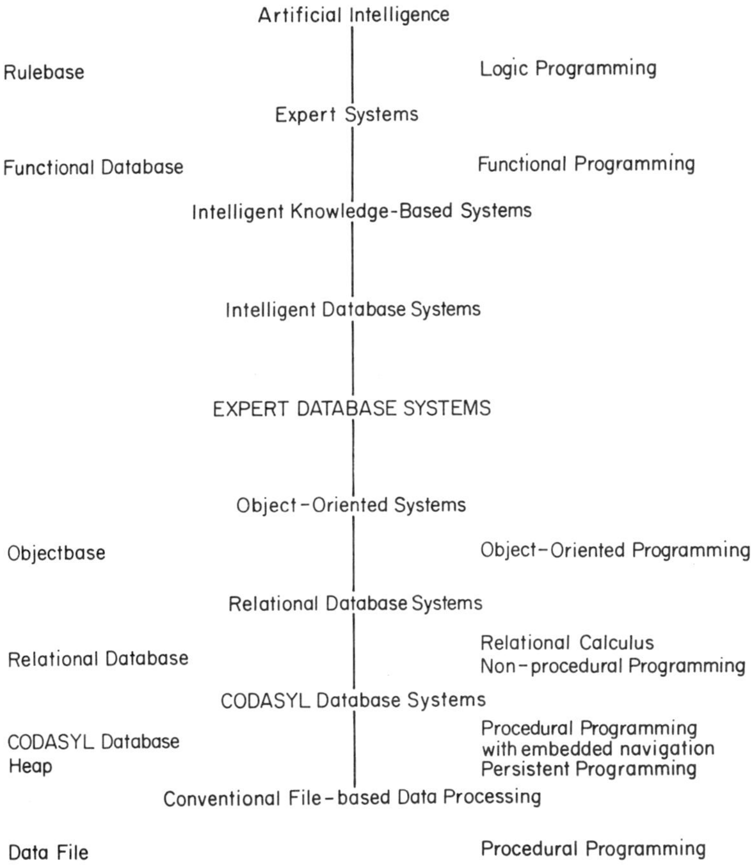

Figure 1 The Jungle

THE THICKETS

Procedural Programming/Data File

This particular thicket is generally well known and understood. It is the area of data processing that has been used conventionally since the fifties, and is taught in schools as well as colleges. However, it has certain characteristics that are worth highlighting because they contribute to the overall evolution of thought towards expert database systems.

There is no underlying theory; the construction of a procedural program to act on a data file (or files) has no basis in theory. There have been many advances in the formal specification of a program, which provides some theoretical foundation for procedural programming, but such formal methods have not yet been used greatly in commercial data processing.

Systems based on procedural programming and data files are usually efficient; they are designed to perform a specific task and are optimised for that task. There are, of course, techniques of using specific file organisations to obtain better performance characteristics. For example, the use of an indexed-sequential organisation will provide good performance for both serial scans of the data and direct access to individual records; a sequentially organised file is likely to outperform the indexed sequential file for serial scans, but will exhibit poor performance for direct access to one record. A randomly organised file (e.g. by the use of a hashing algorithm) will give poor performance for a serial scan, but excellent performance for direct access.

File Organisation \ Type of Access	Serial	Direct
Sequential	Excellent	Bad
Indexed-Sequential	Good	Good
Random (hashed)	Bad	Excellent

Figure 2 File Organisation and Access

Systems in this 'thicket' are non-general; that is they are specific to the application for which they were designed. The objects manipulated by the program are stored; in this way there is a close (and application-specific) relationship between the program and the data file. This relationship is seen in both data content (type and length of variables, for example, mirrored in the file field specifications) and in data structure. In the case of structure it is most clearly seen when within the program one loop exists within another. This indicates a hierarchic data structure, as seen in Figure 3.

```
PROGRAM                                           FILE
Do Until....
     Read Record Type 1                           Record Type 1
          Do Until.....
               Read Record Type 2                 Record Type 2
                                                  Record Type 2
                                                  Record Type 2
          End
End
```

Figure 3 Program and File Structure

Work done in the sixties on this area of data processing led directly to:

(a) concepts of procedural database with the data definition stored with the data as well as in the program 'data definition' section and the idea of the procedural program navigating around the database;
(b) concepts of persistent programming with the idea of 'writing away' the data structures defined, manipulated and changed in the program to a persistent store or heap.

Persistent Programming/Heap

Like the previous 'thicket' this one is characterised by the lack of underlying theory. Systems based on this concept are usually efficient, because the program structure and data structure are matched. The technique depends on extensions to a procedural language providing the operators to 'write away' complete data structures to the persistent store or heap. This means that objects defined in the program, objects created in the execution of the program and objects changed in the execution of the program become persistent (if required). The relationships between data items, or data substructures, are maintained by means of pointers – and so the heap contains not only data but also navigational information – rather like CODASYL database systems.

There is an intrinsic close relationship between program and data repository because the repository just accepts, stores and protects data objects (with their content and structure) when the object is 'written away'.

These systems tend not to be characterised by a high degree of data sharing, and so the concurrency problems of CODASYL or relational database systems do not occur. However, since the objects can be large and complex (large arrays, complete tree-structures) then if there is any likelihood of the need for concurrent access, the granularity (area of data in the repository locked at any one time to prevent concurrent access) is likely to be very large.

Work on these systems has led to many of the characteristics of object-oriented systems, including the matching of program object and repository object, and ideas of inheritance and versions (Atkinson *et al.*, 1983).

Procedural Programming/CODASYL

This 'thicket' is characterised by the work on hierarchic and network database systems (where the adjective describes the type of data structure managed), the culmination of this work being the CODASYL DBTG-standard (CODASYL, 1971).

The work drew on earlier procedural programming/file experience. The major contributions of this work were:

(a) to hold a description of the data – the DDL (Data Definition Language) – separately from both the database (the repository) and from the program(s). This allowed the database content and structure to change (evolve) independently of the programs, and for the programs to be changed (or new programs added) independently of the database content and structure as defined in the DDL (Figure 4). In practice this ideal of full independence was not achieved; any but minor changes required an unload/reload of the database and a recompilation of the programs.
(b) to provide a layered architecture for a database system;
(c) to define a standard set of procedures (with defined procedural calls from a third-generation programming language) for accessing and manipulating the database – the DML (Data Manipulation Language);
(d) to encourage work on data models – the consideration of data independently of the expected processing procedures.

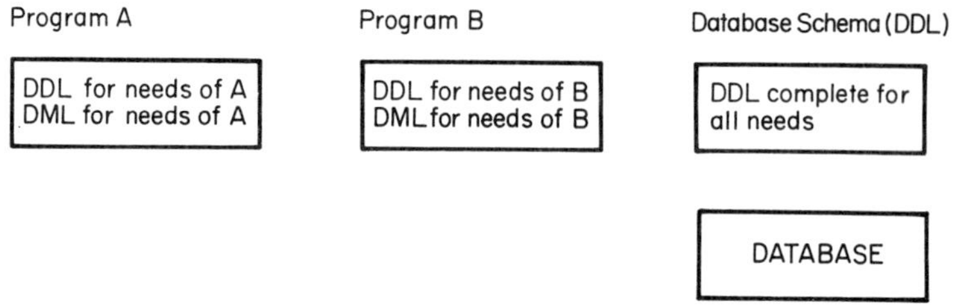

Figure 4 Basic CODASYL Architecture

This work was responsible for a great burst of activity in database technology in the seventies. In particular, the work on the relational model, work on functional databases and the move towards fourth-generation languages were all instigated largely as efforts to overcome the limitations of the CODASYL model. However, without the CODASYL model the limitations – and thus the opportunities for further work – would not have been so well-defined. It is worth noting, in passing, that most existing commercial database systems are still of this type; it is only now that the advantages of later technological advances are starting to outweigh the inertia inbuilt into the use of any system for production applications.

Relational Calculus/Relational Database

This particular thicket has been described exhaustively elsewhere, in particular see the excellent summary in Date (1986). However, there are some highlights which are particularly relevant in the interrelationships between this area of work and others.

The relational database theory incorporates:

(a) a model of data;
(b) an algebra for manipulating that data;
(c) a calculus for expressing requirements of (a) and (b).

The model of data is theoretically based in mathematical formalism; it is an extension to set theory (Codd, 1970). This contrasts strongly with all other data repository models, which are more-or-less pragmatic in design. The more pragmatic are seen in CODASYL and file-based systems; the less pragmatic have some basis either in information theory (persistent and object-oriented repositories) or logic (rulebases).

The algebra consists of a set of well-defined and general operators; that is their purpose is well-defined and they can act on a wide range of data types (certainly all those used in third-generation programming languages) and they act on the data structure as mapped into relations. The relational data model allows the mapping of any data structure into relations so that it can be operated upon by the algebra; there are some problems over alternative mappings of the structure to relations, over the preservation of the original structural semantics after the mapping to relations (referential integrity) and the efficiency of processing complex structures using relational algebra.

The calculus allows the expression of the requirement of the system (the predicate) in terms that are non-procedural. Put simply, it allows the user or programmer to tell the system 'what to get' not 'how to get it'. The calculus finds expression in SQL (Structured Query Language). This is a language that allows not only query, but also update (in the senses of insertion, deletion and amendment).

The importance of the data model is that it provides data independence to a degree hitherto unavailable. Not only is there data-content independence (the data types are independent of the algebra) but also data-structure independence in the sense that new components (columns) can be added to relations (tables), and relations (tables) can be joined on a common key domain. Thus new structural relationships can be created – just as required by the demands of applications in the real world.

Like the CODASYL model, the data definition is stored externally to both the data repository and the programs; however, the data definition is stored in the same form (relations) as the data repository so that the data definition itself can be manipulated by the same algebra as the data repository. This congruent handling of metadata (or data about data) is extremely powerful, and relates to one point of view held on the work in the logic programming domain. In this viewpoint the 'facts' correspond to the data repository (extensional database) and the 'rules' correspond to some characteristics of the data definition (intensional database) and also to some characteristics of the processing.

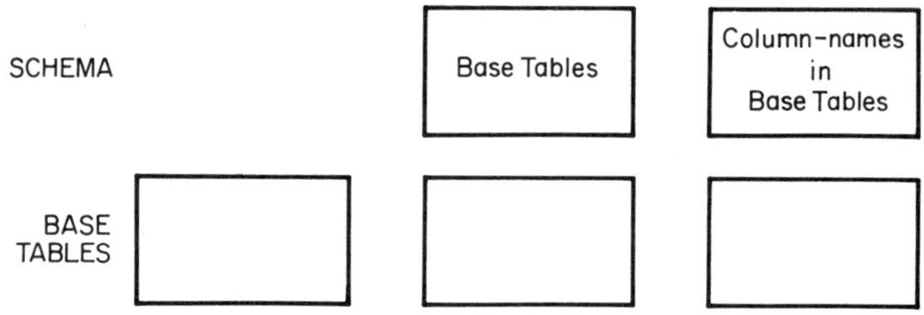

Figure 5 Relational Metadata

There is a further similarity between the relational domain and that of logic programming: the relational domain is characterised by query evaluation and the logic programming domain by unification. The former consists of satisfying the predicate (query) by instances in the database. The latter consists of unifying rules and facts to provide appropriate data instances.

It is in this area that another similarity occurs: efficiency. Relational systems originally were considered inefficient compared with CODASYL systems – and with good reason. A procedural program with navigation for a specific database designed by a skilled analyst and programmed efficiently could outperform the more general relational approach. However, work on query optimisation has managed to utilise the metadata to provide more efficient queries and the performance differential is reduced considerably, and certainly to the level where the tradeoff between staff time for procedural programming and faster run-times and staff time for non-procedural programs and slower run-times is in favour of the latter.

Logic programming also shows inefficiency in operation: the exhaustive traversal of the graph representing the facts and rules is time-consuming.

There is one last area concerned with queries in the relational domain. Relational queries are finite: that is they terminate. In contrast, unification is not finite: it may not terminate. This is because the relational domain does not allow recursion, but the logic programming domain does. Practical implementations in the logic programming domain include an operator ('cut' in PROLOG) to restrict infinite unifications.

Object-Oriented Programming/Objectbase

In recent years this area of study has become very popular. It can trace its roots to three main sources:

(a) Simula;
(b) persistent programming and heaps;
(c) Smalltalk.

Simula is a language designed by staff at the Norwegian Computing Centre and aimed at simulation applications. In fact it is ALGOL-like, with concepts of procedures, variable scope and persistence (Dahl *et al.*, 1968).

Persistent programming and heaps have already been described; it is worth noting, however, that much of the work in this area has been based on extensions to ALGOL (e.g. PS-ALGOL) (Atkinson *et al.*, 1983).

Smalltalk (Goldberg and Robson, 1983) was developed at the Xerox Palo Alto Research Center (PARC) in the late seventies. It included many of the concepts now associated with object-orientation, but also introduced a new kind of user interface – WIMP (window, icon, mouse, pointer or pull-down menus) which gained wide acceptance first on the Apple Macintosh and then on UNIX-based workstations. The importance of the user interface technology is that it allowed the close-coupling of the user's 'mind-model' of the data and required processing with the implementation in terms of data objects and associated processes.

Object-oriented systems are characterised by (Atkinson *et al.*, 1989):

(a) data abstraction and encapsulation;
(b) object identity independent of (changing) properties;
(c) property inheritance;
(d) versions and time;
(e) messages;
(f) overloading;
(g) late binding;
(h) WIMP interactive user interfaces.

The last has been mentioned above. The others are now considered in turn.

Data abstraction and encapsulation has the concept of taking a data structure (however simple or complex) and:

(1) giving it a name;
(2) attaching to it some properties (e.g. data type);

(3) attaching to it some methods or object-specific processing functions;

then treating all of the entity described in (1), (2), (3) above as a whole.

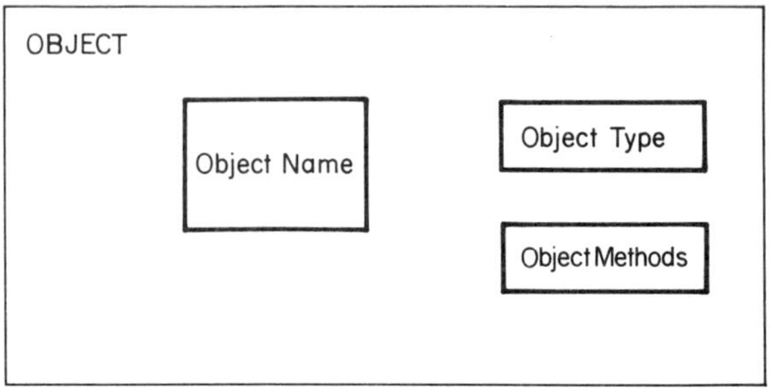

Figure 6 Object-Oriented Object

The object identity being independent of (changing) properties is very important. This means that once an object is identified (by a name) then it can evolve, but still be identified by that name. For example, a person may change properties (height, weight, family name) but is still the same person. Similarly an object may change roles; as a simple example the mailing address attached to a person may change depending on whether the mail is directed to the person in their professional or private capacity (role). Most importantly, the independent object identity simplifies considerably the handling of inheritance and versions.

Property inheritance allows one object (or class of objects) to inherit or take on some or all of the properties of another object (or class of objects). This tends to lead to hierarchies of objects: a road vehicle has the property of needing a licence, while light vehicles (car, van) inherit this property (and others) and use it along with properties specific to the object car and the object van. Incidentally, they also inherit the property 'four-wheeled' from the class of vehicles ('light') to which they belong. Thus properties belonging to one class of objects can be inherited by another class of objects. Interesting problems occur when one class of object can inherit from two or more other classes – the theoretical problems are closely related to those in the database field experienced in the transition from hierarchic to network data structures.

The idea of versions is powerful.There are many applications in engineering, administration and elsewhere where it is important to have a view of the evolution of an object through versions at different stages or points

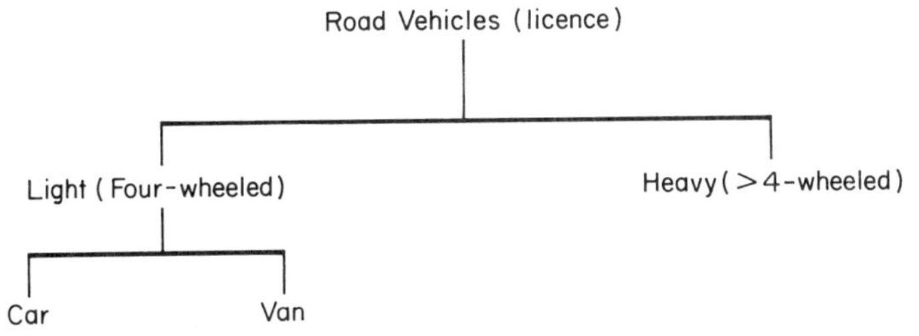

Figure 7 Property Inheritance

in time. Further, the final (or current) version of an object may include sub-objects which are at different version levels within their own version hierarchy. The current engineering assembly for, say, the subwing wheel assembly of an aeroplane may well have the version number 9, but include version 3 of the wheel, version 5 of the braking system, version 7 of the main leg strut, version 8 of the bracing struts, version 2 of the wheel nuts and so on. Later versions of each of these components may be used in other assemblies. Office documents, engineering drawings and many other examples have such natural properties – until the emergence of object-orientation this was only handled with a great deal of difficulty.

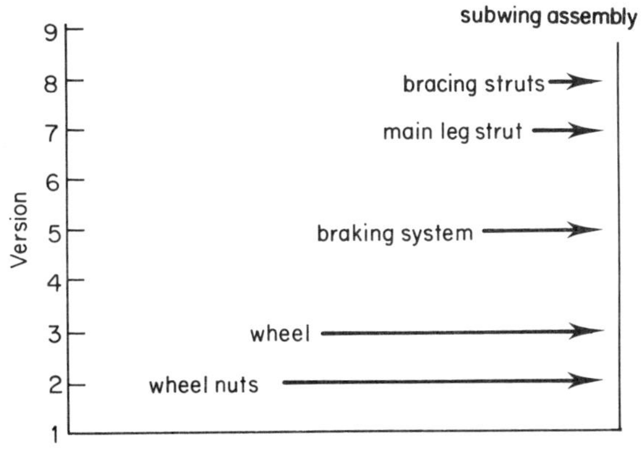

Figure 8 Versions

Messages are the means of communicating between objects. Usually, the message is triggered initially by a change of condition caused by an external interrupt – for example, a change in the temperature. This change of state is communicated to relevant objects which have associated methods (processing) which may fire (be executed) upon this change of condition if it exceeds certain limits. The processing may well cause messages to be sent to other objects. A typical processing chain might be:

(a) external temperature drops five degrees;
(b) associated method recognises this exceeds limits, sends message to heating system;
(c) heating system accepts message, ignites gas under boiler, sends message to water system;
(d) water system accepts message, sends message to pump to start to circulate the hot water round the radiators, sends message to radiators;
(e) radiators monitor ambient temperature in room with associated thermostat, when temperature reaches set limit they send message to radiator valve to shut;
(f) when radiator valve shuts it sends message to pump;
(g) at pump, when all radiator valve messages received it shuts down and sends message to heating system;
(h) heating system accepts message and shuts down.

This chain is not meant to be exhaustive, nor a metacode – it is only meant to illustrate the type of use of methods attached to objects and messages passed between them. This type of system is commonly represented by a Petri-Net (Solvberg, 1986).

Overloading is a concept associated with operators (methods) and data types. Consider the simple statement:

I – J

Figure 9 Overloading

If I and J are of type INTEGER then this is a simple subtraction. If I and J are of type SET, then this is a set difference operation. Thus, overloading is the concept of the operator being dependent on the type(s) of the object(s) being operated upon.

Late binding is otherwise known as run-time binding or execute-time binding. This means that the data structure and content from the data definition is only bound to the program or processing procedure at execute-time. In comparison, for CODASYL database systems, the binding of data definition to program is done at pre-compile time; the output is a third-generation language program with embedded navigational procedure calls, which is then compiled conventionally and executed. Relational systems either use pre-compile-time binding (when embedded SQL statements are placed in a third-generation language) or, in some implementations, execute-time binding for interactive user access.

Late binding is essential for object-orientated systems because the data structures can change dynamically during execution. The later the binding in any procedure/data system, the more dynamic can the data be. However, there is a penalty; the performance is usually worse if late binding is used. The tradeoff is between maximum flexibility and performance.

Object-orientation, with its data-centric view of the world is a very strong influence on expert database systems. It provides solutions to some of the difficult problems of relational database technology such as complex data structures, dynamic data structures, versions, integrity constraints and triggers. However, current systems exhibit relatively poor performance.

Functional Programming/Functional Database

The functional data model (Shipman, 1979) is based on the same concept as the binary relational model, and both may be grouped together as irreducible data models (Date, 1983). The main point of the functional model is that it has the concept of the application of functions over data types. Each relationship between an entity type and a corresponding property type is expressed as a function. For example:

Let E represent the entity Employers. Then we can define:

Ename, a function from E to a character string length 40 and its inverse, nameE
Ecity, a function from E to a character string length 20 and its inverse, cityE

We can now have the functions of the type:

Ename of E of cityE of 'Paris'

which returns names of employers in Paris. The graphic representation might be:

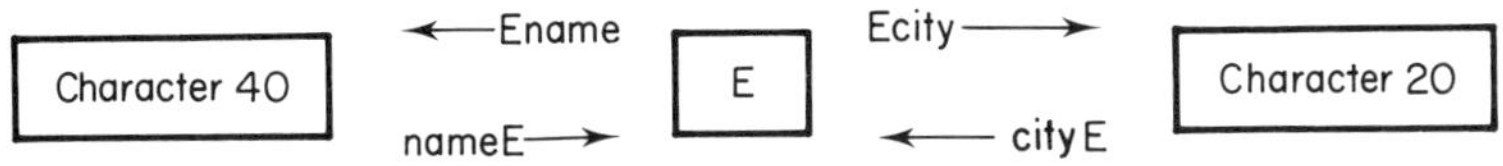

Figure 10 Functional Representation

It is worth noting that:

(a) a graph representation of the data model looks very much like the entity-relation model of Chen (1976), but with functions in place of relations;

(b) the model has some affiliation with the object-oriented approach, where methods can be likened to functions, and objects to entities;

(c) the functional model is intuitively elegant, and acts on the atomic units of data. Furthermore, it encourages a modelling discipline which is graph-oriented – and thus shows some similarity with logic programming;

(d) the use of functions over data types is not unlike the unification process in logic programming, where rules are unified with facts to satisfy goals.

Extended work on the model has led to interesting work on concurrency; there are severe problems because of the potentially long navigation path through the graph from node to node by means of the functional arcs, and the increased chance of one transaction blocking another.

Logic Programming/Rulebase

This 'thicket' or area of work reached wide recognition in the early eighties when, in response to the choice of PROLOG (Clocksin and Mellish, 1981) as the language for the Japanese 'fifth-generation project', research work on logic programming was intensified. However, logic programming finds its roots in the work on Artificial Intelligence, and has links with robotics.

Logic programming is based on the theory of logic (and so possesses an underlying theoretical basis). Logic programming languages handle first-order predicate logic (FOPL) and, in particular, a restricted logic named Horn Clauses. This limits the power to querying, retrieving, deducing and related operations over a static collection of facts using theorem-proving methods on the rules. There is no real provision for integrity-controlled update, although it is possible (by defining integrity constraints as rules) to validate the integrity of a rule-plus-factbase after update. Update is achieved by the use of 'assert' (insert) and 'retract' (delete). Validation of database integrity after update is known to be a computationally expensive task, because there is no necessary internal organisation to the rule-plus-factbase – each rule is independent – and so the concepts of navigation (in the CODASYL database sense) and optimisation (for example, by use of indexes) are irrelevant.

It is worth considering the differences between relational database theory and logic programming theory. In the case of relational database theory, the schema provides the theory, the data in the database (the instances which form the extensional database) provide the model. The model can be updated, but only within the limits defined by the theory (schema) enforced by integrity constraints. In the logic programming domain, there is no schema, and the rules and facts form the theory. (It could be argued that the rules form the theory and the facts the model, but the close association in implementations, and the usual unary instance of a fact in unification with a given rule indicate that both rules and facts form the theory.)

The relationship can be shown diagramatically:

	Relational Database	Logic Programming
Theory	Schema	Rule-and-fact-base
Model	Database	

Figure 11 Relationship between Relational Database and Logic Programming

Furthermore, the theory can be regarded in both cases as the intensional database, and the model as the extensional database.

In the classical logic-programming languages, the rules and facts are stored and manipulated in main memory. This placed an unfortunate restriction (main memory capacity) on the use of these languages. However, work in the late seventies (Gallaire and Minker, 1978) already indicated that there was much benefit in linking together logic programming with database technology. There are some important facilities that are found in database systems, but are lacking in logic programming (and specifically in PROLOG); (Brodie and Jarke in Kerschberg, 1986):

(a) data structures within the database (organised collections of data);
(b) multiple users – PROLOG is a single-user system;
(c) efficient access to large volumes of data or to individual data items;
(d) consistent support of views over base relations;
(e) transactions – and the concepts of concurrency, serialisation and (related) rollback/recovery;
(f) query optimisation both in the compilation phase and in the run-time use of performance assists such as indexes.

Similarly, there are important facilities available in PROLOG which are lacking in database systems:

(a) recursion: PROLOG supports recursion in predicates; existing database management systems do not support either recursive data structures (except in specially built systems) nor in the interpretation of the query language;
(b) inference: PROLOG provides a proof-theoretic evaluation of Horn Clauses (unification) whereas database systems can provide only model-theoretic query evaluation;

(c) dynamic typing: PROLOG does no type checking in assertion and so new types can be added at any time. Conventional database management systems do not provide this facility, although some extended systems do allow dynamic typing (and associated execute-time binding);
(d) backtrack trace: PROLOG can show how it reached certain logical conclusions in the process of unification. A database management system usually just returns the results of the query evaluation without explanation.

There are some features which exist in both PROLOG and conventional relational database management systems to a greater or lesser extent. These are:

(a) ordering: many implementations of relational database management systems have an underlying ordering of tuples within relations on value of primary key – although relational database theory makes ordering irrelevant. In PROLOG the order of clauses is of critical importance because of the way unification traverses the graph of the rule-and-fact base;
(b) wildcarding is common to both domains; PROLOG provides a greater wildcarding facility ('don't care' value in a predicate) than conventional relational database query languages.

THE PROBLEM SPACE

Apices and Virtues

From the descriptions of the 'thickets' above, it is clear that they all have something to contribute to a rather hazy concept which could be called 'expert database systems'. Each of the thickets has advantages, and each has disadvantages. None is the panacea for all data-processing problems.

However, to proceed further it is necessary to reduce the problem space to something manageable. Let us presume that the majority of the advantages of persistent programming and the use of heaps is subsumed within the object-oriented concept. Let us assume that the advantages of the functional data model and functional programming are subsumed partly within the object-oriented concept, and partly in the logic-programming concept. Finally, let us assume that the advantages of CODASYL-type database processing are subsumed within the relational database concept. The other thickets contribute ideas to the ones mentioned above, but none contributes anything not covered by the concepts mentioned above.

Thus we have reduced the problem space to a triangle; the three apices are:

(a) object-orientation;
(b) logic programming;
(c) relational database technology (and in particular query evaluation).

We now need to consider the three apices from the point of view of the virtues of 'expert database' outlined in the Introduction, namely:

(a) efficiency;
(b) flexibility;
(c) expressive power.

This will allow us to consider the respective contributions each apex or end-point should make to a compromise system based on these existing technologies.

Efficiency

Object-orientation provides a flexible data structure, responsive to changes in interconnections between objects and to those changes at different times. However, this very flexibility means that object-oriented systems are expensive in terms of computing resource, and are difficult to optimise. They are characterised by long transactions (e.g. update of an engineering design) and require preservation of versions.

Logic-programming systems use inference. This is computationally expensive because it involves exhaustive traversal of a graph of all related nodes. Worse, since recursion is possible, it is potentially non-terminating. This is the well-known transitive closure problem, which has stimulated a lot of excellent research work, for example see Bancilhon and Ramakrishnan (1986).

Query evaluation acts on a static data structure and so is relatively inexpensive because optimisation of the query can take place (by the compilation process to reduce the impact of a poorly structured statement of requirement by the user) and optimisation of the evaluation can take place by the use of indexes and by the use of large memory buffers.

Thus, it is clear that the virtue of efficiency is best satisfied by query evaluation, but at the expense of flexibility and expressive power.

Flexibility

Object-oriented systems have great flexibility. Because objects are defined, together with their associated type constraints and processing methods, dynamically when needed then the data flexibility is powerful. The processing of objects involves triggers sending messages from one object to another to activate the methods of that object to cause the required effect. Changes in the processing paths can only be achieved by changes in the object type contraints or the methods – but this is a dynamic operation.

Logic-programming systems are flexible with respect to processing. The use of in-query functions in extended logic systems is very powerful, and the ability to choose different strategies for unification (although, in practice, most systems offer only one) provides flexibility in processing. Thus the flexibility is more potential than realised at present. However, the ability to handle complex objects is much less than that of object-oriented systems, and the flexible use of the systems by end-users is difficult to achieve because of the problems of user comprehension of the logic-programming interface. Indeed, powerful front-end expert systems have been developed to help users utilise such systems – and these front ends may, themselves, limit flexibility.

Query evaluation (in relational database systems) can handle only a limited range of data types. Most suppliers of relational DBMSs actually provide extended data types over those found commonly in third-generation programming languages (e.g. type 'date'). It is also worth noting that these extended types provide to the relational DBMS user much more flexibility than that provided by CODASYL DBMSs. The data structure in a relational DBMS is essentially static – certainly when compared with object-oriented and logic-programming systems. It is true that columns may be added dynamically to a table, and new tables created. Further, tables can be joined on a common key dynamically. These aspects of flexibility are one of the main advantages of relational over the earlier CODASYL DBMSs.

Expressive Power

All three end-points of the triangle used as the model have good expressive power. All three are predicate-based rather than procedural – that is, the user states 'what I want' not 'how to get it'.

Object-oriented systems achieve their expressive power by defining functions over objects (or more specifically, object-classes). Thus, all objects whose type constraints and methods satisfy the function will be processed. The result of a user input is a chain of processing sweeping through the object-base from object to object via messages consequent upon the method of one object triggering the message to another. However, the computing resource and elapsed time taken by such processing can be excessive – and the price for the expressive power is found in the computational cost.

Logic-programming systems have the full power of first-order predicate logic (FOPL). Again, the result of a user input is the traversal of the graph of the 'rule-base' from rule to rule (node to node) as unification proceeds. The computational cost can also be high – like in object-oriented systems the price of expressive power is the cost of computation.

Query evaluation in relational DBMSs exhibits limited expressive power. Like in object-oriented systems and logic-programmming systems the expression is by means of predicates, but in general the available operations are limited and for many data-processing applications require supplementing by the use of third-generation programming languages to gain additional functionality.

THE SOLUTION

Having considered the problem-space, it is clear that no one end-point (apex of the triangle) provides a universal solution in the dimensions of efficiency, flexibility and expressive power. Each apical type of system exhibits strength in one of these characteristics, and lesser abilities in the others. It is therefore quite reasonable to look at the possibilities of combining systems with the characteristics of those at the three apices in a mixture to exhibit the required properties. The proportions of each 'apex' will depend on the end-system characteristics required, but as a starting point one could imagine:

(a) taking a relational DBMS as the base component for storage and retrieval because of its characteristic of efficiency;
(b) adding logic-programming characteristics to provide additional expressive power;
(c) adding object-oriented characteristics to provide flexibility.

The terms which seem to be emerging in general use for these combined systems are:

(a + b): Intelligent Database System
(a + c): Extended Database System
(a + b + c): Expert Database System

although it must be emphasised that different authors use these terms to mean different things. The term Advanced Database System is also used widely and may cover any (or all) of the three mentioned above.

Intelligent Database Systems

There are essentially three ways to provide intelligent-database-system capabilities. These are:

(a) add logic (inference) capability to a DBMS;
(b) couple together a database system with a logic-programming system;
(c) add DBMS facilities to a logic-programming system.

Research work has tackled all three possibilities. Option (a) involves the addition of an inference engine and additional data constructs to a DBMS. Work on POSTGRES (Stonebraker and Rowe, 1986) provides a good example.

Option (b) is attractive because the basis of each type of system is in a similar expressive domain – FOPL and relational calculus. However, the problem is the well-known 'impedance mismatch' (discussed in Zaniolo, 1986). This problem is not unique to intelligent database systems using the coupling of logic-programming and database management systems. In fact it is seen clearly in third-generation programming language interfaces to relational DBMS facilities; the query returns a set of tuples which satisfy the predicate but the third-generation programming language expects to work in 'record-at-a-time mode'. This is overcome by the use of the 'cursor' which keeps track of the 'current record in set' – not unlike the equivalent device in CODASYL DBMSs.

Option (c) would require significant amounts of development effort, and in an environment not best-suited to efficient low-level input/output (I/O) operations. Furthermore, the natural data constructs associated with logic programming do not lend themselves easily to efficient handling of simultaneous multi-user access. However, recent work on MegaLog (Bocca, 1990), has shown acceptable performance for a logic-programming system based on an extended PROLOG and with an abstract machine optimised for database activity.

Extended Database Systems

A DBMS could be extended to provide more flexibility in handling data types and structures. Much research work has been concerned with this topic. Early work on POSTGRES (Wong, 1984) was concerned with the addition of geographic data types, while the concept of nesting one relation as a data structure within another relation (Dadam *et al.*, 1986) has been pursued by the team at Heidelberg.

The basic requirements are to provide:

(a) complex data types;
(b) complex data structures;

(c) frames (with methods);
(d) inheritance (with versions);
(e) use of metadata – to assist in query formulation, query compilation and integrity maintenance;
(f) late binding;
(g) overloading.

(a) can be provided by the use of specifically defined functions which can act on specifically named columns. Ideally, the range of type-definitions would be extended (as it has for some commercial relational DBMSs for the type ‘date’). However, the requirement for the data to be processed correctly by the required function, with associated integrity checking, and at the same time to be processed transparently by other operations is not easy to satisfy using a system with relational calculus. Some systems have used relational algebra to overcome this problem – but with the loss of expressive power of the calculus (Jeffery and Gill, 1976; Read, 1986). The compensation is in greater flexibility of both data types and processing.

(b) can be provided by the use of either dynamic joins on demand (an expensive option computationally) or by the maintenance of a table which provides not only a set of tuples showing which tuples in one relation are to be regarded as semi-permanently joined to those in another, but also acts as a performance index.This technique was explored for geological and environmental applications by the system G-EXEC (Jeffery and Gill, 1976).

(c) can be handled by storing the names of procedures (methods) associated with a data object. The names of the procedures are stored with the unique key defining the data object – whether it is a simple- or complex-structured object. There is some similarity with stored, parameterised queries or procedures as used commonly in commercially available relational DBMSs – but the linking with the object-type is the additional essential link.

(d) is not easy to accommodate. The handling of versions can be done in a variety of ways – all involving in some way putting a date/time stamp on the data object. The problems concern the granularity of the stamped object. Inheritance is more difficult because the metadata support of existing relational DBMSs is somewhat lacking. A data dictionary, extended to become a system dictionary with the ability to inherit a set of integrity constraints (both simple type constraints and referential integrity constraints to preserve the integrity of a complex-object) from a pre-defined object would be of great benefit.

(e) is related to (d): a good system dictionary is required to provide the facilities needed for optimisers and interfacing tools to use the metadata.

(f) is a characteristic of dynamic SQL in relational DBMS environments;

it has also been used in many special-purpose relational systems – e.g. G-EXEC (Jeffery and Gill, 1976) and R-EXEC (Read, 1986). The advantage is in flexibility of processing with regard to the data structure and content; the disadvantage is a potential loss of efficiency due to the use of interpreting rather than compiling techniques. In the case of G-EXEC the use of minimal compilation and maximum use of pre-compiled code following command interpretation maintained adequate efficiency.

(g) requires that the operator is type-independent, but that for any particular data type is type-specific. If (c) above is implemented then the use of methods associated with the data object makes this possible.

Expert Database Systems

Smith (1984, in Kerschberg, 1986) defined an Expert Database System as 'A system for developing applications requiring knowledge-directed processing of shared data'.

It is the contention of this paper that if 'shared data' is replaced by 'shared complex data' then this definition provides a good basis for a discussion of expert database systems.

Thus, an expert database system has the efficiency characteristics of a relational DBMS but in addition the capabilities of knowledge representation and expressive power from logic programming, and the flexibility of data type and structure, coupled with type-specific processing from object-orientation.

Advanced Database Systems

As explained above, this term is used loosely to cover expert database systems, extended database systems, intelligent database systems and any combination of them.

THE ISSUES TO BE ADDRESSED

Efficiency

The maintenance of processing efficiency in systems exhibiting the characteristics already defined as desirable is not easy. It is likely to involve the use of indexes to complex objects to expedite their processing – and, in passing, to define their granularity for concurrency. The problems of inheritance can be handled by a good system dictionary at the metadata level, but instantiation is likely to be less than efficient without indexes which use not only primary keys but also indications of versions – and also indicate the inter-tuple links needed to instantiate particular complex objects.

Recursion is a major problem for efficiency; techniques for efficient handling of the transitive closure problem appear regularly (see Bancilhon and Ramakrishnan, 1986) and it is clear that the problem will be solved satisfactorily. The optimisation of queries involving complex data types, versions and recursion will require sophisticated optimisers – probably based on rules.

Integrity

The major issues here concern validation and concurrency. The problems of validating input data, or input amendments to data, are well known and understood for simple data types and data structures. However, complex data types and structures will require not only the classical validation techniques (type check, value check, range check, existence check) but also checks concerned with the values in other parts of the data structure and logic based on the structure of the object itself. Referential integrity is only the simplest starting point into this complex subject.

As objects are larger and more complex, then the granularity for locking tends to grow larger (else there is a risk of an integrity violation). In the extreme case a complete data structure is 'taken for change' so that concurrent users can only read the version as it was before changes started – and the changed object may not be replaced in the database for a long period of time. This problem is well known in the application areas of office systems (documents) and engineering systems (design drawings and specifications).

Flexibility

The desire for flexibility leads to the need to provide an object-based view of the data. This implies the provision of support for complex objects with the problems as identified above. It also implies the use of methods in frames attached to the object – and a solution to this problem has only been sketched above. The provision of versions implies a new set of integrity constraints for version control – the use of sub-components of complex objects to build a new complex object from different versions raises serious problems of integrity maintenance.

The use of methods in frames provides great processing flexibility, but places an increased processing load on the system used to enforce the constraints or rules used to define integrity. The associated concept of triggers, fired when a state-change is detected by a method associated with an object-type, provides great dynamic processing capability but again places responsibility for integrity firmly with the methods enforcing the type-checking. If before- and after-update checking is done this can be very time-consuming and expensive in computing resource. However, if this checking is not done it is possible that the integrity of the database will be lost.

Hardware Assists

The construction of an expert database system of necessity involves choices or compromises between the needs of flexibility and expressive power on the one hand, and of efficiency on the other. The balance between these aspects will depend on the application and its particular needs. However, there is one factor which can change the balance-point dramatically – the use of hardware assists.

The use of special-purpose hardware for database handling is not new. CAFS (a product from ICL in the UK) provides fast access to disks while the work of David Hsiao (Hsiao, 1983) has explored multi-processor bus-type architectures. The emergence of commercial products such as the Britton-Lee IDM500 and the Teradata DB1012 have provided significantly increased performance capabilities for conventional relational DBMSs.

The real question is whether the advances in hardware can shift the balance-point such that a user can have the advantages of flexibility and expressive power while still experiencing satisfactory performance (based on efficiency).

It is the final conclusion of this paper that without hardware assists, expert database systems will not provide production facilities, but will remain as research toys.

REFERENCES AND SELECTED BIBLIOGRAPHY

Atkinson, M., Bayley, P. J., Chilsom, K., Cockshutt, W. and Morrison, R. (1983). An approach to persistent programming. *Computer Journal* 26, 4.

Atkinson, M. P., Bocca, J. B., Elsey, T. J., Fiddian, N. J., Flower, M., Gray, P. M. D., Gray, W. A., Hepp, P., Johnson, R. G., Milne, W., Norrie, M., Omololu, A. O., Oxborrow, E. A., Shave, M. R. J., Smith, A. M., Stocker, P. M. and Walker, J. (1984). The Proteus distributed database system. *Proceedings BNCOD3*, pp. 225–46, Cambridge University Press.

Atkinson, M., Bancilhon, F., DeWitt, D., Dittrich, K., Maier, D. and Zdonik, S. (1989). The Object-Oriented Database System Manifesto (a political pamphlet). *Proceedings, DOOD89.*

Babb, E. (1979). Implementing a relational database by means of specialised hardware. *ACM TODS* 4, no 1.

Bancilhon, F. and Ramakrishnan, R. (1986). An amateur's introduction to recursive query processing strategies. *Proceedings, ACM-SIGMOD Conference.*

Bertino, E., Rabitti, F. and Thanos, C. (1988). MULTOS: a document server for distributed office systems. *Proceedings EDBT '88.* Springer.

Bocca, J. (1990). MegaLog: a platform for developing knowledge base management systems. ECRC Internal KB Report 75.

Cardenas, A. F. (1985). *Data Base Management Systems.* 2nd edn. Allyn & Bacon.

Carey, M. J., DeWitt, D. J., Frank, D., Graefe, G., Muralikrishna, M., Richardson, J. E. and Shekita, E. J. (1986). The architecture of the EXODUS extensible DBMS. *Proceedings International Workshop on Object Oriented Database Systems, Washington* (ed. K. R. Dittrich, and U. Dayal), pp. 52–65. IEEE Computer Society Press.

Ceri, S. and Pelagatti, G. (1984). *Distributed Databases: Principles and Systems.* McGraw-Hill.

Chen, P. P.-S. (1976). The entity–relationship model – towards a unified view of data. *ACM TODS* 1, No 1.

Clocksin, W. F. and Mellish, C. S. (1981). *Programming in Prolog.* Springer.

CODASYL (1971). *Data Base Task Group (DBTG) Report 1971.* ACM, New York, April.

Codd, E. F. (1970). A relational model for large shared data banks. *CACM* 13, no 6, June.

Codd, E. F. (1971). Normalized data base structure: a brief tutorial. *Proceedings, 1971 ACM-SIGFIDET Workshop on Data Descriptions, Access and Control, San Diego, California, Nov 11–12.*

Codd, E. F. (1972). Further normalization of the data base relational model. *Courant Computer Science Symposium Vol. 6 Data Base Systems. New York, 1971.* Prentice-Hall.

Codd, E. F. (1974). Recent investigations in relational data base systems. *Proceedings 1974 IFIP Conference, Stockholm, Sweden, August 5–10, 1974.* North-Holland.

Codd, E. F. (1979). Extending the database relational model to capture more meaning. *ACM TODS* 4, no 4.

Dadam, P., Kuspert, K., Andersen, F., Blanken, H., Erbe, R., Gunauer, J., Lum, V., Pistor, P. and Walch, G. (1986). A DBMS prototype to support extended NF2 relations: an integrated view on flat tables and hierarchies. *Proceedings ACM SIGMOD 1986.* pp. 356–67.

Dahl, O., Myrhaug, B. and Nygaard, K. (1968). *Simula 67 Common Base Language*. Norwegian Computing Centre S-2.

Date, C. J. (1981). *An Introduction to Database Systems*, 3rd edn. Addison-Wesley.

Date, C. J. (1981a). Referential integrity. *Proc. 7th International Conference on Very Large Data Bases.*

Date, C. J. (1983). *An Introduction to Database Systems, Volume II.* Addison-Wesley.

Date, C. J. (1984). *Database: A Primer*. Addison-Wesley.

Date, C. J. (1986). *An Introduction to Database Systems*, 4th edn. Addison-Wesley.

Date, C. J. (1986a). *Relational Writings*. Addison-Wesley.

Date, C. J. (1987). *A Guide to Ingres*. Addison-Wesley.

Date, C. J. (1987a) *A Guide to the SQL Standard*. Addison-Wesley.

Date, C. J. (1988). *A Guide to DB2*. Addison-Wesley.

Deen, S. M. (1985), *Principles and Practice of Database Systems*. Macmillan.

DeWitt, D. J. (1979). Direct – a multiprocessor organisation for supporting relational database management systems. *IEEE Transactions on Computers* 1–28, 61–75.

DeWitt, D. J. and Boral, H. (eds) (1985). *Database Machines: Fourth International Workshop*. Springer.

Dittrich, K. R. (1986). Object-oriented database systems: the notion and the issues. *Proceedings of the International Workshop on Object-Oriented Database Systems* (ed. K. R. Dittrich and U. Dayal). IEEE Computer Society Press.

Dittrich, K. R. and Dayal, U. (eds) (1986). *Proceedings of the International Workshop on Object-Oriented Database Systems*. IEEE Computer Society Press.

Gallaire, H. and Minker, J. (eds) (1978). *Logic and Databases*. Plenum Press, New York.

Gardarin, G. (1984). Database machines. *Institution Proceedings Davos, 1984*. IBM Europe Institute, Davos.

Goldberg, A. and Robson, D. (1983). *Smalltalk-80: The Language and its Implementation*. Addison-Wesley.

Gray, P. M. D., Moffat, D. S. and Paton, N. W. (1988). A Prolog interface to a functional data model database. *Proceedings EDBT '88*. Springer.

Held, G. D., Stonebraker, M. R. and Wong, E. (1975). INGRES: a relational data base system. *Proceedings National Computing Conference, Anaheim, California, May 1975.*

Hsiao, D. (1983). *Advanced Data Base Machine Architecture*. Prentice-Hall.

Jeffery, K. G. (1985). Databases and office automation. *Proceedings BNCOD4*, pp. 215–29. Cambridge University Press.

Jeffery, K. G. and Gill, E. M. (1976). The design and philosophy of the G-EXEC system. *Computers and Geosciences* 2, 345–6.

Jeffery, K. G., Lay, J. and Curtis, T. (1989a). A logic-based system for data validation. *Proceedings BNCOD7*. Cambridge University Press.

Jeffery, K. G., Lay, J. O., Miquel, J. F., Zardan, S., Naldi, F. and Vannini-Parenti, I. (1989b). IDEAS: a system for international exchange and access to data for science. *Information Management* 25, 6, 703–11.

Kerschberg, L. (ed.) (1986). Expert database systems. *Proceedings of the First International Workshop on Expert Database Systems, 1984*. Benjamin-Cummings.

Kerschberg, L. (ed.) (1987). Expert database systems. *Proceedings of the First International Conference on Expert Database Systems, 1986*. Benjamin-Cummings.

Kerschberg, L. (ed.) (1989). Expert database systems. *Proceedings of the Second International Conference on Expert Database Systems 1988*. Benjamin-Cummings.

Kowalski, R. (1981). Logic as a data base language. Technical report, Imperial College, London.

Kowalski, R. (1984). Logic as a database language. *Proceedings BNCOD3*, pp. 103–32. Cambridge University Press.

van der Lans, R. F. (1988). *Introduction to SQL*. Addison-Wesley.

Lindsay, B., McPherson, J. and Pirahesh, H. (1987). A data management extension architecture. *Proceedings ACM SIGMOD 1987*. pp. 210–26.

Lingat, J.-Y., Nobecourt, N. and Rolland, C. (1987). Behaviour management in database applications. *Proceedings VLDB 1987*, pp. 185–96.

Litwin, W. (1988). From databsase systems to multidatabase systems. *Proceedings, BNCOD6*, pp. 161–88. Cambridge University Press.

Morgenstern, M. (1986). The role of constraints in databases, expert systems and knowledge representation. *Proceedings of the First International Workshop on Expert Database Systems, 1984* (ed.) L. Kerschberg), pp. 351–68. Benjamin-Cummings.

Read, B. J. (1986). A relational data handling system for scientists. *Proceedings BNCOD5*, pp. 23–42. Cambridge University Press.

Rowe, L. and Stonebraker, M. (1987). The POSTGRES data model. *Proceedings VLDB 1987*, pp. 83–96.

Schmidt, J. W. (1977). Some high-level language constructs for data of type relation. *ACM TODS* 2, 3, 247–61.

Senko, M. E., Altman, E. B., Astrahan, M. M. and Felder, M. (1973). Data structure and accessing in data base systems. *IBM Systems Journal* 12, 1, 30–93.

Sharman, G. C. H. (1975). A new model of relational data base and high level languages. Technical report TR.12.136, IBM Hursley Park Laboratory, England.

Sharman, G. C. H. (1987). *Introduction to Database on Microcomputers*. Addison-Wesley.

Shipman, D. (1979). The functional data model and the data language

DAPLEX. *SIGMOD 79 Conference*. Revised version in *ACM TODS* 6, 140–73.

Smith, J. M., Bernstein, P. A., Dayal, U., Goodman, N., Landers, T., Lin, K. W. T. and Wong, E. (1981) MULTIBASE – integrating heterogeneous distributed database systems. *Proceedings 1981 National Computer Conference, June.*

Solvberg, A. (1986). Behaviour-specification in an information systems analysis context. *Proceedings BNCOD5*, pp. 71–86. Cambridge University Press.

Stocker, P. M., Gray, P. M. D. and Atkinson, M. P. (1984). *Databases: Role and Structure*. Cambridge University Press.

Stonebraker, M. and Rowe, L. (1986). The design of POSTGRES. *Proc. ACM SIGMOD 1986*, pp. 340–55.

Wong, E. (1984). Semantic enhancement to QUEL. *Institution Proceedings, Davos, 1984*. IBM Europe Institute, Davos.

Yost, R. (1984). R*. *Institution Proceedings, Davos, 1984*. IBM Europe Institute, Davos.

Zaniolo, C. (1986). Prolog: a database language for all seasons. *Proceedings of the First International Workshop on Expert Database Systems, 1984* (ed. L. Kerschberg). Benjamin-Cummings.

Zloof, M. (1975). Query by example. *Proceedings, National Computing Conference, Anaheim, California, May 1975.*

2
Extensible Database Systems

B. LINGS, Y. JIN, N. ADABLAH AND L. FOSTER

Department of Computer Science, University of Exeter, Exeter EX4 4PT

1. INTRODUCTION

1.1. The Motivation for Extensibility

Current-generation database management systems are designed to support business applications, typified by information needs requiring a few standard data types and many instances of each type. The application domains are uniform enough for a single, fixed database management system to give efficient, controlled, shared access to the data. There are, however, emerging needs for the application of database technology in a number of domains which have very different characteristics from traditional applications. These include spatial databases, knowledge bases, multi-media systems, engineering applications for CAD/CAM and VLSI data, and scientific and statistical applications. These needs have prompted a new direction for database systems research. Compared with the more conventional applications such as business-transaction processing and record keeping, these novel applications have very different requirements which demand unusual storage structures and query-processing algorithms, and require data models and data languages that admit new constructs, such as novel data types and operations [5].

In particular, novel data storage systems have had to be invented in order to tackle the problem of the efficient storage of these complex objects [9]. The importance of this particular issue, as we shall see, is reflected in the fact that, in most of the new systems being proposed, the storage component forms a core on which the rest of the system is based. This core is either fully fixed or at least has a fixed interface with fully defined semantics. The new data types (e.g. geometric data types for CAD/CAM or latitude and longitude position data type for mapping applications) can be simulated by conventional, built-in data types, but in most cases this leads to verbose and confusing queries, as well as very poor performance [16, 17]. The reason for

Expert Database Systems
ISBN 0-12-382255-6

this is that the semantics of the domain in which the query is initiated will be poorly represented, or unrepresentable, in the relational model. Hence the query will have to be transformed into the relational domain, making it difficult to understand. Also the system will know little about the underlying semantics of the query, so its optimization is likely to be very poor.

Definition of new data types may necessitate the definition of new access methods. Further, better access methods may become available that would be more efficient at indexing and accessing some existing data types. For instance K-D-B trees [13] and R-trees [8] are appropriate access methods for point and polygon data, respectively, that became available after the introduction of many graphical database systems. Extensible DBMSs are not only being designed to allow the addition of new access methods, but also aim to provide interfaces that will make such additions easy for users. This is not a simple task: the introduction of new access methods is a complex operation in all the proposed systems, as it carries with it the need to interface such access methods into the rest of the system (including the query optimizer). The simplicity with which extensions can be made to a DBMS is likely to be a governing criterion for its success.

1.2. The Concept of Flexibility

The concept of extensible database management systems has been introduced by researchers to tackle the problem of providing efficient database support for non-traditional applications. From the literature so far available (e.g. for DASDBS, EXODUS, GENESIS, ORION, POSTGRES, STARBURST), it is apparent that there are several approaches to extensibility [5, 11, 19]. Here are three different views that have been put forward:

> These systems ... are essentially software busses where modules with desirable DBMS capabilities can be plugged or unplugged in a matter of hours or days at virtually no cost to produce a customised DBMS. [1]

> the goal is to provide a collection of kernel DBMS facilities plus software tools to facilitate the semi-automatic generation of high performance application-specific DBMSs for new applications. [6]

> the idea is to extend the relational model developed by Codd with general mechanisms that can be used to simulate a variety of semantic data modeling constructs. The mechanisms include (1) abstract data types (ADTs), (2) data of type procedure, and (3) rules. [14]

The different approaches can be viewed as representing different points on a spectrum of extensibility.

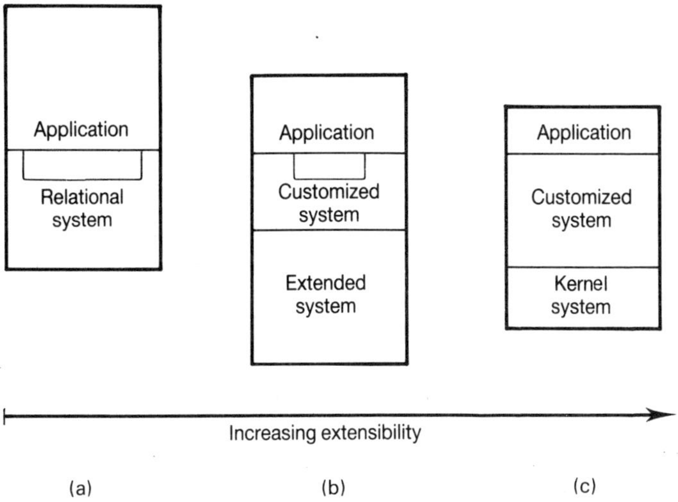

Figure 1 The Spectrum of Extensibility

Conventional relational databases are at one end of this spectrum. These systems are poor with respect to semantic richness in the model, inflexible with respect to query optimization and access methods, and restrictive in their storage management. Extensible systems of all kinds attempt, to greater or lesser extents, to increase the functionality and flexibility of all components of a database management system. The degree to which they do so is governed primarily by the implied complexity of the resultant systems. In order to control this complexity, the systems reflect the state of the art with respect to software engineering practice. Systems are designed in a highly modular way, and the modules are customizable where possible by parameterization.

Figure 1 represents one way of partitioning the spectrum into three areas representing current systems and two broad categories of extensible systems. These two categories can be distinguished as single-model systems and multi-model systems, or alternatively as full-function systems and tool-kit systems [10].

In Figure 1(a) an application is depicted which uses a standard relational database management system. The interface between the two is virtually untailored, and therefore is depicted as narrow. There is said to be a great impedance mismatch between the application and the system model. This means that operations in the application domain must undergo a complex mapping to the database domain with all the inherent complexity and performance loss.

In Figure 1(b) a full-function system is provided, with a much richer semantic model. Objects in the domain can be more closely modelled, and the resulting interface is broader. However, the application must still use the given (all be it richer) model so the interface is not ideal and some complexity and inefficiency will remain. For example, the query optimizer may be very restrictive in how it can be tuned for the new domain, and the new model may not fully support aspects of the domain model. Further, there may be inefficiencies due to other components of the system: the buffer management may be suboptimal for the domain or the transaction manager may be less than suitable.

In Figure 1(c) a tool-kit system is envisaged. In this case a kernel database management system is provided, but not a full-function system. A model can be selected and parsers and optimizers generated which are domain-specific, and tools are provided for this complex software engineering task. Other aspects of the system may be equally flexible: the system may provide alternative buffer managers, for example. The ultimate goal of such a system is to have a library of reusable components which are plug-compatible with a skeleton system.

Whatever the approach taken, the potential of extensible DBMSs is well recognized:

> Extendibility is one of the few ideas that everyone agrees are good ones. Hence many of the new prototypes under construction are doing something in this area. [19]

1.3. The Role of the DBI

With the concept of extensible DBMSs comes the role of the database implementor (DBI). This role becomes apparent in most of the proposals cited above as one involving tasks in the design and implementation of DBMSs that are too complex to be catered for within the ANSI/SPARC roles [20] of DBA, EA and user. Although most proposals have not clearly identified this role and few have fully identified the corresponding tasks, it is implicit in all proposals.

> In a conventional database environment it is customary to consider the roles of two different classes of individuals: the database administrator and the user. In EXODUS, a third type of individual is required to customize EXODUS into an application-specific database system. While we referred to this individual as a 'user' in the preceding paragraphs, he or she is not a user in the normal sense (i.e., an end user, such as a bank teller or a cartographer). Internally, we refer to this 'user' of the EXODUS facilities as a 'database implementor' or DBI. [6]

> The ANSI/SPARC role of database users, who write and execute transactions, and the DBA, who designs and writes database schemas, remain unchanged. Extensible DBMSs, such as GENESIS, require an additional party, the DBI, who is responsible for the construction and customization of a DBMS. [3]

This paper attempts to analyse extensibility through this new role, because ultimately the success of new systems will depend entirely on how supportable the role is. To highlight its scope, we examine what is involved in making extensions to a DBMS in the next section. In section 3 we examine some current proposals of extensible DBMS which take differing views on extensibility, but between them cover what we consider to be the major issues in the concept of extensibility. In section 4 we present an analysis in terms of a structured environment aimed at facilitating the implementation and support of extensible database management systems by the DBI.

2. EXTENSIBLE ASPECTS OF DBMS

2.1. Extending Functionality

For a given DBMS, we are mainly interested in its functionality and extensibility. Functionality refers to the DBMS as delivered to users. In contrast, extensibility refers to the extent to which the DBMS is capable of being 'extended' by users, i.e. the DBI is able to add new or alternative features to the original system.

DBI-provided components can be either directly used by a generic mechanism (algorithm) at run-time or compiled to generate a customized system that supports the new functionality required. As will be seen, extensibility is closely related to parameterization. For example, it may be possible to register a newly added access method by making an entry in a table, so a table-driven optimizer can make use of it. Such new components must be mapped to the object class on which the algorithm is defined. This would involve specifying for each component those properties on which the algorithm depends. This allows the algorithm to be fixed, and the overall system complexity to be less, but extensibility can only be achieved to a relative extent that is constrained by the definition of the generic algorithm.

The interface to all database management system components should ideally reflect the properties common to a complete class of algorithms which may be used in their implementation, and should be derived minimally with reference to this known set. This is referred to as the simplest common interface (SCI) principle in [2]. Use of the SCI principle caters for interchangeability of components, but relies on the derivability of a manageable SCI without artificial constraints on the generality of the class of algorithms supported. Some systems therefore do not use the SCI principle but instead define simple, fixed interfaces which constrain system design; the claim is that the net simplification of the overall system will outweigh in its advantages any implementation constraints.

No absolute extensibility can be contemplated, and it is as yet unclear how orthogonal many of the components of a system can be made and to what extent parameterization and the SCI principle can be used as the means of providing simple but powerful DBI customization. Some researchers take the view that the long term-goal of database research, and of the systems which follow from it, is to completely decouple DBMS components and thereby provide simple, engineered solutions to the provision of efficient, tailored database systems. Others believe that the resultant complexity of interfaces will dominate such systems, overriding the advantages of module independence, and that both short- and long-term advantage are gained by the close coupling of certain components. An example of this is the close coupling of the trigger and locking mechanisms in POSTGRES [17].

2.2. Some Specific Issues

Extensible DBMS research has addressed a number of issues with the aim of increasing the flexibility available in customizing systems. In some cases (for example, the storage manager) it is almost universally acknowledged that flexibility must be compromised for simplicity: too many components rely on decisions made at this level. In other cases only the degree of flexibility is in question, representing differences of opinion on how inherently complex the interface to a certain component is: the classic software engineering problem of the degree to which modules can be decoupled. There are many open research questions in this area.

In this section we look at several important facets of the overall database management system architecture which are contenders for extensibility, and note the spectrum of choices made for different systems. We limit our attention to a few of the major issues: choice of data model, transaction management, buffer management, storage structure, access methods and query optimization. Some of these issues are inherently non-orthogonal and so cannot be tailored simply and independently. We discuss the general issues below: we become more system-specific in section 3.

2.2.1. DATA MODEL

We consider the four elements of data models distinguished by [21]: data types, relationships, constraints and operations. In general, a simple data type (i.e. one that has no structure as far as the model is concerned) can be defined, together with corresponding operations, without requirements on the model which would impact the DBMS. The addition of complex data types and new operators can be achieved by making the query optimizer and run-time system table driven off a data structure containing the known types and operators [19]. In this case when new types are added to the table, a form of extensibility is achieved. However, it is not easy to achieve extensibility in the case of relationships, constraints and operations on complex objects (e.g. performing a join operation on relations in the relational model). The fact that relationships are often implied in a model can pose a real problem. This is clearly seen when attempting to represent a network structure in a system supporting a hierarchical model. In the case of constraints, these may be either explicitly stated or implicit in the model. In the implicit case we have the potential problem of over-generalization. This is a clear limitation to extensibility based upon a single model. Because the semantics of both relationships and constraints is deeply embedded in the whole structure of the model, it is difficult to achieve extensibility whilst efficiently supporting the model.

Any adherence to a single model will potentially lead to an impedance mismatch with some application domain. This can be overcome in one of two ways: by generalizing the model or by allowing discretion in the choice of a model.

The first approach is in line with providing full function systems. The model adopted varies, but may be extended relational, functional or object-oriented. Proponents of the extended relational approach can argue with conviction that it is based on a well founded theory which has been amply tested in practice, and that the relaxation of certain constraints on the relational model provides a systematic and controlled way of increasing flexibility. The burden of proof is then on detractors to demonstrate the inadequacy of the approach, for it is they who are proposing a marked deviation from the current line of development. Those in favour of the functional approach can again argue that there is a well founded underlying theory, but there is less by way of practical demonstration of its efficacy. In fact in GENESIS [4, 22] the pure functional approach adopted by DAPLEX [4] has been adapted to a production system to provide a more consistent user interface. Another aspect of the functional/production approach is that many of the relationships and constraints which are primary features of other models, such as inheritance, become derived features. This is an advantage if the rest of the system is flexible enough to allow the definition of efficient support for their exploitation. This is a strong argument for adoption of the tool-kit approach to extensibility for such a model (which is then being treated as a meta-model). Proponents of the object-oriented approach suffer from the fact that there is as yet no definition of what is meant by an object-oriented database system, so it lacks the clarity of the other proposals. In fact a central feature of object-oriented systems, inheritance, has no universally accepted semantics.

Whichever single model is adopted, the approach does have advantages. The model forms a fixed point in the web of mappings which allows for simplification of query optimizers, external to internal transformers and user interface languages (DML and DDL) with their associated translators. If these advantages are fully exploited, however, many of the other levels of the DBMS become less flexible: the addition of access methods or the tuning of query optimizers may be very complex or severely constrained.

It can be argued that there is a trade-off with respect to the choice of model for a single-model system. The simpler the model the greater the impedance mismatch is likely to be with applications software, but the richer the model the more complex will be the system and the less efficient its implementation. This is one of the major justifications for multi-model systems: they can be tuned to a specific application-oriented model.

To make the data model aspect of a DBMS more extensible, i.e. to cater for multiple models, it is necessary to design the system in a more semantic-free way. This, in turn, requires the concepts underlying the system to be more abstract in terms of data modelling. A mechanism is needed to accommodate those semantics of data models which will be defined by the DBI. In a simple case, this mechanism can be a table-driven algorithm. The more complex cases may involve generating a model-dependent algorithm as, for example, in the case of a query optimizer. For this reason, in an extensible DBMS some semantics of the data model are explicitly expressed as pieces of knowledge provided by the DBI, while in a conventional DBMS, most of the semantics are coded in the DBMS itself.

The concepts of a data model are represented by means of a data language (including both DDL and DML). How to deal with the extensibility of a data model both syntactically and semantically is a major challenge in the area of extensible DBMSs. Most multi-model systems envisage substantial tool support for the generation of translators, including powerful, enhanced languages for the expression of database semantics. It must be acknowledged, though, that the support of a generated model in terms of help facilities and manuals will still be a major task in the provision of a tailored system. This is an issue we return to in section 5.

2.2.2. TRANSACTION MANAGEMENT AND BUFFER MANAGEMENT

There is obviously a need to provide concurrency control at the level of a complex object. There is a problem when such objects are not directly supported by the model, as protocols must be enforced outside the direct control of the system (probably in application software) in order to guarantee object integrity. Strategies for concurrency control and recovery are usually data-model independent. Systems will therefore either provide a suitably general mechanism or provide several strategy options within the system. Only one such option can be safely used in any system where a global deadlock algorithm is incorporated [18]. Different applications require different strategies of transaction management. However, fragments of code implementing a transaction management protocol are dispersed at various points in the software, particularly in access methods. Because of this, it is difficult (or costly) to support even a few options unless some generating facilities are available for producing new pieces of software that implement the chosen protocols. In contrast, it will be relatively easy to provide several choices of buffer management so that high system performance can be achieved.

2.2.3. STORAGE STRUCTURE

In a conventional DBMS, the mapping from conceptual level to internal level is coded within the DBMS because the structure and semantics of both levels are already known and newly constructed data structures are expressed in terms of built-in types. But in extensible DBMS, neither level is necessarily fixed. Mechanisms for new simple data types and data relationships may be introduced independently of any existing structures, and the underlying storage structure manager may change as well. Hence, the mapping problem can become very complicated unless strict interface control is maintained.

Storage structures are usually data-model independent and designed in connection with transaction management and buffer management. It is desirable to make them generic enough to support a wide domain of applications for reasons of simplicity. It may be very difficult to generate automatically an application-specific storage structure manager. Also, the complexity of the whole system increases rapidly with a dynamic storage structure because there are many other components on top of it, relying heavily on the functions it provides. It becomes imperative that we have a trade-off between extensibility and simplicity. The more components that become extensible, the wider the domain that can be supported, but on the other hand, the higher is the complexity of the system. The complexity may reach a level at which it becomes very hard or even impractical to control, so a careful balance is needed.

In reaching this balance some systems will provide a storage manager which is not flexible enough to cater fully for a given application. Rather than complicate the storage structure level by making its interface too complex, a system may have, built in, a capability for using external storage managers. In this situation, an object for which efficient storage and retrieval is not supported would be represented in the database system by an instance whose value is a reference to the stored object in an alternate storage system. This is obviously not an ideal situation, as there are also implications for other features such as the recovery manager. In POSTGRES, for example, it is suggested [18] that the transaction manager could be provided with hooks so that external storage managers can be notified of transaction-specific information (start and end of transactions and rollback information).

2.2.4. ACCESS METHODS

Access methods provide associative access to databases which is important for system performance. The requirement for access methods differs from application to application, as indicated above. And as new access methods continue to be introduced as a result of research and development, it becomes very important to have a mechanism to allow the right access method to be chosen or a newly developed one to be added into the system. The provision for access-method introduction in a system will depend on the designers' expectations with respect to an SCI for access methods and how frequently they are likely to be changed. If it is assumed that the introduction of a new access method will be a rare event then there is less need to simplify the task.

Implementing new access methods involves writing the algorithms in a high-level language and interfacing with other system components such as storage structure, buffer management, transaction manager, etc. This is recognized as an inherently complex task [18]. There will be a defined access-method interface protocol so that the method can be used by other components such as the query planner and the query-processing routines. If the interface is kept simple and fixed, decoupling from these subsystems is high.

2.2.5. QUERY OPTIMIZATION

Query optimization is invariably based on graph transformation, and there are two basic parts to a system: equivalence transformations and cost functions. These are related to many other aspects such as the data model and access methods. Hence, query optimization is potentially very dynamic. An optimization algorithm may be table-driven, with new operators being provided with a parameterized profile which dictates how they will be manipulated. This can be taken to an extreme, where very few parameters are allowed and these mirror exactly those properties relevant to relational optimizers. Using a table-driven method, a query optimizer can, within the limits dictated by the parameterization, take advantage of the new data types and new access methods to produce more efficient access plans. However, for more and more diverse domains of application it can be argued that no static optimizer will meet efficiency requirements due to the limitations of the data model underlying it. Consequently, automatic generation of a domain-sensitive query optimizer is highly desirable. This may be achieved by adding a rule capability to the query optimizer.

Obviously, the extensibility of a DBMS as a whole system depends on how flexible each of the above aspects is and how they affect each other.

3. TWO CURRENT PROPOSALS

As indicated above, there are a number of proposals on extensible DBMSs. Here we examine only POSTGRES and EXODUS in any detail because we believe they are two typical approaches which, between them, address most of the major issues on extensibility.

3.1. Overview of POSTGRES and EXODUS

The approach of POSTGRES is to build a full-function DBMS using a single data model, namely an extended relational model. Complex objects are supported by including the concepts of shared subobjects, abstract data types and attributes of type procedure. POSTGRES adopts the philosophy that simple is best, and wherever there is a trade-off between simplicity and flexibility more emphasis is placed on the former. This leads to an economy of design which makes both implementation and use of POSTGRES much simpler than in many competitor systems. Against this is set the criticism that efficiency must be compromised and flexibility limited. The latter is caused by two design decisions. The first has already been mentioned, namely the use of close coupling of modules resulting in the presentation of a complex interface to the DBI for some extensions. The second is the strict definition of interfaces for access methods and operators. In POSTGRES, access methods are only allowed for indexing operations, that is, to allow more efficient selection of subsets of tuples in a relation. This is true whatever the type of the object, as it is believed that the concept of indexing and the abstract operations of selection and join are universal in their applicability. This conformance to the relational model allows a query optimizer which is specific to the relational model and has a fixed, table-driven algorithm. Hence new operators which are to be used by the system, either for indexing or as a parameter to an existing access method, must have specific parameters defined. For example, a comparison operator may need an inverse to be defined and may also require the identification of which functions are to be used for selection and join when these are based on that operation. It must also have statistical information declared, for use by the query optimizer in costing query strategies. Hence, on introducing a new operator, several entries into system tables must be made and code must be made available for the various implementations of the operator.

POSTGRES supports active databases via triggers, alerters and inferencing, and provides user extensibility via new functions, data types, operators, aggregates and access methods, which may be written in high-level languages, and then introduced into the system. Inheritance, recursion, historical data and version control are also supported. Crash recovery is simplified by not overwriting data but 'vacuuming' out-of-date tuples to an archive store.

While POSTGRES provides limited extensibility, EXODUS is pursuing a more ambitious approach to an extensible database system. The idea is to design an extensible system intended to handle all new application domains. In fact it is not a single DBMS, but a collection of kernel DBMS facilities plus software tools to allow an implementor to generate high-performance, application-specific DBMSs for new applications in a semi-automatic way. EXODUS includes two components that require little or no change from application to application: one is the storage object manager, a flexible storage manager that provides concurrent and recoverable access to storage objects of arbitrary size; the other is the dependency manager, a class-based schema-management subsystem whose repertoire of base-types can be extended by the DBI and through which the mapping from logical level to physical level can be implemented. In addition, EXODUS provides libraries of database system components that are likely to be widely applicable, including components for access methods, version management and simple operations. It is based on a philosophy of module decoupling. The corresponding system layers are constructed by the DBI through a combination of borrowing components from the libraries and writing new components. To simplify the writing of new components, the E database implementation language is provided largely to shield the DBI from the details of internal object formats, buffer management, concurrency control and recovery protocols. Access methods and operators are schema-independent. At run time the schema information can be obtained from the dependency manager. EXODUS also provides a number of transaction-management protocol stubs and buffer management hints for the DBI to select. At the upper level of the system, EXODUS provides a generator that produces a query optimizer and compiler for algebraic languages from a description of the available operations, methods and their cost formulas, and a collection of transformation rules. To make use of the generator, all application-specific data languages must be transferred by their parsers into a unique target language – the set-algebraic tree, with the content of the nodes being dynamic. Tools for generating application-specific front-end software are also planned.

3.2. The DBI Role in these Systems

EXODUS and POSTGRES offer interesting contrasts in the role of the DBI. Although POSTGRES is already a complete DBMS which a DBI may enhance, whereas the DBI must actually build the DBMS using EXODUS, it is still valuable to compare the specific DBI tasks both to see the relative extent of them and to see how each component of the DBI's task is affected by the differing philosophies behind the systems.

Although the role of a DBI is not discussed explicitly in the POSTGRES literature [14, 16, 17], there is considerable comment on what users and other parties may do with that system to achieve extensibility. We shall use 'DBI' when referring to users or other parties in this context.

Since POSTGRES imposes a framework for the data model, the DBMS starts with many built-in data types and operators. The DBI may augment these. In terms of the data model, a DBI may implement new data types beyond the usually fixed-length, simple types of the relational model, and these can be used as types for columns of any relation in the database. The DBI may create a new atomic data type by using the abstract data type, or ADT, facility to specify a type name, the length of the internal representation, procedures for converting the external representation to internal and vice versa. Optionally, the DBI may specify a default value, procedures to handle conversion of data between formats of different machines, and whether the data type should be passed by value to operators and functions. An operator may be included by writing a procedure to evaluate the operation. This may be a complex task and is discussed in [18]. New comparison operators make new indexes possible. Inheritance may be specified with an inherits-clause. New structured data types are also available to the DBI through the specification of arrays which may be of variable length, the writing of a sequence of POSTQUEL commands which results in the data types returned by each of the retrieval commands in the sequence, and data types returned by procedures written in conventional programming languages. The registration of such procedures is dealt with in [15].

In POSTGRES the DBI may also provide new access methods. This may involve writing a collection of procedures that correspond to a POSTGRES-defined access method interface. Every new method must be registered so that it can be implemented and queries optimized. To facilitate optimization, the DBI must provide selectivity factors which estimate the expected number of records satisfying certain conditions and must indicate whether certain join methods are feasible. According to [18], this is a very complex task, only to be undertaken by an expert.

Because of the relational framework there is no opportunity for the DBI to eliminate relations or relational operators from the data model, nor to add new relational operators if such would be desired. One gets all the overhead of the relational model whether or not it is needed.

In the references cited, no suggestion is made of developing a library of procedures for future reuse by DBIs.

Those who perform the traditional ANSI/SPARC roles of EA, DBA, or AA, need to be able to interpret what the DBI has written in POSTQUEL and be furnished appropriate documentation by the DBI.

In sharp contrast to POSTGRES, EXODUS does not provide a complete DBMS ready for DBI enhancement [6, 7, 12]. Instead, EXODUS introduces the idea of a software engineering environment which supports a DBI so that a complete DBMS may be built as quickly as possible. Once the customised DBMS is completed, the role of the DBI ends.

EXODUS offers no data model nor does it place any constraints on what might be developed. The DBI may use EXODUS tools to generate components which support the DDL and DML of the model. Some data types and operators are provided by EXODUS. If others are defined by the DBI, these definitions are compiled along with the furnished dependency-manager source code to produce the dependency manager itself. The DBI must code one or more methods for each new operator. Hence, the semantics of new data types and operators is entirely embedded within the DBI's code.

At the low end of the system, EXODUS provides a storage object manager as noted above. This manager provides a procedural interface, so that calls to it may be issued in the E language code. Also, the DBI is allowed to issue hints which influence options used by the storage object manager.

In the EXODUS architecture, the operator methods and the access methods sit above the storage object manager. As with new operator methods, the DBI must use the E language to write code for any new access methods. However, the DBI may also use an existing access method for a new data type if that type has the appropriate properties. For example, B-trees might be used for a new data type on which an ordering had been defined.

Query optimization is central to the EXODUS architecture. The query optimizer and compiler component are generated using EXODUS tools. 'To produce an optimizer for an application-specific database system, the

DBI must supply a description of the target query language, a list of the methods that can be used to implement each operator, a cost formula for each operator, and a collection of transformation rules.' [6]

This list of tasks for the DBI in building an EXODUS system shows that the role is a larger and more complex one than is the equivalent role in POSTGRES, particularly in the performance aspects of the DBMS. Furthermore, much of it is done at the programming language level. This means that an EA or a DBA trying to interpret what new data types, operators, or access methods were available would either have to be proficient in reading E code, or be dependent on supporting documentation by the DBI.

Unlike POSTGRES, EXODUS does explicitly suggest that a DBI's library would allow the reuse of coded components in future DBMSs.

For none of the current proposals is there a clear development of the role which builds a DBMS for a particular application domain. The order in which the DBI's tasks must be done is not clear, nor is it obvious what dependencies may exist between these tasks.

3.3. Some Specific Comparisons

In [17] Stonebraker postulates that 'a complete extended type system should allow:

1) the definition of user-defined data types
2) the definition of new operators for these data types
3) the implementation of new access methods for data types
4) optimized query processing for commands containing new data types and operators'

To facilitate these aspects an extensible database system must provide the DBI with tools and guidelines for the introduction of each of these into a DBMS. We look at each in turn.

3.3.1. USER-DEFINED TYPES AND OPERATIONS

As EXODUS is designed to support multiple models, its type manager must be model-independent. In fact it caters for generalized class hierarchies with multiple inheritance. It has built-in provision in its kernel for the standard base types of integer, real, char and object identifier. It also has a provision for the record, array, set and bag type constructors. A system can be customized by adding new base types and operations, using the programming language E. This uses the abstract data type concepts of C++. There is also the possibility of adding new constructor types and their operations, though the implication here is that the task would be more complex – necessitating the addition of information concerning query optimization.

It is envisaged that the type manager for each derived DBMS will be fixed, generated from the kernel definitions and the DBI's ADT definition. There is therefore no dynamic binding. This separates the DBI capability from that of other users. In POSTGRES, however, any user can dynamically create new base types, the definition facility provided being similar in scope to that of EXODUS. The problem noted about the dynamic aspect of the definitions is that of security: adding operation implementation code can compromise the database as the compiled code will be dynamically linked in with the rest of the DBMS and there would be the possibility of corruption. Such code could be made safe, but at a cost to efficiency.

Being an extended relational system, the situation with respect to constructors in POSTGRES is rather different. In fact the constructors available are fixed but very flexible. Arrays (both fixed and variable length) are provided, but otherwise the relation is the only EXODUS-style constructor. However, by the provision of procedures as data types POSTGRES effectively gives a further powerful constructor option. Any POSTQUEL query can be stored as the value of a procedure attribute.

3.3.2. NEW ACCESS METHODS

Providing access methods is recognized as a difficult task in both POSTGRES and EXODUS, particularly when no specific restraint is placed on them. In [6] Stonebraker is quoted as stating that 70% of the code involved in introducing a new access method concerns issues other than the access method algorithm itself. This other code provides mappings to the storage structure and controls interactions with the buffer manager, concurrency control and recovery manager. In acknowledging the complexity of this task, the POSTGRES approach is not to give a unified DBI interface for the overall task, nor to simplify it specifically through the architecture of the system. This philosophy is largely coloured by the expectation that the task will be undertaken very infrequently, and then by experts.

EXODUS, through its E language, attempts to reduce the task to writing the specific 30% concerned with the actual access method algorithm and then providing 'a few declarative "hints"' [6] to the translator. E therefore gives a simplified abstraction of the lower levels of the EXODUS DBMS. Whether such an approach can give performance approaching that of 'hand coding' is an open question, but it is reasonable to suppose that it is, at least in essence, the only realistic way of catering for access method introduction by any other than an expert DBMS engineer, and is also likely to be the more resilient approach should changes be made to any of the lower levels.

3.3.3. OPTIMIZING QUERY PROCESSING

The EXODUS query optimizer is generated when a full DBMS is specified. The generator accepts rule-based input which defines the set of operators for the model, the set of access methods available, transformation rules for query trees and implementation rules, which map operators to access methods. The first type of rule captures the rewrite rules expressing the algebraic properties of the operators, and is therefore similar in style to axioms in an algebraic specification system.

For both types of rule the query optimizer will first match a rule, to check whether it matches a condition found in the query tree, and then will check any condition which may be attached to the rule. These conditions are of arbitrary complexity, and must be written in c (the implementation language for the rule system). Arguments to rules can also be modified by DBI-provided procedures indicated in the rule (for example a sort routine may be available for an argument in an implementation rule).

Hill-climbing AI techniques are used in the query optimizer, and the overall system has been demonstrated to be very effective in producing good query evaluation strategies [7]. By contrast POSTGRES, as has been noted, adopts a fixed, table-driven optimizer and therefore does not need an optimizer generator. When new operators are defined there are several parameters to be specified which together form the information to be used by the query optimizer. The first of these refers to an operation's associativity and commutativity, and whether a negator is available. This information allows for transformation of the query tree. Efficient implementation is effected by the various parameters which influence the applicability of the various join methods provided by POSTGRES. The lack of provision for new operations on constructors obviously simplifies things considerably, and there is not seen to be a need for more complex rules of either kind.

The simplified procedure for registering operators obviously has benefits with respect to the DBI's task, but whether its inflexibility could be a problem in some application domains is an open question. Certainly the query transformation process is a key element in efficient DBMSs, so the EXODUS approach may well have advantages in some domains.

3.4. Summary

In POSTGRES, except for functions, data types, operators, aggregates and access methods, all aspects and the framework are basically fixed with their semantics known. Thus, POSTGRES is based on a conventional relational DBMS, following a very practical approach. Due to the known structure and semantics, the designers of POSTGRES are able to build it in a delicate and efficient way. In particular, the components of the system can be interrelated in a complex way, e.g. the alerters and triggers can be implemented by extension of a locking system which is also dependent on the tuple storage structure for keeping locking information. On the other hand, its extensibility is limited. It cannot directly support data models other than relational. Although it should be possible to determine equivalence relationships and equivalence-preserving mappings between data models, performance and simplicity may suffer. It is felt that allowing users to define an alternative storage manager for POSTGRES is a task far too complex to attempt, so it is anticipated that some users may create new storage managers external to the system. Some hooks may be provided in POSTGRES to facilitate this.

A non-trivial loader is provided to load DBI-defined routines (access methods, aggregate functions etc.) into the DBMS address space. A difficulty with these routines is that they may easily crash the DBMS by overwriting the DBMS data structure accidentally. With regard to adding a new access method, the DBI has to cope with the interface to buffer management, transaction management and storage structure. This may prove to be a very difficult task. The design of a simple interface to these services is still an open research question. Finally, because POSTGRES is a comprehensive system, its demand for computer resources may be high, so it may not be practical for small systems or those requiring very high performance. This concern is mooted in [18] where direct use of access methods for low overhead is suggested, bypassing layers of the database management system and going directly to the low-level routines.

Supporting multi-data models, the approach of EXODUS appears promising in achieving high extensibility and very efficient target systems. But on the other hand, there remains a problem of how to organize the kernel facilities, generators, tools and libraries in a consistent way and to provide DBIs with a clear conceptual interface. The DBI's task seems quite heavy. The DBMSs generated may differ from each other in various aspects such as data models, data languages and so on. However, for any one of these DBMSs, its data type modelling ability relies on the dependency manager. In EXODUS the dependency manager is fixed. The reasons for this might have been: (1) it is generic enough to meet most modelling requirements, (2) the mapping problem is greatly simplified by fixing the dependency manager. In fact, both the dependency manager and the storage manager of EXODUS are core components. This makes the mapping problem reduce to a conventional one. In the E database implementation language a persistent variable has one-to-one correspondence with a storage object. The EXODUS storage manager can be considered as the target machine of

E. E also functions as a unique communication interface among the dependency manager, access methods and operators. The optimizer generator is rule-based and produces an optimizer based on algebraic transformation. The transformation is designed to map a query tree generated by the user-interface routines into an equivalent tree which represents a better query evaluation plan. Further, the abstract operations in the initial tree will have been replaced by specific access methods. The rule-based nature of the query optimizer allows greater flexibility than a fixed, table-driven system. The optimizer can be more closely tuned to the particular operators and methods available in the system, and the rule set can also be augmented to reflect complex transformations which may short-cut some existing strategies. The query optimizer is a central part of the DBMS and it has been found that efficiency here is very important. Early experiments with Prolog as the implementation language for the rule base were unsuccessful [7].

The multi-model approach increases complexity because of the need to maintain data model independence wherever possible. It may prove to be very difficult to develop data-model-independent techniques to interface programs to application-specific database systems, as is noted in [6]. Furthermore, the dependency manager in EXODUS can actually manage only part of a schema, because the other part, including constraint requirements and relationships between data objects, may be data model dependent. Thus, some other mechanism may be needed in co-operation with the dependency manager to cope with this difficulty.

4. THE DBI ENVIRONMENT

The tasks to be performed by a database implementor are, as is now apparent, many and varied. Some are of a relatively simple nature: comparable with the definition of new types in Ada, for example. Others, normally those expected to be performed rather less frequently, are to be contemplated only by experts in database systems design. We have found it useful to consider the total environment in which a database implementor might work, in order to consider the whole breadth of tasks for which this role is responsible. This includes the tasks of database creation, communication with the DBA and EA, documentation and maintenance. In this section we describe aspects of this environment and relate it to the standard ANSI/SPARC model of database architecture.

4.1. Overview

The environment in which a DBI will work will vary according to the particular extensibility characteristics of the system to be used; in particular whether the tool to be used is a DBMS generator (multi-model extensibility) or a full DBMS with enhancements catered for by table-driven, generic components (single-model extensibility). However, the characteristics of given environments will only differ in the degree of flexibility permitted by the system being used in each case, not in any fundamental way. Hence it is meaningful to postulate a general model of the DBI environment. We believe it is useful to do this for two reasons. Firstly, it would help in specifying a clear role for the DBI and how other roles interact and are delimited. Secondly, it would give some structure to the environment, making it possible to compare proposals with respect to the DBI role. After all, claims are made that a DBMS should be configurable for a specific domain within weeks [3] or at most months [5]. It is impossible to assess such claims without a unifying framework for discussion. Further, such a framework would also allow an analysis of why certain limitations on flexibility are common to all proposals, and how the maintenance function might be made manageable. Within maintenance we include the function of providing new access methods and enriched semantics for a system which is already in use.

Figure 2 enhances an ANSI/SPARC three-schema framework to incorporate extensibility. There are two major environments represented in addition to the application environment: the Research and Development environment, where new access methods, data models, buffer management schemes etc. are produced and characterized; and the Software Engineering, or Database, environment, where reusable components are stored in a library and made available for configuring a DBMS. Crossing the divide involves the development of implementations of techniques from the R&D domain with interfaces which adhere to the standards defined for the extensible system. This will be an ongoing activity.

Once in the SE domain, tools and components can be utilized in the development of: a DBMS data model, which will be used for logical schema specification; a DBMS implementation model, which will provide implementation options to the DBA for database tuning; and a runtime environment, which will incorporate buffer management schemes and a query optimizer amongst other facilities. The data model and implementation model must have a human-readable form, as they will be used by the EA and DBA respectively.

The DBI role is significantly simplified in a single-model system. For example, in POSTGRES the DBMS data model is specified, meaning that language parsers and the type manager are part of the core system and so do not need DBI involvement. Similarly, most of the runtime environment is fixed: the query optimizer is table-driven and the storage model is fixed.

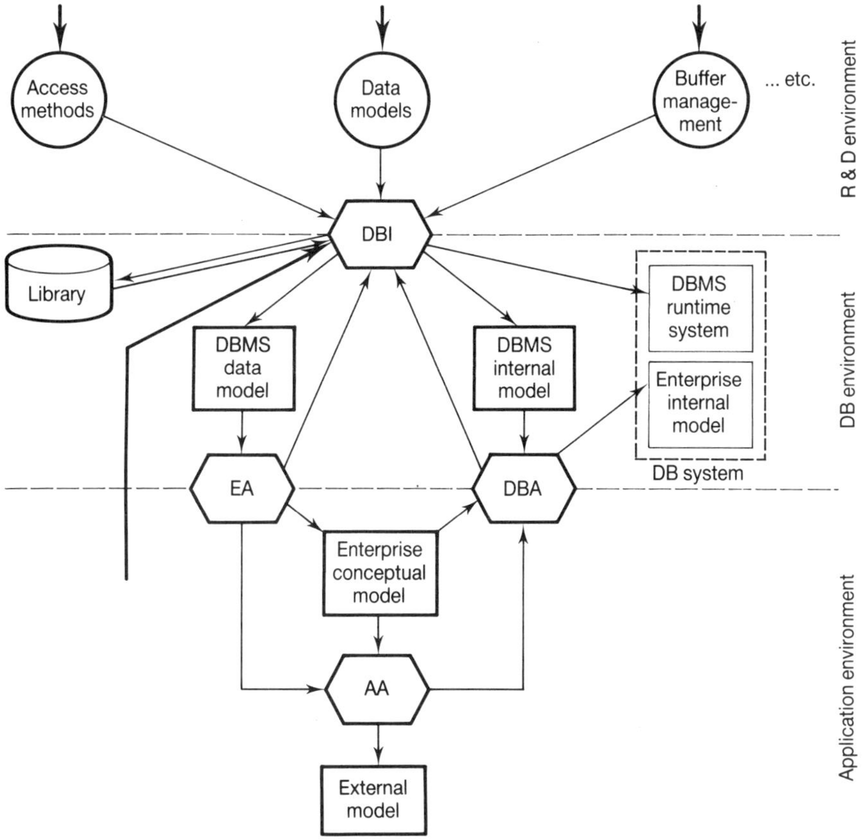

Figure 2 The Context of the DBI

The price to pay is the inflexibility inherent in table-driven systems. For example, EXODUS allows for a rule-base to be used for query optimization, but POSTGRES insists on a fixed algorithm with only operator priorities variable.

4.2. Operational Aspects

One major problem with respect to extensible systems is the maintenance of database systems thus generated. It is of little use to define a system by the code which comprises it, so high-level descriptions of a system, which can act as system documentation, must be generated. With a fixed DBMS the cost-overhead can be spread over the many copies to be used. For a domain-specific DBMS, particularly one developed using a multi-model

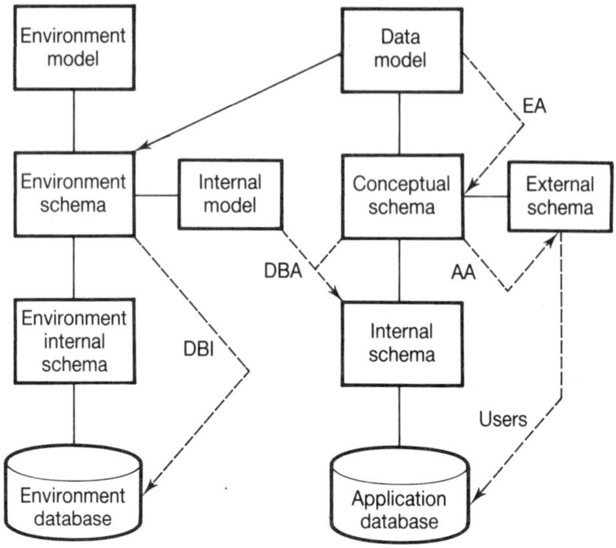

Figure 3 Database Support for the DBI role

tool, this is potentially a major problem. There is an obvious need for a sophisticated CASE tool to manage what will effectively be a meta-dictionary for each system. An example architecture, which is effectively an active database system, is shown in Figure 3. It is beyond the scope of this paper to develop the CASE architecture, but certain characteristics can be indicated.

When a DBI wishes to utilize a new data structure (for example R+ trees) he must first register it by defining it in the environment database (the meta-dictionary part) and installing supporting code, with a standard interface, in the library part. Query optimization issues will have to be addressed, and performance profiles defined. An active system could ensure that all of these tasks are performed before the DBA can access the new structure. Once properly inserted into the environment database, the DBA is at liberty to use the R+ tree to support operations on an existing object type. This will be done by modifying the entry for that type in the internal schema and activating it. This will be no different from tuning a current relational system by deciding to index on a previously unindexed attribute.

Because of the problems which would be generated, storage structures and lock managers may be fixed for all DBMSs generated. This may lead to users going outside the system for supporting unusual applications efficiently. For example, a new storage structure manager could be created outside a POSTGRES database system in order to utilize a specialized storage structure. Crash recovery and lock management must now be handled separately by the DBI. Forcing such complex aspects outside particular systems is the price to pay for simplicity in the general case, but this price may be high in terms of development and maintenance.

4.3. The Position of the DBI

It would be useful if those producing extensible systems were to clarify reasonable expectations of the technology: is it for customizing within an enterprise, or primarily for the production of a variety of 'off the shelf' packages? A further goal may be the efficient production of a portable DBMS, for restricted domains. Another aspect is that there appears to be no fixed idea in the literature of where the database implementor is to be situated with respect to an enterprise which has a special database need. Two obvious possibilities are outlined below.

It is possible that the role envisaged would best suit a specialist software house, which would then configure systems either for 'off the shelf' or customized sale. Systems once developed would be firm, and changes or enhancements fairly costly but by no means out of the question. In this scenario the development time is not very critical, but a significant improvement over current DBMS development would be expected. Complex database issues could reasonably be expected to fall within the expertise of the software house, so the construction of complex query optimizers and interfacing to transaction management modules would not be considered unreasonable. All in all the great flexibility offered by tool-kit systems would seem appropriate here.

Alternatively, if the DBI is at the enterprise level it would be expected that development time would be shorter and the costs significantly less. Maintenance would have to be very manageable, so some flexibility could be sacrificed to this aim. Certainly POSTGRES would appear to be suitable as a development vehicle at this level. It is unlikely that new access methods could be successfully added, but tasks relating to novel data types and their interfacing to current access methods should prove acceptable.

One final point can be made about the DBI role, and that is that it in effect comprises three roles in its full generality. The first is a software engineering role, where a database system is to be configured from pre-existing modules in the standard library for an extensible system. This may be achieved either by option selection or by binding built-in hooks to library modules. The second role is that of librarian, not only looking after the library catalogue but constructing new entries as methods from the R&D environment are tailored to the requirements of the particular extensible system. The third role is the most complex, namely the tailoring of implementations of access methods, buffer management schemes etc. to allow entry into the library catalogue. As an extensible system develops, the first role will dominate: the library will become relatively stable as good new techniques are not developed frequently. This scenario leads to the (possibly optimistic) claims of the GENESIS group with respect to database system configuration times.

5. CONCLUSIONS

There is ample evidence that current relational database management systems are unable to support efficiently and effectively the growing demands being made for database support in non-traditional application areas. It is equally clear that extensibility of some degree is necessary in order to cater for these new requirements. What is unclear is whether any particular approach to extensibility will emerge as dominant in the future. In fact, we have tried to look at developments in the extensibility area as points on a spectrum of flexibility, the ultimate perhaps being the software bus concept of completely decoupled modules with a library of alternatives ready for selection based on criteria determined by the application domains. It seems that, whatever the eventual architecture, there will be a need both for full-function, single-model systems and multi-model systems, the latter for very specialized areas or those with strict efficiency requirements. There seems no reason why such systems should not share a common architecture.

The role of the DBI has emerged from research into extensible systems. We have attempted to clarify this role and to examine, from the standpoint of the DBI, the various styles of extensible systems proposed. This has led to an identification of some of the major complexities within these systems; to a further refinement of the role of DBI by identifying the scope and complexity of certain duties; and to the development of a framework which extends the ANSI/SPARC architecture to include the DBI alongside the Enterprise and Database Administrators.

There are a number of complexities with respect to extensibility. The design of simple interfaces to some system components is still an open question, and the complete decoupling of modules may not be feasible. Further, the introduction of DBI code can result in database crashes, unless all such code can be isolated to run as a process in a separate address space. This means that the DBI role may well be the limiting factor in the utilization of extensible systems, with the dependence between tasks a major aspect.

The definition and maintenance of extensible database management systems is a major software engineering task. A powerful supporting CASE environment will be required if the goal of a flexible and easily configurable application-oriented database system is to be achieved. We conclude that it is an important task to develop a common architecture for extensible systems, to refine further the duties of the DBI in a way which makes the role as clear as that of EA and DBA, and to construct a general CASE environment suitable for supporting this role.

REFERENCES

1. D. S. Batory, 'GENESIS: A Project to Develop an Extensible Database System', in *Proc. International Workshop on Object-Oriented Database Systems*, Sept. 1986.
2. D. S. Batory, 'Principles of database management system extensibility', *Database Engineering*, vol. 10, pp. 32–46, June, 1987.
3. D. S. Batory, J. R. Barnett, J. F. Garza, and K. P. Smith, 'GENESIS: An extensible database management system', *IEEE TOSE*, vol. 14, pp. 1711–1729, Nov. 1988.
4. D. S. Batory, T. Y. Leung, and T. E. Wise, 'Implementation concepts for an extensible data model and data language', *ACM TODB*, vol. 13, pp. 232–262, September 1988.
5. M. J. Carey and D. J. Dewitt, 'Extensible Database Systems', in *On Knowledge Base Management Systems – Integrating AI and DB Technologies*, ed. J. Myopoulos, pp. 315–330 , Springer-Verlag, New York, 1986.
6. M. J. Carey, D. J DeWitt, *et al.*, 'The Architecture of EXODUS Extensible DBMS', in *Proc. Int. Workshop on O-O Database Syst.*, pp. 52–65, Sept. 1986.
7. G. Graefe and D. J. DeWitt, 'The EXODUS optimizer generator', in *Proc. ACM SIGMOD 1987 Annual Conf.*, ed. I. Traiger, pp. 160–172, 1987.
8. A. Guttman, 'R-Tree: A Dynamic Index Structure for Spatial Searching', in *Proceedings of the 1984 ACM SIGMOD Conference*, Boston, Ma., 1984.
9. R. Lorie, 'Complex objects and their use in Design Transactions', in *Proc. Engineering Design Application Stream of ACM-IEEE Database Week*, San Jose, CA., May 1983.
10. Laguna Beach Participants, 'Future Directions in DBMS Research', *SIGMOD RECORD*, vol. 18, no. 1, Mar. 1989.
11. H.-B. Paul, H.-J. Schek, M. H. Scholl, G. Weikum, and U. Deppisch, 'Architecture and Implementation of the Darmstadt Database Kernel System', in *Proceedings for ACM SIGMOD 1987 Annual Conference*, pp. 196–207, 1987.

12. J. E. Richardson and M. J. Carey, 'Programming Constructs for Database System Implementation in EXODUS', in *Proc. ACM SIGMOD 1987 Annual Conf.*, ed. I. Traiger, pp. 208–219, 1987.
13. J. Robinson, 'The K-D-B Tree: A Search Structure for Large Multidimensional Indexes', in *Proc. ACM-SIGMOD Conf. on the Management of Data*, Ann Arbor, Mich., May 1981.
14. L. A. Rowe and M. R. Stonebraker, 'The POSTGRES Data Model', in *Proceedings of the 13th VLDB Conference*, Morgan Kaufman, Brighton, 1987.
15. M. Stonebraker, 'Object Management in POSTGRES Using Procedures', in *Proc. Int. Wkshp on Object-Oriented Database Systems*, pp. 66–72, Asilomar, CA, Sep., 1986.
16. M. Stonebraker and L.A. Rowe, 'The Design of POSTGRES', in *Proc. 1986 ACM-SIGMOD Conference on Management of Data*, pp. 340–355, Washington, D.C., May, 1986.
17. M. Stonebraker, 'Inclusion of New Types in Relational Data Base Systems', in *Proc. Second International Conference on Data Base Engineering*, pp. 480–487, Feb. 1986.
18. M. Stonebraker, J. Anton, and M. Hirohama, 'Extendability in POSTGRES', *Database Engineering*, vol. 10, pp. 16–23, June, 1987.
19. M. Stonebraker, 'Extendibility', in *Readings in Database Systems*, pp. 477–479, Morgan Kaufman, 1988.
20. D. C. Tsichritzis and A. Klug, 'Report on the Study Group on Database Management Systems', *Information Systems*, vol. 3, pp. 173–191, 1978.
21. D. C. Tsichritzis and F. H. Lochovsky, in *Data Models*, Prentice-Hall, Englewood Cliffs, 1982.
22. D. Shipman, 'The Functional Data Model and the Data Language DAPLEX', *ACM TODS*, vol. 6, pp. 140–173, 1981.

3
Combining Functional and Logic Programming in Expert Database Systems

P. M. D. GRAY

Computing Science Department, University of Aberdeen, Aberdeen AB9 1FX

INTRODUCTION

Expert systems with moderately large numbers of rules, can be compiled in LISP or Prolog and held in memory. Also, the comparatively small numbers of facts can just be represented as lists in memory. However, these techniques no longer suffice once people start to tackle problems with much larger collections of data. The first attempts (Jarke & Vassiliou 1984) just tried a simple coupling to an existing relational database by passing the string representation of an SQL query in one direction and retrieving a set of answers in the other. It was simple to implement, but people are now finding the limitations of relational databases, in particular the awkwardness of the standard relational query language SQL (which is not a full programming language), and the lack of data-modelling constructs in a relational schema compared with a frame-based schema. This chapter argues that what is needed instead is a system that can describe networks of objects and store and manipulate them in a database, together with a high-level navigational query language to replace SQL. We shall be looking for a suitable combination of logic and functional programming languages to achieve this.

We start by examining the *Functional Data Model* (FDM) of Shipman (1979), together with the associated Daplex programming language. Shipman's system is based on fundamental ideas of modelling entities and relationships developed by Chen (1976) which are now widely used in Systems Analysis. It also combines these very elegantly with computation

Expert Database Systems
ISBN 0-12-382255-6

expressed as evaluation of expressions involving functions and sets. Ultimately, it is based on Zermelo–Fraenkel set expressions. However, the basic variables are not sets, as in Codd's relational algebra, but objects representing entities and attribute values. Thus we are concerned with the application of functions to stored values, held in list structures. We should note that when these structures get very large they have to be held on disc and efficiently indexed as described by Atkinson *et al.* (1984). However, that is not the subject of this chapter, which is concerned with the schema for such structures, and with a style of querying which owes much to functional programming.

Database query languages are based either on the predicate calculus or on the lambda calculus, the two classic models of computation. Poulovassilis (1988) has developed an elegant functional data language, FDL, which is based entirely on functional programming and list abstraction, but otherwise looks similar to FDM. We shall explore instead a role for *Logic Programming* in the implementation of a functional data model. The advantages are in the use of high-level interpreters written in Prolog which can search for sets of objects, subject to constraints. This suits expert systems work better than the functional programming paradigm, as it is more closely related to the use of backward-chaining frame-based systems, as found in AI tools.

Another approach (Zaniolo 1986, Tsur & Zaniolo 1986) has been to build the new logic language LDL which handles complex term structures involving function symbols as though they were proper data structures, and is able to unify over sets. However, their work is aimed mainly at bulk database queries. Thus it translates from Prolog into the set-based operations of an extended relational algebra. Although this is a good approach for some problems, we shall argue that a navigational approach is more suitable for expert systems, so that the system can take control of the search. The architecture which we shall explore provides this.

Finally, we shall consider how to extend the FDM, so that it has many of the features of an *Object-Oriented Database* (Dittrich 1988, Bancilhon 1988). This type of database breaks away from the relational model and takes seriously the handling of complex data structures and lists, with procedures being stored in the database instead of in monolithic user application programs. However, the programming languages used with such databases tend to be based on C++, using the usual iteration and assignment constructs, instead of on the declarative style of logic or functional programming. Nevertheless, their use of *Abstract Data Types* to encapsulate knowledge and cluster information with an object is important. This coincides with a similar move in AI towards frames as data structures clustering a variety of information about an object, together with selected rules to use for various operations, in place of the large uniform 'flat' rule-bases of MYCIN and R1. It parallels the move away from 'flat files' of tuples in relational databases and towards structured object databases.

In this chapter we shall attempt to show that a synthesis of these ideas (Functional Data Model, Logic Programming and Object-Oriented Database) is possible and that it provides exciting new possibilities for Expert Database Systems.

MODELLING ENTITIES AND RELATIONSHIPS IN FDM

The Functional Data Model (Shipman 1979) developed from the Entity-Relational Model of Chen (1976). At about the same time a number of so-called Semantic Data Models (Hammer & MacLeod 1978) were proposed. These arose from dissatisfaction with the relational data model of Codd (1970), which presented data simply as tables or 'flat files'. Any notion of hierarchy was concealed by the uniform tabular format. Smith and Smith (1977) pointed out that this was misleading and that there were important implied relationships between the tables making up a relational database, by virtue of references to the same data items.

The FDM emphasises the notion of *relationships*, not just between data items, but between the underlying *entities* concerned. Thus, instead of a relationship between a name 'F Smith' and a company name 'IBM' appearing side by side in the same table, the FDM sees a relationship between an entity *Fred* of type Person whose name is 'F Smith', and the company he works for, which is another entity, but of type 'Corporation' and whose company name is 'IBM' (see Figure 1). This is not splitting hairs! The introduction of entities has important consequences.

The first effect of introducing entities is to provide an object about which one can cluster information. For example, Fred may take part in several different relationships. In a relational database such information is scattered over different tables. In an FDM database it is logically collected together with an object, which has a unique internal *object identifier* (*OID*) by which it is known to the database system. This identifier corresponds to a 'surrogate' number as used in some relational systems (Codd 1979). It is assigned when the entity is created or first introduced, and cannot be changed. It is similar to the ideas of object identity as used in object-oriented programming, which we shall discuss later. It allows us to change the external name by which a person or company is known, whilst keeping all its associated data.

The second effect of introducing entities is that it provides an extended type description. In relational theory a person's name is just a string – an

PNAME	COMPANY
F.Smith	IBM
A.N.Other	IBM
F.Bloggs	CR Smith

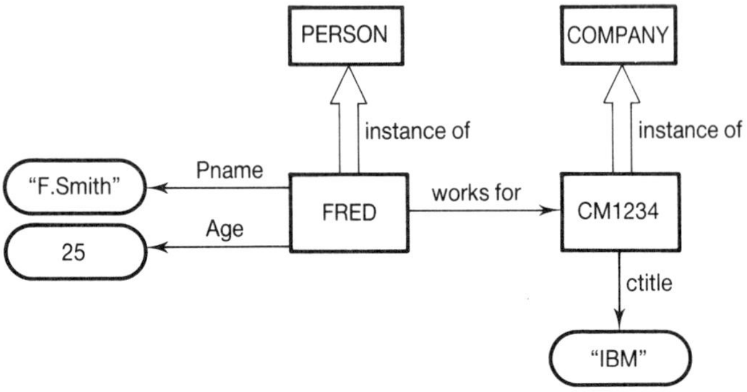

Figure 1

ordered sequence of characters. However, in the FDM a relationship must be between valid entity identifiers of the appropriate type – in this case one of type person and one of type corporation. A person 'C R Smith' could have the same name as a company, but there would still be no confusion, since we know the underlying entity type.

Objects and Attributes

There is an interesting connection between FDM and early systems used in AI, for example, SAIL (Feldman & Rovner 1969). This was based on the fundamental storage unit of an *object-attribute-value* triple (the same idea that is present in hardware triple stores). Data on attributes are usually of scalar or atomic type, for example:

Fred-age-25, Fred-sex-'male', Fred-born-(11,2,40)

These represent different attributes of Fred, and all have printable values, even though one is compound (the date of birth). However, the *value* can also be an object identifier, in which case the *attribute* generalises to a *relationship*, and thus we have an *object-relationship-object* triple. For example:

Fred-likes-julie, Fred-sonof-harry, Fred-worksfor-ibm.

SAIL allowed one to build up a network of interrelated data connected by such relationships; it was an early form of semantic net, but without the inheritance of class descriptions. It was based on a notion of objects (or entities) and their relationships.

Functional Syntax

The Functional Data Model also allows one to store attributes and relationships of objects. The big difference is that it provides a uniform syntax and type description for working with derived or computed data as well as with stored data. In order to do this it represents both attributes and relationships as kinds of *functions on* entity objects.

We can easily see how to view attributes as functions. It is easy to read 'age of Fred' as 'age(Fred)' and to treat the resulting value, '25', as the result of applying the 'age' function, instead of extracting a stored value from the record for Fred.

For those who are used to thinking of functions as being restricted to obtaining results by calculation (like sine or square root), we must recall that functions can equally well obtain their results by looking up tables. The main idea behind functions is one of *dependency*. Giving the input parameter determines the output result; it does not matter *how* the result is obtained! Once we have understood this, we can see how function application provides a uniform syntax for denoting the dependent result value. The same syntax can be used whether the result is obtained by table look-up or by calculation.

However, in the case of relationships, the use of a functional syntax does obscure the symmetry. Thus, instead of just saying married(Fred, julie) we have the two alternative statements:

julie = wife(Fred) and Fred = husband(julie)

(This is discussed further when we consider the use of Prolog.) However, it is a small price to pay for the convenience of functional syntax. Furthermore, in practice we usually know one object and wish to find the related one, and thus we know whether we need to use a function on the source entity, or its inverse on the target entity. Thus the use of a functional syntax is quite natural unless we are stating or checking a constraint.

The greatest advantage of functions is in the use of applicative syntax. Thus it is much easier to write

age(Bill) = age(father(mother(Fred))) − 3

than the equivalent relational expression:

age(Bill,N) and mother(Fred,X) and father(X,Y) and age(Y,Z)
and N is Z-3

because the use of functions in expressions saves us naming intermediate results.

Many-Valued Functions

Some relationships are multi-valued, so the corresponding function must deliver multiple results. Since, in mathematical parlance, a function should deliver a single value, we need to treat the entire multiple result as a single set of values, or more conveniently, as a list of values. Consider:

courses(Fred) = {C1, C5, C9a}

which delivers a set containing the identifiers of three entities representing courses taken by Fred.

The names of these courses are of course obtained by applying the appropriate function: for example, cname(C1) gives 'chemistry'. What happens if we apply a function such as cname to the set as a whole? For example:

cname(courses(Fred)) = {'chemistry', 'music', 'physics'}

Thus we get a set (list) of three strings, which is as we should expect. However, what if the function we apply is itself multi-valued? Consider, for example the function *taking* which is the inverse of the function courses, and gives those students who take a given course. Thus if we ask for the students taking the same course as Fred we shall get the *union* of the identifiers of the students taking each of the three courses, e.g.

$$\text{taking(courses(Fred))} = \{\text{Fred}, s3\} \cup \{\text{Fred}\} \cup \{\text{Fred}, s3, s6\} = \{\text{Fred}, s3, s6\}$$

In general, if f and g are multi-valued functions the result is defined as:

$$f(g(X)) = \{\ Y \mid (\exists Z)\ Z \text{ is in } g(X) \text{ and } Y \text{ is in } f(Z)\}$$

This also allows f(Z) to be undefined for some values of Z, in which case it just returns the empty set. However, if f is single-valued, then FDM insists that it return a value for every element to which it is applied in the set g(X); if it is undefined for any such value, then f(g(X)) is also undefined.

This solution is workable, but it means that we have lost some of the simplicity of single-valued functions with unique inverses. It also makes for technical problems, since we now have results of variable length, possibly huge sets containing all the entities in the database!

Schema Declarations

Having introduced the idea of functions let us look at a typical FDM schema in more detail.

The examples below are taken from a schema on university courses. Consider the following extract which introduces the entity types *student* and *course* and the functions on them:

declare person( ) ↠ entity
declare sex(person) → string
declare dob(person) → date

declare student( ) ↠ person
declare matricyear(student) → integer

declare course( ) ↠ entity
declare cname(course) → string

declare courses(student) ↠ course
declare taking(course) ↠ student

The declaration course( ) ↠ entity introduces a new entity type *course.* It also introduces the multi-valued function of the same name (and no arguments) which delivers the set of all instances of this entity type which have been stored in the database. The following declarations introduce functions defined on the entity type. In general, single arrows denote single-valued functions and double-headed arrows denote multi-valued functions. Functions corresponding to *attributes* are defined to have scalar values, for example, cname(course) → string. Functions corresponding to *relationships* are defined to deliver entity identifiers as result, e.g.

courses(student) ↠ course

As seen above, the function *courses* is multi-valued. We can also have a single-valued function representing a relationship, for example, courses may have a unique organiser:

organiser (course) → staff

Subtypes

When we come to look at students and staff we see the declarations:

declare person ( ) ↠ entity
declare student ( ) ↠ person
declare staff ( ) ↠ person

This declares students and staff as specialisations of persons. As before, both student and staff are names of entity types. They can also be used to enumerate the entities which are instances of students and staff respectively. All of these entities will be persons, and therefore all functions applicable to persons are applicable to them. We say that students are *subtypes* of person and they *inherit* the functions defined on persons. However, students have extra functions defined on them, which are not applicable to all persons in general, for example, courses(student) defines the courses being taken. It is possible to refine subtypes further; for example, to refine students into mature students, overseas students and others.

When a new person entity is introduced it will usually be assigned to a given subtype (staff or student). In general this will last for a long time. However, it is possible for a person to be re-assigned to another subtype. Thus FDM has operations to *exclude* an entity from a subtype and to *include* it into another subtype. When this is done, any values of attributes or relationships pertaining only to the former subtype are, of course, removed. However, it will still retain all attributes and relationships pertaining to its membership of the supertype.

There may be extra constraints on subtypes. For example, we may declare subtypes to be *non-overlapping*, in which case one cannot include a member in one subtype before excluding it from the former subtype.

These ideas are also present in the *class* concept from object-oriented systems, which is discussed later.

Keys

Besides giving the functions on a type we may also define a uniqueness constraint, to enable us to identify a particular member. Typically there are some scalar-valued functions on an entity (i.e. attributes) which have a unique inverse. Given the value of such an attribute, one can obtain the internal identifier of the one and only corresponding entity. For example, from the social security number one can identify a person.

Sometimes one needs a concatenation of several attributes to identify an entity. For example, town-name, county-name and country-name may all be needed to identify a location uniquely. Sometimes one needs the identifier of a related entity; a son may be identified by a combination of his name with mother's maiden name (as in Spain).

Thus, in the database schema, a key clause can be given which gives a unique way of identifying an entity from the data. Further, it is possible to create an index which gives a quick way of finding an entity identifier from the key. This is very valuable when loading bulk data, because the key can be used to cross-reference entities already loaded. Furthermore, one should not include internal entity identifiers in external data since it is easy to make mistakes in them. It is also much easier to refer to the person who is son of John and Mary and born in December 1980 than to object #22179983564! In fact, FDM deliberately does not allow one to print internal identifiers of entities. We should note that the use of apparently meaningless identifiers led to the unpopularity of the early Binary Relational Model. It was also a problem for attempts like RM/T (Codd 1979) which included surrogate identifiers in relational databases.

A contentious issue concerns whether an object should have its key values always given at creation time, as argued by Paton and Gray (1988). The advantage is that it guarantees what Date calls *key integrity*. Thus one can ensure that a new entity can never be created which is later found to match an existing one. However, this rule does allow one to have null values for non-key attributes, which can be entered later. Null values occur in real data, but it is best to restrict them to non-key attributes.

We should note that, in the case of subtypes, the key of any subtype is just the same as the key of its highest supertype. This follows because we need to be able to enumerate all instances of the supertype, and each of them must have a different value for the supertype key. Consequently, the extra attribute and relationship information that is provided for subtypes is not needed for purposes of establishing uniqueness.

The key mechanism can also be used to enforce *referential integrity* when loading data. This means that it should not be possible to have a dangling reference. Thus when data is to be stored on a relationship between one entity and another, then it must identify the other entity by its key. Either the entity already exists, and can be found by its key or else, if it does not exist in the database, it can at once be created, since all that is needed is the key information. Finally, if an attempt is made subsequently to delete the other entity then this cannot be done unless the relationship has first been deleted.

Value Entities

A problem of Shipman's original FDM was that everything which was not a simple atomic type had to be an entity. This is inconvenient for things like birth dates or the co-ordinates of points. Such things are best represented as aggregates of atomic or similar values. We have introduced the notion of a *value-entity*, represented internally by a tuple. Such entities have a type, and their components can be found by applying functions. However, it is not usual to enumerate all their instances (and it is expensive to implement); nor do they need a key mechanism, since their components taken together identify them – they stand for themselves. A date is a good example of a value-entity; it can be declared thus:

declare date( ) ->> value-entity
declare year(date) -> integer

declare month(date) —> string
declare day(date) —> integer
{NO key declaration}

Inverses

It is convenient when declaring a function to have the system automatically declare the inverse function, which has the name of the original function with 'inv' appended. It follows that whenever one function is updated, the inverse is updated also. In principle, one could compute the inverse function at run time by generate and test, but in practice it is convenient to store the inverse and update it. This also speeds up checks on deletion.

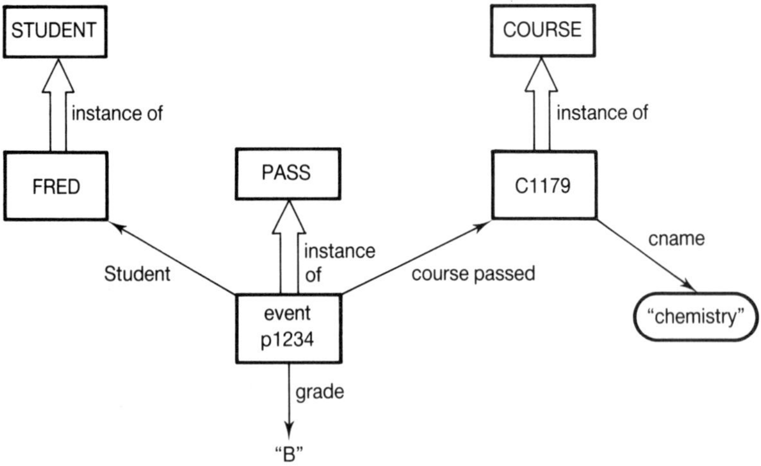

Figure 2

Relationship Entities

Some relationships are so complicated that they themselves have attributes. For example, if a student gets a 'grade' for taking a course, then we cannot attach the grade attribute just to the course or to the student entity alone, since it depends on both. The solution is to declare a new entity type *pass* representing an *event*, in this case the successful graduation or completion of the course with a grade. This entity (Figure 2) then has three functions on it: grade(pass), coursepassed(pass) and student(pass). These functions are all single-valued but they have multi-valued inverses.

The key of such a pass would be declared as

keyof (pass) is keyof (student), keyof (coursepassed)

representing the fact that the grade of pass depends on both student and the course passed.

It should be clear that each instance of the entity pass in some sense represents an instance of a relationship. However, it is confusing to say that ‘a relationship can be an entity’; it is better to say that ‘we treat a relationship with an attached property as an entity’. In general, such ‘relationship entities’ are distinguished from other entities by having very few attributes, and by having the keys of several other entities as part of their key. Instead of just having a relationship represented by a function and its inverse, it is now represented by a composition of functions involving the relationship entity. For example, the courses passed by Fred now become coursepassed(passes(Fred)), where passes(student) is the inverse of student(pass); we could instead write coursepassed(studentinv(Fred)).

Operations on Entities

So far, we have concentrated mainly on the declaration of entity types. Let us now consider the permissible operations on entity types. Interestingly, the FDM treats entity types much like an abstract data type. The properties of the type are implied by the available functions. No information is given on the internal representation of entities. It is in fact possible to store the data as Entity-Attribute-Value triples (remembering that a Value may be a list of entities), but this is not the only way.

All entities have certain generic operations on them.

The first is to *enumerate* all entities of the type:

for each X in student do ...

The second is to *find* an entity from its key value:

for the s in student such that fname(s) = ‘Fred’ and sname(s) = ‘Smith’

The third is to *apply* a function to an entity, thus forming an applicative expression:

print cname(courses(Fred))

The fourth is to *update* a single-valued function:

let matricyear(Fred) := 1989

The fifth is to *add or delete items* from a multi-valued function:

include {the c in course such that cname(c) = 'chemistry'} in courses(Fred)

exclude {cnameinv('math'), cnameinv('french')} from courses(Fred)

The sixth is to *create* another entity of the type:

create a new x in student
with key(x) = 'John', 'Smith'

The last is to *delete* an entity instance:

delete the c in course such that cname(c) = 'Latin'

Note the use of the qualifying phrase *such that* which is followed by a boolean expression with equality and inequality comparisons; this expression may include functions applied to any objects identified by variables currently in scope.

Metadata Operations

The operations just considered work on instances of pre-declared types. In order to introduce new types we must make a declaration of a schema extension, which adds new entity types, or adds new functions to existing entity types, or adds new subtypes as specialisations of existing ones. It is also possible to drop an entity type if all instances have been deleted, and likewise to drop a function type. For example, in P/FDM (Paton and Gray 1988a) one can declare:

```
extend module University
   declare country( ) ->> entity
   declare nationality(person) -> country
   declare overseas( ) ->> student
   declare passportno(overseas) -> integer
end-module
```

These operations are important for real databases, which need to evolve. They pose implementation problems where the implementor, as in early CODASYL network database systems, represents an entity by a record with a fixed number of slots, one for each attribute or relationship. This made it almost impossible for the schema to evolve. Some relational databases had similar restrictions on extending the number of columns of a relation; it could only be done by re-loading the whole database. The fact that this was not necessary was shown by the NDB system (Winterbottom & Sharman 1979), based on binary relations. Extra binary relations could be added at any time to a populated database without affecting performance or requiring re-loading. Since binary relations are just triples of the form (relation-name, object, value), FDM can use similar techniques (allowing for multiple values).

Another valuable feature introduced in NDB, and also in the FDM implementation of Kulkarni and Atkinson (1986) is to have data on the available entity types and functions itself included as part of the database and used in database queries. This is done by having a pseudo-entity named *etypes*, which has one instance for each actual entity type, and which has attributes recording the names and classes of entity types. There is also a pseudo-entity *ftypes* which lists the function names and types of each actual function type. It is then possible to ask questions like:

```
for each f in ftypes such that ename(domain(f)) = 'person'
  print name(f)
```

The data recorded in etypes and ftypes is data *about* other data in the database, i.e. *metadata*. It can only be updated by the database system at the time that entity types are created and deleted. The user is not allowed to update it directly, but it can, of course, be queried as if it were normal data. However, it only delivers the *names* of functions, not the functions themselves. We should note that FDM only allows variables to represent actual entity instances or atomic values, but not functions. Thus the query language is not a higher-order functional language like Miranda.

QUERY LANGUAGE AND NAVIGATION

Queries in the Functional Model can be expressed in a language called Daplex from which we have already seen extracts. A query is expressed in terms of iteration by nested loops. A typical example would have the form:

```
for each E1 in entity1          such that pred1(E1)
  for each E2 in h(E1)          such that pred2(E1, E2)
    for each E3 in entity3          such that pred3(E1, E2, E3)
      print f1(E1), f2(f3(f4(E2))),...
```

One starts by enumerating over an entity type, or by selecting particular instances through the *such that* clause. Here *pred1* is a boolean expression which may involve functions and quantifiers, for example:

```
f1(E1) = 3 and some C in f2(E1) has f3(f4(C)) = 'a'
          or at least 5 K in f4(f2(E1)) have f6(K) > f1(E1)
```

We call this style of query *navigational* since it follows pointers from entity to entity supplied by the FDM functions. We are iterating over sets in a tuple-at-a-time fashion instead of doing bulk operations on sets as in a relational algebra. In consequence it is much easier for the programmer to include calls to extra functions for computation.

The innermost loop can either print the result of an arbitrary combination of functions applied to an entity, or instead do an assignment or update operation. An interesting possibility is that it creates a set of entity instances to hold the results. This set can then be the basis of a follow-on query.

This creation of a set makes the query formally equivalent to a ZF expression as used by Turner (1985) in KRC and Miranda. This is the usual Zermelo–Fraenkel set notation, except that certain elements are used as *generators* for values of variables, by binding them successively to values in another set.

In Turner's notation the preceding Daplex query would be written as:

$$\{r(X,Y) \mid E1 \leftarrow entity1,\ pred1(E1),\ E2 \leftarrow h(E1),\ pred2(E1,E2),\\ E3 \leftarrow entity3,\ pred3(E1,E2,E3),\ X = f1(E1),\ Y = f2(f3(f4(E2)))\}$$

Here the left-arrows can be read as 'is member of' and act as generators. Thus we see that what appears to be a rather Fortran-like loop structure can instead be considered as a declarative notation for a set of results.

Relationship to SQL

The relational model uses query languages that are *set-based*; for example, SQL derives sets of results from sets of data values. It uses the classic operations of set intersection, generalised set intersection (join), set union, set difference, restriction and projection (Gray 1984). The advantage of such a language is that it does not specify the access paths for the sets, and so it can be optimised. In the case of data on disc, the most important optimisations are the use of indexes to speed selections, and the re-ordering and batching of operations so that groups of data that are clustered together on disc are treated together, so as to avoid repeated accesses. Where an expert system is coupled to a relational database via an SQL optimiser we shall call this *set-based coupling* to distinguish it from *navigational coupling* (Gray, Archibald and Lunn 1989), in which the expert system takes much tighter control of the search, and maintains a number of pointers or cursors into the database.

However, the advent of systems with larger memories means that many more data items can be held in store, which then acts as an enormous buffer. This reduces the importance of batched operations and makes it possible for a query language based on navigation, like Daplex, to retrieve data from a large database in times comparable with SQL. Effectively,

Daplex uses its functions for direct access, which is even faster than SQL's use of indexes, and it does not lose much by the absence of bulk operations, like sorting and merging of sets.

At the same time, Daplex can carry out arbitrary computations with defined functions which can be used both inside predicates to select data and also to compute printed results, which is something SQL cannot easily do. We shall expand on this below when we consider storage of procedures in the database.

Another point to remember is that FDM can be used very effectively for personal databases, for use by designers. Such databases do not need the heavy overhead imposed by locking and efficient transaction management.

EXTENSION TO OBJECT-BASED OR FRAME-BASED SYSTEMS

A system based on entities can easily be adapted to a more object-based form of computation, and there are several advantages in so doing. As remarked earlier, the FDM says nothing about how entities should be represented internally. It treats them like an abstract data type (ADT), whose properties are represented entirely by the functions on it.

In case this is unfamiliar to the reader, consider the example of a boolean value. The functions defined on it are (read, write and, or, not). The values TRUE and FALSE may be represented by 1 and 0, or by the characters T and F, or by the bit patterns all-ones and zero, or even (as in LISP) by the atom NIL and anything else! We do not need to know the internal representation, as long as the functions are written to produce the expected results. Some of the bit-pattern representations produce results very efficiently, but they may not be convenient. The main thing is that the user should not *assume* that the represention are zero and one, and thus do his own negation by subtraction from one! The user *must* always use the functions provided on the object, and all other functions must be written in terms of these. In this way we can *hide* the internal representation of an object, which both allows re-structuring for efficiency and protects us from many software bugs.

Exactly the same principles apply to entities. Better still, we can arrange that defined functions are stored with the class descriptor for the entity class, as in an OODB. This means that they are stored in the database, so that they can be shared, instead of being locked up in application code.

Another advantage of treating entities as ADTs is that it widens the variety of data that can be stored. In particular, one can store pictorial and graphic information, and use a function to display it. Such facilities are very necessary for CAD/CAM applications, which are suited to object-oriented databases much better than to relational ones.

Once function definitions are stored in a database it makes sense to store them with a class descriptor object, instead of replicating copies with each instance. In FDM, class descriptor objects are used to contain sub-type information and to maintain the extent of the class via a data structure (tree or table) that records the object identifiers of all instances. Hence defined functions should be stored in the descriptor. Where such a class is a sub-type of another class, it makes sense to inherit the stored function definition from the superclass descriptor instead of repeating it. Thus the classic object-oriented programming structure fits well with an extended FDM.

There is a problem, however, with multi-argument functions. FDM normally deals with functions on a single entity. The original design allowed for functions to have several arguments, provided they were all entities, as an alternative way of storing relationships. For example, one could define a function grade(student,course) which takes two entities and returns a scalar result. The function as implemented would have to search a number of stored facts, looking for the appropriate combination of student and course, and return the associated grade. However, the restriction to entities is unnecessary. In P/FDM (Paton and Gray 1988), which is an object-oriented extension of FDM, we have found it useful to allow arguments to be either entities or scalars. In particular, where one is dealing with an ordered sequence, as in the amino-acid residues forming the chain of a protein molecule, it is useful to have a function absolutepos(chain, N) which returns the entity representing the Nth residue. Such a function is stored with the class descriptor for chains. An obvious extension is to allow functions to have any number of arguments, but to store the definition with the descriptor for the first argument, which must be an entity. The remaining argument(s) provides a list of additional values to be supplied when the function is called.

Where a function needs to return several different types of result, then one must define an entity type to hold such results. The entity type can however be a value-entity, as referred to earlier.

With these extensions we achieve many of the most important features of object-oriented programming, as summarised by Bancilhon (1988).

> First is *encapsulation*, the hiding of internal representation.
> Second is *object identity*, the provision of a reference to a shared structure.
> Third is *inheritance* of function and procedure definitions.
> Fourth is the storage of functions with data, instead of in application code.

Comparison with Frame-Based Systems

We shall now consider the use of frames in AI tools, because they are closely related to objects. Although first introduced to handle problems of natural-language sentence recognition, they have grown into a technique for the organisation and maintenance of systems with very large numbers of rules. Rules are not as independent as people would have you think. Adding an extra rule to an enormous rule base can have results which are almost unpredictable, especially in forward-chaining systems which modify working memory destructively. Thus, in order to ensure that a rule was used in the right context, people started adding extra preconditions which made it become unwieldy, and lost the essential simplicity of the rule-based approach. In consequence, they started to look for ways to cluster rules together and associate them into classes.

Frames are a generalisation of records containing a variable number of named slots, which in turn may contain many different kinds of information. Frames can be used to represent entities and events and, as such, are a form of object. It is usual to cluster frames in classes in order to inherit common facts and properties from the class descriptor and its superclasses. Thus rules now refer to frames, just as if one was passing a whole array or record as a parameter to a procedure. The slots in these frames behave like variable parameters in the rules, which makes the rules both more concise and more expressive. The frames may, in turn, directly reference other rules through 'if-needed' demons or triggers. Thus these systems have moved away from a flat knowledge base of declarative rules towards a network view where rules are clustered around objects, and referenced from them. This increases the complexity and changes the kind of database that is needed.

The early Prolog systems were based on a flat space of clauses, and so they could easily use relations, which are effectively just flat files of tuples. However, frames are not quite like tuples.

(i) Typically an AI knowledge base has a very large number of different types of frame, with only a few instances of each. By contrast, commercial database systems usually have less than a hundred types of relation, with many thousands or millions of instances of each.

(ii) Not all frames which are instances of the same class need to have the same number of slots (attributes)! This runs totally contrary to relational database theory. AI systems that interface to relational databases get round this by allowing one to retrieve tuples from the database into newly created frames with the appropriate fixed number of slots, using an SQL query to select the tuples. However, this does not solve the problem of storing arbitrary types of frame back into the database.

(iii) Frames have complex metadata. In Knowledge Craft big frames have little frames attached to them (like little fleas!). Slots can have many facets attached. They can also have meta-slots containing documentation, or descriptions of restrictions on relationships, or pointers to attached procedures to be triggered. None of this fits with normal form relations.

(iv) Frames can inherit slot values and meta-slots from more than one hierarchy. The standard one is the 'isa' or 'ako' (a kind of) link, but frame languages like CRL (Sathi, Fox and Greenberg 1985) permit one to nominate other relationships with a user-defined transitivity to be used for inheritance links.

The consequence of all this is the general unsuitability of relations for storing AI knowledge, as discovered by Abarbanel and Williams (1986). We shall argue that object storage is very suitable for frames (Campbell & Gray 1988), and that having Prolog as a top-level language provides many of the features required by AI systems.

USING PROLOG TO IMPLEMENT FUNCTIONAL MODELS

Prolog has the ability to store facts and relationships and to search through stored data for suitable instances. Thus it is a very suitable language for implementing database applications. Furthermore, it has the ability to compute data that will satisfy constraints expressed as Prolog procedures. Thus it can be used to represent stored procedures, which can be stored with data in the database, as required for implementing FDM.

At first sight, the main difference between Prolog and Functional views of data is a syntactic one, very like the difference between FDM and the relational model. Thus, the atomic unit in Prolog is a fact or ground unit clause which is asserted to be true (like a relational tuple). Thus 'loves(fred, mary)' is an assertion that fred loves mary, which is either true or false. In other words it is a boolean.

If instead we want to say that fred loves mary's sister, then we have to introduce a quantifier, thus:

(Exists S) sister(S, mary) and loves(fred, S)

Here fred and mary are constants, denoting unique objects in the 'universe of discourse' or world that is being modelled. The letter S is a variable denoting an unnamed object in the same universe which satisfies both relationships. If in Prolog we wish to ask a question about whether such a person (S) exists, then we write, similarly:

?- sister(S, mary), loves(fred, S).

The Prolog system will then search for data to satisfy this. First it looks to see if there are any facts of the form e.g. sister(sue, mary) and it then tests to see if there is a corresponding fact loves(fred, sue). If one is found then it prints 'Yes, S = sue'. If not, it looks for other facts, e.g. sister (helen, mary) and tests these, until it finds a value for S; otherwise it prints 'No' and is said to fail. This is formally equivalent to testing that fred is in the set denoted by the FDM expression:

lover(sister(mary)).

Note that both sister and lover are potentially multi-valued functions, unlike standard mathematical functions. In FDM, the result would be the set of persons who were lovers of sisters of Mary. In Prolog this result can be achieved by using the built-in function 'setof' and representing (Exists S) by S^ :

?- setof(L, S^(sister(S, mary), loves(L, S)), Result), write(Result), nl.

Here the working variable 'Result' contains the list of values of L (it may be empty), which satisfy the constraints. Thus we see that the use of Zermelo–Fraenkel set abstraction provides the link between the logical and functional views of the problem

lover(sister(mary)) = { L | (Exists S) sister(S,mary), loves(L,S)}

If we invert the function then the relational expression is similar, but with variables in different positions:

sister(loved(fred)) = { M | (Exists S) sister(S,M), loves(fred,S)}

The 'setof' expression to evaluate this in Prolog is very similar. Note that S was an *input* argument of 'loves' in the previous case, but it is an *output* in this case. The use of unification for parameter matching in Prolog enables us to write both cases the same way, without knowing until run-time which parameter values will be provided (in fact both could be). By contrast, in FDM, we must provide values for arguments of functions, and we must say whether we wish to use a function or its inverse.

Darlington, Field and Pull (1985) take a novel approach to overcome this problem in the functional programming language HOPE. They allow logic variables to be introduced within the context of a ZF expression and for unification to take place in this context. They argue that this removes one of the main disadvantages of functional languages and that functional languages are already superior to logic languages in the matter of strong type-checking and use of higher-order functions.

Prolog and ADTs

We shall now look at the types of the variables in Prolog facts like 'loves(fred, mary)'. As it stands they are atoms. They could also be strings, as in a relational database. However, there is no reason why they should not be entities represented as abstract data types! If we represent these entities by some kind of unique internal identifier, which we shall write as digits prefaced by a hash sign, we should have for example:

```
loves (#2297, #3146)
sister (#3146, #3392)
name (#2297, fred)
name (#3392, mary)
age (#3392, 24)
sex (#3392, 'F')
```

The difference from before is that we can no longer print the internal identifiers; instead we look up and print external identifiers through the 'name' relationship. Now that we have entity identifiers we can store other attributes for them, just as we do in the functional model: for example, age and sex attributes for persons, as above. Thus the object-attribute-value triples referred to earlier for storing FDM facts can be replaced by Prolog facts of the form

```
   attribute-name (object-id, value)
or relationship-name (object-id, object-id)
   [where object-id begins with a # sign]
```

The next stage is to treat the internal identifiers as a special kind of object identifier. We can then associate these object identifiers with object storage on disc, by using database hashing techniques to locate the disc address of an object directly from its identifier. The attribute values can then be stored with the objects just as in a commercial database record. We also need indexes from those attribute values which are keys on to the corresponding object identifiers. Using this representation, based on classic database techniques, we can find values to satisfy any Prolog database goal (such as 'loves' or 'name') very efficiently. For example, to find the attribute value of an object, we use the object identifier to locate the place on disc where the attribute values of the object are stored, and extract them and unify them with the corresponding argument. Where the attribute value is an object, or list of objects, representing a relationship, we can follow its identifier to retrieve its attributes from disc and so on. We are just using the navigation and pointer-following techniques of the original network databases. Effectively, the Prolog goal is satisfied by executing a procedure, written in a systems programming language such as C, which does the disc access. The procedure must satisfy the definition of the Abstract Data Type, but the internal details of the choice of object identifier and how the objects are stored on disc are left to the implementor. It would be perfectly possible to have some kind of hardware triple store or object store (Harland 1988) instead.

Comparison with Relational Storage

Database storage techniques are needed once one is dealing with large numbers of facts. The simplest technique is to use commercial relational databases to store facts, which would be held in Prolog as unit clauses with multiple fields. Each unit clause is stored as a tuple in a relation. One then uses the indexing features of a relational database to find clauses. In this representation, entity relations, where each tuple contains all the attribute values of a single entity, are not dissimilar to a table of objects, and it provides a simple way to scan the whole table and find all the entities.

However, relationship relations are treated very differently in the two systems. In an object representation, the relationship information is held with the object, just like another attribute value. In a relational representation, the relationship information is held as a separate table, which has to be searched. In one case the information about loves(X,Y) is held with each object X, in the other case all information about who loves who is held in a table separate from other information about persons. Unfortunately, the storage of many-to-many relationships is technically more complex for objects, since one has to store a variable-length list of related objects, instead of just adding more fixed-length X-Y tuples on to a table. (However, Prolog storage schemes have to deal with this anyway, since Prolog allows lists as values.)

The other technical problem for object storage is that one needs to maintain a list of all entities of a particular type, and this list can be very short or very long. One solution is to use a B-tree, which can also be used to find an entity given its key. Thus, besides enumerating the entire range of entities, it can also enumerate entities lying within a range of key values.

Interfacing Prolog to FDM

We have thus established that if Prolog is used with object storage, then it can implement all the functionality required by FDM. The secret lies in binding Prolog variables to entities, represented as objects of a particular abstract data type. All the basic operations in the FDM which were listed earlier can then be implemented in C on the database storage system used for the objects, and interfaced to Prolog as procedures. In P/FDM, an interface is provided whereby Daplex queries and updates can be parsed (in Prolog) and used to generate a conjunction of Prolog goals calling out to the basic object methods. Thus entities can be stored, enumerated, retrieved by key and their attributes and relationships found. Where multiple values are required, they can be represented by Prolog lists, representing sets. Any sequence of functions applied can be computed by satisfying a conjunction of Prolog goals. The advantage of all this, as we shall see, is that we have available all the power of Prolog search techniques and all the generality of Prolog computation available to work on the stored data. Prolog can also be used for query optimisation, translation and parsing.

Use of Backtracking like Lazy Evaluation

When the answer to a query is multi-valued it is not always sensible to use the 'setof' operation to construct a list of values. Prolog provides a natural method, based on backtracking, to explore a space of solutions and this has many of the advantages of lazy evaluation, as used in functional systems. In particular, it saves one from constructing a very large set, when the user may be satisfied by seeing the first few items. Also it saves one from storing large intermediate results, when for example one just wants to compute a sum-total, and enables one to use techniques similar to stream processing.

Any Prolog goal which can succeed in multiple ways can be made to re-succeed, binding new values to variables, by executing a subsequent goal which fails. For example, one can look for a student aged over 24 by

```
?-student(X), age(X,A), A > 24, name(X,N), write(N), nl.
```

Here X is bound to successive student entities. If the goal A > 24 fails then student(X) is retried until it succeeds with another student for whom A > 24 succeeds, and the corresponding student name is printed.

One can force this to keep backtracking by executing the special goal *fail*, which never succeeds, and thus print a complete list of names:

```
?- student(X), age(X,A), A > 24, name(X,N), write(N), nl, fail.
```

Instead, one could construct a list by using 'setof', which is slower because it needs to check for duplicates, even though they do not occur in this example:

```
?- setof(N, X^A^(student(X), age(X,A), name(X,N), A > 24), L),
write(L).
```

Similarly, one can keep presenting solutions to a user so long as they type m, meaning more:

```
?- student(X), age(X,A), name(X,N), write([N,A]),nl,
read(More), not(More = m).
```

Here, if the value read from the keyboard is m, then the last goal fails and causes backtracking as with 'fail'.

STORING KNOWLEDGE AS PROLOG PROCEDURES

Let us now consider more closely the storage of Prolog procedures in a database. Prolog procedures provide a very simple and elegant means of computation. Their syntax is very simple. The only operators needed are AND (,) OR (;) IS-DEFINED-AS (:-) and the use of brackets for parameters, and commas and square brackets for lists. There are no declarations for local variables. Better still, there are no references by name to global variables, and no destructive assignments to local variables. These are the things which complicate code in a Pascal-style language, and make it hard to move it from one context to another. By contrast, Prolog procedures tend to be self-contained; information can only be passed into or out from them through parameters. Parameters are passed by reference, but an existing value cannot be changed. A parameter with no value can be given a value, but neither it nor any parameter equal to it can subsequently be changed.

Because Prolog procedures are made of few operators, they can, just like LISP functions, be treated as data structures with the operators as functors. In fact, a Prolog procedure is represented just as the functor ':-' applied to two data structures, representing the head and the body respectively. These are in turn represented by data structures for other functors and arguments and so on, forming a tree structure. Thus it is relatively easy to store Prolog procedures in a database that is capable of holding list and tree structures, and it is much easier than storing C or Pascal procedures. It is also possible to store a procedure in text form, in which case the structure for the procedure is built dynamically when it is accessed from disc and parsed. It may then be possible to cache such structures.

We now return to an idea that keeps recurring in AI: the idea of Knowledge represented as Procedures, or as Rules. This ties up with the basic idea of a database, which is as a cross-referenced store of validated data, which can be shared by multiple users. Now we have the possibility of storing and sharing procedures! This greatly extends the types of knowledge we can store.

High-Level Programming Architectures for Databases with Procedures

Two possible architectures suggest themselves, one based on frames and the other based on object-oriented programming, as suggested earlier. These are closely related. The frame-based idea comes from AI and is apparent in many tools (Fikes and Kehler 1985). Here procedures are mostly to be found on *property lists*, or as *attached procedures* to be fired (like demons) when the user attempts to get a value of a component, or to change a value in a frame. In this way they can also be used to enforce integrity constraints.

By contrast, in an object-oriented architecture, the emphasis is on specialisation of procedures through an inheritance network. However, the notion of specialisation is more in keeping with strong typing than is the use of inheritance in frames. Procedures are treated as *methods* and stored with the class descriptor. Thus one sends a message to an object and treats it almost as a procedure call, where the body of the procedure is hidden inside the object. This is different from the notion of procedures being invoked as the side effect of an action in frame-based programming.

The most significant difference is in the style of top-level program that works with a database containing procedures. In an object-oriented database, this is the classic style of programming using state change and possibly some kind of simulation. The main advantage of the architecture is in the re-use of procedure code, specialised in various ways, and in the binding of procedure code to the components of objects considered as variables, instead of being restricted to variables allocated off a stack.

By contrast, using frame-based programming, we have the basis of a new architecture for Expert Systems (Gray 1988). In this case the top-level program can be an interpreter using forward or backward chaining, which is either searching for data values to satisfy certain constraints (as in database queries) or which may even derive and construct complex new frame structures to satisfy these constraints. This is very much the paradigm used by Prolog in list construction, but with backtracking to allow the exploration of alternative solutions as part of list structures. This technique is the basis of the very powerful Definite Clause Grammar Rules of Pereira and Warren (1980), written in Prolog. These scan a text string and produce trees representing alternative parses by backtracking.

This paradigm can also be applied to a large network of objects in a functional data model database in place of a sequence of characters in a text string. Furthermore, some of the Prolog goals can be satisfied by calling up Prolog method procedures which are stored in the database with the entity descriptors, just as described earlier. In this way, useful knowledge on *how* to find things, possibly as alternative methods to be tried by backtracking, can be stored in the database; such methods can call other ones, and so on recursively.

Prolog methods can do calculations with real numbers. They can take as parameters data structures, such as value entities, representing shapes and coordinates of three-dimensional objects. Modern Prolog implementations can even call out to function code written in C or Fortran to do some of the calculations. This is a very effective division of labour between interpreted Prolog code to do exploratory reasoning, and compiled algorithmic code to do iterative calculations.

The results of this kind of computation will in general be Prolog list structures, or could even be collections of new objects containing calculated and discovered values. To save time, these objects can in turn be stored in the database. This technique has proved very useful in the protein structure database work (Paton & Gray 1988). It is a very effective way for expert database systems to work.

Comparison with Logic Programming

Surprisingly, most of the publications on Prolog have concentrated on its use for logic programming. In consequence, they have ignored the possibilities of using Prolog with data structures, since data structures involve expressions using function symbols, and these have certain implications for completeness proofs! Also, they have concentrated on the correspondence between unit ground clauses in Prolog and relational tuples. But relational tuples in Codd's first normal form never contain list structures! Once again this is a reason for the apparent lack of interest in the use of Prolog with complex data structures.

One of the original key ideas of expert systems was that a programmer should not write a program which had effectively compiled into it a preplanned set of execution paths for a set of queries foreseen by the programmer. Instead, the user should be able to ask queries not foreseen by the programmer, and the interpreter should be clever enough to find an execution path through the available knowledge to solve the query. Simple rule-based systems have had partial success, but have proved to be too limited in this respect. With the architecture outlined above, clever interpreters should be able to read meta-information held with objects and choose appropriate methods from the database. It is a step nearer the aim of expert systems.

Conclusions and Summary

We started with the need to organise large numbers of facts for efficient querying and computation of results. We saw the need for a schema which allowed one to model entities and relationships between them, and to declare the types of functions producing derived results. We have gone deeply into the Functional Data Model and seen examples of schema, and of the Daplex query language. We then saw how Daplex queries can be viewed as Zermelo–Fraenkel set expressions, and how these in turn can be represented in Prolog, taking objects as arguments. The use of unification and backtracking in Prolog to manipulate a network of objects is seen as the basis of a new Expert Database Systems architecture. We have compared it with architectures of existing frame-based AI systems, and with object-oriented database work arising out of programming language research, and seen it as a valuable synthesis of the two.

REFERENCES

Abarbanel, R. M. and Williams, M. D. (1986), 'A Relational Representation for Knowledge Bases', *Proc. First International Conf. on Expert Database Systems*, L. Kerschberg (ed.), Addison-Wesley, p. 139.

Atkinson, M. P., Bailey, P., Cockshott, W. P., Chisholm, K. J. and Morrison, R. (1984), 'Progress with Persistent Programming' in *Databases – Role and Structure*, Stocker, Gray and Atkinson (eds), Cambridge Univ. Press, pp. 245–310.

Bancilhon, F. (1988), 'Object-Oriented Database Systems', *Proc. 7th ACM SIGART-SIGMOD-SIGACT Symposium on Principles of Database Systems (Austin)*, ACM Publications, pp. 1–11.

Campbell, C. W. and Gray, P. M. D. (1988), 'PROOFS: an experimental Frame-Based Programming System implemented in Prolog', *Proc. UK IT'88 Confce (Swansea)*, IEE Publications, Hitchin, 143–147.

Chen P. S. (1976), 'The Entity-Relational Model – towards a unified view of data', *ACM Trans. on Database Systems* (1), 9–36.

Codd, E. F. (1970), 'A relational model of data for large shared databanks', *CACM* (13), 377–387.

Codd, E. F. (1979), 'Extending the relational model to capture more meaning', *ACM Trans. Database Systems (Dec. 1979)*, 397.

Darlington, J., Field, A. J. and Pull, H. (1985), 'The Unification of Functional and Logic Languages', research report, Imperial College, London.

Dittrich, K. (1988), *Advances in Object-Oriented Database Systems*, Springer-Verlag.

Feldman, J. A. and Rovner, P. D. (1969), 'An ALGOL-based associative language', *CACM* (8), 439–449.

Fikes, R. and Kehler, T. (1985), 'The role of frame-based representation in reasoning', *CACM* (28), 904–920.

Gallaire, H. (1983), 'Logic Data Bases vs Deductive Data Bases', *Proc. Logic Programming Workshop 1983*, L. M. Pereira (ed.), Univ. Nova de Lisbon.

Gray, P. M. D. (1984), *Logic, Algebra and Databases*, Ellis-Horwood, Chichester.

Gray, P. M. D. (1988), 'Expert Systems and Object-Oriented Databases: Evolving a new Software Architecture' in *Research and Development in Expert Systems V*, Kelly and Rector (eds), Cambridge Univ. Press, pp. 284–295.

Gray, P. M. D. and Lucas, R. J. (1988), *PROLOG and DATABASES: Implementations and New Directions*, Ellis-Horwood (Wiley).

Gray, P. M. D., Moffat, D. S. and Paton, N. W. (1988), 'A Prolog Interface to a Functional Data Model Database', in *Advances in Database Technology – EDBT'88*, J. W. Schmidt, S. Ceri and M. Missikoff (eds), Springer-Verlag, pp. 34–48.

Gray, P. M. D., Archibald, I. J. and Lunn, K. (1989), 'Interfacing a knowledge-based system to a large database', *Knowledge Engineering Review* (4), 31–51.

Hammer, M. M. and McLeod, D. J. (1978), 'The semantic data model: a modelling mechanism for database applications', *Proc. ACM SIGMOD78 Confce (Austin)*, 26–35.

Harland, D. M. (1988), *REKURSIV Object-Oriented Computer Architecture*, Ellis Horwood/Wiley.

Jarke, M. and Vassiliou, Y. (1984), 'Coupling expert systems and database management systems' in *Artificial Intelligence Applications for Business*, W. Reitman (ed.), Ablex, pp. 65–86.

Kulkarni, K. G. and Atkinson, M. P. (1986), 'EFDM: Extended Functional Data Model', *Computer Journal* (29), 38–46.

Paton, N. W. and Gray, P. M. D. (1988a), 'An Object-Oriented database for storage and analysis of protein structure data' in *PROLOG and DATABASES*, P. M. D. Gray and R. J. Lucas (eds) (op cit), pp. 251–266.

Pereira, F. C. N. and Warren, D. H. D. (1980), 'Definite clause grammars for language analysis', *Artificial Intelligence*, (13), 231–278.

Poulovassilis, A. (1988), 'FDL: An Integration of the Functional Data Model and the Functional Computational Model' in *Proc. Sixth British National Confce on Databases (BNCOD6)*, W. A. Gray (ed.), Cambridge Univ. Press, pp. 215–236.

Sathi, A., Fox, M. S. and Greenberg, M. (1985), 'Representation of Activity Knowledge for Project Management', *IEEE Trans. Pattern Analysis and Machine Intelligence*, 531–552.

Shipman, D. (1979), 'The Functional Data Model and the Data Language DAPLEX', *Proc. ACM SIGMOD79 Confce (Boston)*, revised and printed in *ACM Trans. Database Systems* (6), 140–173.

Smith, J. M. and Smith, D. C. P. (1977), 'Database abstractions: Aggregation and generalization', *ACM Trans. Database Syst.* (2), 105–133.

Tsur, S. (1988), 'LDL – A technology for the realization of tightly coupled expert systems', *IEEE Expert 3 (Fall 1988)*, 41–51.

Tsur, S. and Zaniolo, C. (1986), 'LDL: A Logic-Based Data Language', *Proc. 12th International VLDB Confce (Tokyo)*, Morgan Kauffman.

Turner, D. A. (1985), 'Miranda: A non-strict functional language with polymorphic types' in *Functional Programming Languages and Computer Architecture*, J. P. Jouannaud (ed.), Springer-Verlag.

Winterbottom, N. and Sharman, G. C. H. (1979), 'NDB: Non-Programmer Database Facility', Report TR.12.79, IBM(UK) Labs, Winchester.

Zaniolo, C. (1986), 'Safety and Compilation of Non-Recursive Horn Clauses', *Proc. 1st International Conf. on Expert Database Systems*, L. Kerschberg (ed.), Univ. S. Carolina.

4
The Role of a Repository Manager in Deductive Database Systems

CAROL SMALL,[1] ALEXANDRA POULOVASSILIS[2] AND MIR DERAKHSHAN[3]

[1]*Department of Computer Science, Birkbeck College, Malet Street, London WC1E 7HX*
[2]*Department of Computing, King's College London, Strand, London WC2R 2LS*
[3]*SQL Software Ltd, Latton Bush Centre, Harlow, Essex CM18 7BL*

0. INTRODUCTION

Deductive database systems lie at the confluence of two independent but related areas of technology: those of database management systems (DBMSs) and declarative, or referentially transparent, programming languages (DPLs) (logic-based languages, such as Prolog [Clo81], and functional languages such as Miranda[1] [Tur86]). The logic-based approach to deductive database systems has long been a focus of interest [Gal78, Gal84], and descriptions of proposed and implemented systems have appeared with increasing frequency [Ker86, Gra88b]. With a few exceptions [Bat88, Gra88a, Kul86, Pou90], considerably less attention has been given to the functional approach.

A hackneyed but pertinent observation is that DPLs typically deal with a small body of transient data (i.e. data existing only for the duration of the program) with highly complicated structure, whilst DBMSs typically deal with a large body of semi-permanent data (i.e. data existing until modified or deleted) of relatively simple structure. For example, a credit card database may contain details of several hundred thousand retail outlets accepting the card, details of several million card holders, and details of several milliard transactions. In sharp contrast, a large Prolog database for

[1]Miranda is a trademark of Research Software Ltd.

Expert Database Systems
ISBN 0-12-382255-6

protein topology will contain only tens of thousands of rules. Deductive database systems, by incorporating features from both, aim to provide the expressive power of DPLs whilst retaining the ability to deal with large volumes of information. In Section 1 below the advantages that follow from this integration are considered.

A deductive database system comprises two principal components: a repository manager, which is the sub-system responsible for the storage and retrieval of data and the movement of data between memory and secondary storage devices, and which provides concurrency and error recovery facilities, and an inference engine, which uses rules (such as clauses in a logic-based system, or function definitions in a functional system) to infer implied data from data which is explicitly stored. Deductive database systems can be classified according to the way in which these two components are coupled, as either loosely coupled systems in which an existing DBMS is used as a 'back-end' for an existing DPL, or as tightly coupled systems in which either a DPL is extended with an integrated database component or a DBMS is extended with deductive capabilities. The relative merits of these approaches are examined in Section 2.

The remainder of the paper is concerned primarily with the structure of the repository manager/inference engine interface. Based upon the discussion in Section 2 on the relative merits of integration strategies, Section 3 discusses the operations the repository manager should support: that it should provide a minimal instruction set, that every field be treated as a key field, that the retrieval operations be lazy, and that it be able to provide a good estimate of the cost of the query before it is executed. In the later part of Section 3 we consider the use of a binary relational repository manager, or 'triple store', as a repository for a deductive database system. The section concludes by discussing some possible software implementations of binary relational repository managers, and describes how implementations based upon grid file methods can provide cost estimates for queries.

In Section 4 we consider how a deductive database system may utilise the binary relational repository manager outlined in Section 3. Rather than add to the plethora of papers describing the integration of Prolog and a database sub-system, we choose instead to describe the implementation of a functional database language. To this end we show how function definitions can be decomposed into sets of triples for storage, how the repository manager can assist in the process of pattern matching, and how the lazy retrieval of records by the repository manager can assist the lazy evaluation of expressions by the functional database system. In the final section of the paper we give our concluding remarks and outline some future research issues.

1. MOTIVATION

This section considers the advantages which accrue from the integration of DBMSs and DPLs. Although all of the points considered apply equally to both the logic-based and functional approaches, the logic-based approach is preferred for purposes of illustration, since we believe that this will be most familiar to the majority of readers. The advantages are as follows:

- More sophisticated view mechanisms can be provided for DBMSs. Consider, for example, an acyclic cable-routing network in which 'link(x,y,z)' denotes that there is a link between nodes x and y of length z metres, and the relation 'connection(x,y,z)' is defined as the transitive closure of the link relation:

  connection(X,Y,Z) :- link(X,Y,Z).
  connection(X,Y, + (Z_1, Z_2)) :- link(X,T,Z_1),
  connection(T,Y,Z_2).

  Thus, one node, y, is connected to another, x, either if y is linked to x or if y is connected to a node t which is in turn linked to x.
- Default assumptions can be made in the absence of information, thus providing a form of data compaction and faster data entry. Defaults can be defined in a functional language by use of overlapping patterns [Pou90] and in a logic-based language by use of 'extra-logical' features (such as the 'cut' in Prolog) or by use of default rules (in an extended logic-based language [Rei80, Sma88]). In contrast, current DBMSs provide only rudimentary methods for specifying default values in the schema or sub-schema, and rely upon application programs to provide default information based upon more complex criteria.
- The DBMS can be used as a cache for the storage of intermediate results. For example, materialisation of the 'connection' relation (defined above) requires the computation of the transitive closure of the 'link' relation each time 'connection' is evaluated. Since this may be costly, the operation could be undertaken just once and the results stored temporarily in the database for subsequent re-use.
- Current DPL systems require the entire program to be loaded into memory prior to execution, and do not access secondary storage (except indirectly via operating system paging); hence the size of a program is in general limited by the system swap space. In contrast, DBMSs incorporate a buffer management sub-system, and hence integration of the two systems will allow several orders of magnitude more rules than at present.

- The DBMS may support range queries. Consider once again the 'link' relation defined above. The following Prolog query requests details of links which are between 10 and 25 metres in length:

  ?- link(X,Y,Z), $\geqslant$ (Z,10), $\leqslant$ (Z,25).

  If the DBMS uses a storage structure such as the grid file [Nie84] the query can be translated into a single retrieval request, as described by Hinrichs [Hin85]:

  readGF(link(X,Y,Z,range(Z,10,25)))

  which results in a search of only that part of the database containing 'link' records with a value in their third column in the range 10 to 25.

2. INTEGRATION STRATEGIES

Two principal strategies have emerged for the implementation of deductive database systems: loose and tight coupling.

A *loosely coupled* system is one in which an existing DPL is extended with procedures to allow communication with an existing DBMS. For example, PROSQL/DS [Cha86] permits Prolog to access SQL databases, EFDM [Kul86] is an extension of DAPLEX which uses PS-Algol to maintain persistent data on secondary storage, and FQL [Bun79] is an integration of the Functional Data Model and a CODASYL database system. This approach has proved to be attractive in the short term, primarily because a working system can be constructed with minimal effort, and has the additional benefit that existing databases, which may have been developed at considerable cost, can be accessed. It is unlikely, however, that loosely coupled systems will prove successful in the longer term, since:

- The approach leads to redundant functionality. For example, DBMSs typically offer view facilities which are less expressive than those offered by DPLs, whilst DPLs adopt a relatively primitive form of rule indexing compared to that offered by DBMSs.
- There is a source-to-source conversion overhead. For example, a Prolog system accessing an SQL database must convert its term structures to an SQL query format, and convert back the response from the SQL system.
- DBMSs are generally 'set-based', in the sense that they return the set of answers satisfying a query and provide poor performance when access is on a record level, whilst DPLs are typically 'tuple-based', in the sense that they adopt some form of lazy evaluation,

returning the answers to a query one at a time. For example, consider the evaluation of a query to retrieve the quantity and price of books whose classification is 'history', which can be expressed as a Prolog query:

```
?- classification(Book,history), quantity(Book,Quantity),
   price(Book,Price).
```

And as a relational algebra expression:

```
JOIN price AND
  (JOIN quantity AND
    (SELECT classification WHERE class = history))
```

A DBMS, when processing the relational algebra expression, will retrieve the pages containing the classification and quantity records to compute the innermost join and then retrieve the pages containing the price records to compute the final result. A Prolog interpreter, on the other hand, will retrieve a single classification record, then a single quantity record, and then a single price record before backtracking to find further answers. Unlike the processing of the relational algebra expression, the same page may be brought into memory on numerous occasions due to the backtracking nature of the interpreter, incurring a heavy I/O penalty.

- Queries posed with respect to a DPL tend to be less predictable in nature than those posed against a database system. For example, any of the following queries can be evaluated by Prolog:

```
?- parent(a,b).          ?- parent(X,Y).
?- parent(a,X).          ?- parent(X,X).
?- parent(X,b).
```

In contrast, traditional database philosophy has been for the database administrator to define indexes which match expected query patterns, an approach which is quite reasonable since retrieval is normally via menu-driven interfaces, or application programs which can navigate the database to make use of those indexes which are available. Consequently, the use of an existing database system will provide a fast response to a query for which appropriate indexes exist, but a prohibitively slow response to one for which no indexes exist (if the query is allowed at all).

However, although DPL query patterns are in general unpredictable in nature it may be the case that some particular query patterns will not occur as a result of the restrictions of the computational model. For example, in a system based upon pure first-order logic the predicate component of an atom will always be known, and consequently in such a system the query

?- X(a,b).

cannot be expressed. As a further example, in a logic-based system using the negation as failure rule, only ground negative goals will be evaluated to avoid floundering. In summary, DBMSs require the definition of allowable access paths to data, whereas DPLs potentially require any form of access to data but may be able to state those access paths which will not be required.

In contrast, *tightly coupled* systems integrate more closely the DBMS and DPL components, and cover a spectrum ranging from those systems which extend a DPL with a 'storage manager' (such as MU-Prolog [Nai83]), to those which extend a DBMS with a deductive component (such as DEDUCE-2 [Cha78], MRPPS [Min78], and LDL [Tsu86]). In general, the former provide the full computational power of the DPL, whilst the latter support only a restricted form of deductive reasoning. It is clear, in the light of the foregoing, that tightly coupled systems will in the longer term prove more successful, and it is to the structure of such systems that we now turn our attention.

3. THE REPOSITORY MANAGER

3.0 Introduction

A deductive database system comprises two components, an *inference engine* which undertakes the evaluation of queries and a *repository manager* which controls the storage and retrieval of data. Since it is the inference engine which must control query processing, it is important that the repository manager should place no unnecessary restrictions upon the ability of the inference engine to access data. In Section 3.1 below we consider the features that the repository manager should support based upon the points raised in Section 2, and in Section 3.2 we consider the use of a binary relational repository manager.

3.1 Functionality of the Repository Manager

The repository manager should provide only a *minimal instruction set* in order to avoid redundant functionality [Sha88]. Hence the repository manager should not provide view or constraint enforcement facilities since these must of necessity be provided by the inference engine. Thus the sole responsibility of the repository manager should be for the storage and retrieval of tuples, together with facilities for concurrency and recovery. A consequence of this is that it be *semantic-free* [Mar84], in the sense that it should associate no meaning with the stored tuples, since the schema information which provides the semantics for those tuples will be the property of the inference component of the system.

Since the queries posed against a deductive database are unpredictable in nature, the repository manager should treat every field of a tuple as a *key field*. When identifying a set of n-tuples for retrieval any combination of the fields can be either specified or unspecified, thus giving rise to 2^n possible query patterns. For example:

Q1 retrieve (<is_a, ?, link>)
Q2 retrieve (<?, ?, ?>)

Q1 identifies for retrieval the set of all 3-tuples with a value in the first field of 'is_a', and a value in the third field of 'link', whilst Q2 will result in the retrieval of all 3-tuples. Nevertheless, although any form of access to the repository should be permitted, information regarding the relative frequency or importance of a query can be used to optimise query response time whilst guaranteeing a 'minimum' standard of performance for infrequent or less important queries.

The retrieval operations supported by the repository manager should be *lazy*: in other words, the tuples matching a given query pattern should only be retrieved as required by the inference engine. The advantages of a lazy retrieval strategy over a strict strategy are that:

- no intermediate work space is required to store the matched tuples;
- there is considerable saving in computational cost when the inference engine requires only a small subset of the tuples matching the retrieval pattern – in fact, our experience in the implementation of both logic-based and functional deductive database systems indicates that such cases are very frequent;
- since a number of retrieval sets may exist simultaneously, the designer of the inference engine enjoys greater flexibility in coding tasks which require the processing of inter-relating queries.

The repository manager should be able to provide a *cost estimate* of a query before it is executed. To locate the tuples satisfying a query one or more disk pages must be searched. Since the number of disk accesses is the primary factor governing the overall cost of answering a query, a good estimate of the relative cost of processing two queries can be found by comparing the number of disk accesses which would have to be made to process each. Such information can prove invaluable to the inference engine when there are choices to be made in the search for answers to a query. For example, an SLD theorem prover uses a selection function to choose the literal within a query upon which resolution is to occur, and the soundness and completeness results for SLD-resolution (see Lloyd [Llo87]) show that any such function can be used, including one in which the most ground literal is selected or (as in this case) one which will cause the fewest possible disk pages to be searched.

In addition to facts, the repository is also a store for rules, integrity constraints and meta-data. For many applications the ratio of rules and constraints to facts is very low, and they are likely to be retrieved with far greater frequency than individual facts (this is especially true in the case of recursively defined rules). Furthermore, each rule and constraint may be decomposed into a large number of tuples for storage in the repository, and hence may be costly to retrieve. For these reasons, it is essential that the repository manager provides a caching mechanism for the most frequent retrieval requests.

Finally, it is worth remembering that a database is a repository for information which is both integrated and shared. The term 'integrated' indicates that a database comprises information from several distinct, but usually related, application areas with reduced redundant information, whilst the term 'shared' suggests that a variety of users have access to the same data. Furthermore, it is useful for different users to have access to the same database concurrently, and hence most large database systems have some form of concurrency control. Little consideration has been given to the incorporation of these aspects into deductive database systems, and thus the use of the term 'database' in the phrase 'deductive database systems' can (at present) be seen to be something of a misnomer.

3.2 Binary Relational Repository Managers

In this section we consider the use of a binary relational repository manager (or triple store) [Fro82]. The operations we require such a repository manager to support are summarised in Figure 1.

A triple store is a set of binary relationships or triples, where each triple is an ordered 3 – tuple such as:

⟨length, link_1, 20⟩

No semantics are attached to the triples by the repository manager, although to a logic-based inference engine a triple may be perceived as a binary atom such as

length (link_1, 20)

In the definitions below we use the following notation:

- TS denotes the triple store before execution of the operation.
- TS′ denotes the triple store after execution of the operation.
- a triple is a 3-tuple $\langle t_1, t_2, t_3 \rangle$ of data values.
- a saf (simple associative form) is a 3-tuple $\langle a_1, a_2, a_3 \rangle$ such that $\forall i$, $1 \leqslant i \leqslant 3$, a_i is either a data value or '?'.
- $\text{match}(\langle a_1, a_2, a_3 \rangle, TS) = \{\langle t_1, t_2, t_3 \rangle \in TS \mid \forall i, 1 \leqslant i \leqslant 3, t_i = a_i \text{ or } a_i = \text{'?'}\}$.

The required repository manager operations are:

- insert_triple(triple). $TS' = TS \cup \{\text{triple}\}$.
- delete_triple(triple). $TS' = TS - \{\text{triple}\}$.
- fetch_triple(saf). An arbitrary element of match(saf,TS) is returned.
- open_virtual_file(saf). The elements of match(saf,TS) are (conceptually) copied to a temporary file and an identifier for the file is returned.
- read_virtual_file(id). A triple in the (conceptual) file identified by id is selected, removed from the file and returned to the calling program.
- close_virtual_file(id). Housekeeping operations are performed to free any storage associated with the (conceptual) file identified by id.
- query_cost(saf). An estimate of the cost of retrieving the triples matching saf, based upon the number of pages which would have to be accessed, is returned.

Figure 1 Repository Manager Operations

whilst to a functional inference engine a triple may be perceived as representing the value of a unary function at some point in its domain, such as

length (link_1) = 20

COMPLEX OBJECTS

It is well known [Bra76] that any n-ary relationship can be re-expressed as n + 1 triples. For example, the ternary relationship

link (node_1, node_2, 20)

can be represented by the following triples, through the explicit representation of the aggregation entity link_1:

⟨is__a, link_1, link⟩
⟨from, link_1, node__1⟩
⟨to, link_1, node__2⟩
⟨length, link_1, 20⟩

More generally, a triple store can be used to store arbitrarily complex structures. Conversely, a triple store is minimal in the sense that some triples cannot be converted into sets of 2-tuples for storage.

LAZY RETRIEVAL

The binary relational repository manager above provides three operations for accessing sets of triples. The first, *open_virtual_file*, identifies a set of triples to be retrieved. Conceptually, as a result of this operation, the triples which match the specified saf are copied into a file, and an identifier to the file is returned to the application. In practice (and hence the term *virtual* file), the triples matching the saf are not copied, but rather information is recorded which details the disk pages on which the triples matching the saf can be found, and which is sufficient to ensure that all triples can subsequently be retrieved, one at a time, via the operation *read_virtual_file*. A number of virtual files can be open simultaneously, the maximum number being system-dependent. Finally, when all triples matching the specified saf have been processed, or when no further triples are required, the operation *close_virtual_file* is used to release any resources associated with the virtual file.

COST ESTIMATION

From the requirement that every field of a triple be treated as a key field we note that the problem of implementing the repository manager is equivalent to that of implementing a three-dimensional file organisation with two important requirements: firstly, that the file organisation method should adapt gracefully to the number of triples stored, and secondly that the method allow 'tuning' based upon information provided by the DBA or the system log. The first requirement excludes implementations based upon static multi-dimensional file structures such as multiple-key hashing schemes [Riv76], and the second excludes those based upon dynamic structures which allow tuning only at the expense of a total re-organisation of the stored data, such as multi-dimensional B-trees [Sch82].

Grid file methods, described by Nievergelt *et al.* [Nie84], and superseded by [Hin85, Fre87], offer high potential for performance tuning. These methods, with the exception of the BANG file [Fre87], divide the *data space* (that is, $D \times D \times D$ where D is the domain from which data values are drawn) into disjoint hyper-rectangular subspaces, or *regions*. Associated with each region is a unique *data page* wherein are stored the records corresponding to points in that region, and information on the association between regions and data pages is held in a *directory*. The directory comprises three linear scales, one for each dimension, and a three-dimensional

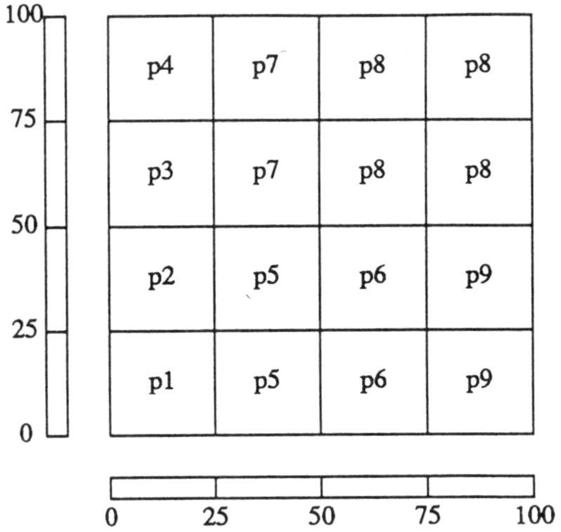

Figure 2 A 2-dimensional grid file directory

array which we term the *grid array*. The linear scales define the points at which the data space is partitioned, and each element of the grid array is a pointer to a data page. The union of the subspaces represented by directory elements pointing to the same data page makes up a region. For example, Figure 2 gives an example of a two-dimensional grid file, in which the domain is [0,100) and hence the data space is [0,100) × [0,100). The subspaces of the top right-hand quadrant of the directory form a region which is associated with the data page p8.

For the case of three dimensions, the *search space* for a query will take the form of a *point*, a *line* or a *plane*, depending upon whether three, two or only one field is specified (by convention we assume that there is no requirement to process a query in which no fields are specified, which would result in the retrieval of the entire contents of the triple store). The data pages which contain the possible matches to a query are those which correspond to regions which intersect with the query search space. Thus, in the above example, page p6 must be searched to process the query ⟨20,70⟩, and pages p8 and p9 must be searched to process the query ⟨?,92⟩. Note that a point query requires a search of only a single data page irrespective of the configuration of the regions over the data space, but that in contrast a line or plane query will require a search of a number of data pages depending upon the partition configuration. Thus, an estimate of the cost of processing a query can be ascertained by reference to the directory information only, the estimate being based upon the number of data pages which would have to be searched to satisfy the query. We note that access to the directory itself may itself incur some I/O cost.

TUNING

When the insertion of a record causes splitting because the data page on to which it should be placed is full, a *splitting policy* determines the dimension at which the region and its associated data page are split into two. Once the dimension is determined the region is split exactly into two halves in that dimension, a new data page is allocated and triples are redistributed between the overflowing data page and the newly allocated data page, and finally the directory is updated to reflect the new state. Thus, in Figure 2, if the splitting policy determines that the region associated with data page p8 is to be split along the x co-ordinate then a new data page (say p10) is allocated, tuples in p8 with an x value in the interval [75,100) are moved into p10, and the two elements of the right-hand half of the top right-hand quadrant of the directory are updated to contain p10. Occasionally the splitting of a region will cause a refinement of the directory, as would occur if the region associated with data page p1 were to be split in either dimension, for example.

Figure 3 3 different partitionings of the same 2-dimensional data space

A line or plane query can take one of six different forms, each form corresponding to the combination of specified fields. The *occurrence frequency* of a form is the probability that a query is of that form, and the *reference frequency* of a form is the probability distribution for the specified values in a query of that form. These values can be ascertained either from the DBA or from the system log. As observed above, the cost of a query is a function of the partition configuration of the regions at the time the query is processed, and this in turn is a function of the insertion and deletion history and of the splitting policy used. Consider, for example, the three different partitionings into 16 regions of the same two-dimensional data space shown in Figure 3. The first configuration in Figure 3 achieves symmetrical processing for queries which only specify a single field since the same number of data pages, in this case 4, will be searched for all such queries. However, the second configuration is completely biased towards queries which only specify the y dimension since only 1 data page will be searched as opposed to 16 for a query specifying only the x dimension. Similarly, the third configuration is completely biased towards queries which specify only the x dimension.

The average query response time in an application is largely governed by the time taken to process the most typical queries, and thus a goal should be to partition the data space such that the configuration minimises this average, whilst taking into account the need to maintain a certain standard of performance for less frequent queries. An expression for the cost of processing of an arbitrary query given the partition configuration of the regions is given by Derakhshan [Der89], who shows how this expression, together with the occurrence and reference frequency probability distributions can be used to minimise average query costs whenever a split occurs.

CONCURRENCY CONTROL

In a multi-user environment the triple store requires the use of a *scheduler* which ensures that operations from transactions executing concurrently do not interfere with each other. Two main classes of concurrency control may be distinguished: locking and optimistic control. *Locking* ensures correct execution of transactions by requiring each transaction to acquire access rights to data before undertaking an operation. Conversely, under *optimistic control* each transaction performs its updates on a private copy of data and the transaction is validated by ensuring that the original data is not also being accessed by a concurrently executing transaction before writing out the updated data [Dat85].

In the context of general database systems a number of different object types can be locked – fields, records, pages, files etc. In contrast, in the context of triple stores, locking is particularly simple since there is only one kind of object to lock – a saf – and each lock can range in granularity from the whole database (⟨?, ?, ?⟩) to a specific tuple (⟨a, b, c⟩). However, Sharman and Winterbottom [Sha88] report that as a consequence of the decomposition of n-ary records into a number of triples the scheduler may have to maintain an order of magnitude more locks than normal record locking, causing the scheduler to become the dominant resource overhead and hence seriously degrading system performance.

Locking is a pessimistic form of concurrency control since it assumes that there *will* be contention amongst transactions, whilst optimistic control assumes that there will *not* be contention. Thus locking methods are preferable for update-intensive systems whilst optimistic control methods are superior for query-intensive systems. The relevance of these methods to deductive database systems is an open question and will clearly be dependent upon the actual application. However, we feel that in contrast to conventional database applications, typical deductive database applications are likely to be query-intensive since each query may result in the generation of numerous sub-queries for its processing. As supporting evidence for this conjecture we cite the provision of only the most rudimentary of update facilities by many current deductive systems.

4. A FUNCTIONAL DATABASE SYSTEM

4.0 Introduction

In this section we consider how a functional database language may utilise the repository manager outlined in Section 3 above. In Section 4.1 we present a brief outline of some of the features of a functional database language which is syntactically similar to functional programming languages but is extended with some of the features necessary for its use as a database language rather than as a programming language. The remainder of this section is concerned with possible implementations of such a database language. Unless indicated to the contrary, details of the italicised terms may be found in the volumes by Peyton-Jones [Pey87] and Field and Harrison [Fie88].

As we shall see in the sequel, a query is an expression which is evaluated by repeatedly selecting and simplifying a reducible sub-expression, or *redex*. There are two major components to such an evaluation algorithm: the order in which redexes are selected for reduction (*reduction order*), and the process of selecting the appropriate function definition to enable the reduction of a redex (*pattern matching*). These two components are mutually recursive: to evaluate a redex may require the pattern matcher to select the appropriate function definition, but in order for this to occur the pattern matcher may require a redex to be evaluated.

In Section 4.2 we discuss the issues related to pattern matching, describe how data definition statements can be formed into a tree, and also how a pattern matcher can navigate this tree to select the appropriate function definition. Then, in Section 4.3, we briefly describe how the right-hand side of a data definition statement can be translated into a combinator expression and stored in the form of a graph in the repository, and also describe two optimisation techniques. Finally, in Section 4.4, we consider the issue of redex reduction order, and discuss the relative merits of 'lazy' and 'eager' evaluation strategies.

4.1 The Database Language

The statements of the language fall into two classes: schema definition statements (which include function type declarations, and the definition of new data types), and data definition statements. The statements of Figure 4 are used for the purposes of illustration.

```
 1 tax_rate : → num;
 2 deductions : num → num;
 3 factorial : num → num
 4 map : (α → β) → (list α) → (list β);
 5 tree :: Leaf | Node num tree tree;
 6 list α :: Nil | Cons α (list α);
 7 twice : num → num;
 8 tax_rate = .30;
 9 deductions x = *x tax_rate;
10 factorial 0 = 0;
11 factorial x = *x (factorial( − x 1));
12 map f Nil = Nil;
13 map f (Cons x y) = Cons (f x)(map f y);
14 twice = *2;
```

Figure 4

SCHEMA DEFINITION

A number of primitive types are provided such as num(ber), char(acter) and bool(ean). The type $t_1 \rightarrow t_2$ is the type of a function with argument of type t_1 and result of type t_2. Thus, statement (1) declares the function 'tax_rate' to take no arguments and to return a number, whilst statement (2) defines the function 'deductions' to be of type num → num – i.e. to take a number and to return a number. In addition, user-defined structured types can be introduced by means of algebraic type definitions. An example of such a definition occurs at statement (5), which introduces a new sum type 'tree', a 0-ary *constructor* function 'Leaf' of type tree, and a constructor function 'Node' of type num → tree → tree → tree. In other words, Node when provided with a number and two trees will construct an object of type tree, an example of such an object being

Node 5 (Node 2 Leaf Leaf) (Node 8 Leaf Leaf)

Polymorphic type definitions can be introduced through use of the type variables, α, β, γ etc. Thus the definition of a list (6) introduces a number of different list types, such as 'list num', 'list tree', 'list (list bool)', 'list (num → num)' and so forth.

Thus far we have considered only type declarations of computational functions which involve system-defined types, or types constructed solely from them. The purpose of a database system, however, is to model some subset of the world which, following the functional data model [Shi81], we perceive as consisting of *entities* and *functions* relating the entities. We therefore require the ability to introduce new entity types such as:

employee :: entity;
department :: entity;

Functions relating employees to the department in which they work and to their salaries can thus be declared as:

works_in : employee → department;
salary : employee → num;

DATA DEFINITION

The purpose of a data definition statement is to give a value to a function. A number of primitive functions are provided such as the usual arithmetic (+, −, *, etc.), boolean (<, >, =, etc.) and conditional (if, case) functions. The right-hand side of a function definition is an *expression* which is:

- a variable, constant, function or constructor function;
- an application of the form $e_1\,e_2$, where both e_1 and e_2 are themselves expressions; or
- a bracketed expression of the form (e), where e is itself an expression.

The left-hand side of a function definition comprises the name of the function being defined followed by zero or more formal parameters. Each formal parameter is a *pattern*, which is an expression containing no functions. We assume for simplicity that the left-hand side contains no repeated variables. Of course, the types of the formal parameters and the right-hand side of the definition must accord with the type declaration for the function.

For example, referring to Figure 4, 'tax_rate' is a function taking no arguments and returning the value '0.30', whilst 'factorial' when applied to a non-negative number, n, returns n! Notice that functions can be partially applied, that is, supplied with fewer than their required number of arguments. For example, the function 'twice' partially applies the * function to a single argument, and so returns a function from num to num which doubles its argument. Furthermore, functions are first-class objects and can be passed as arguments to other functions. Thus the evaluation of:

map twice (Cons 1 (Cons 2 Nil))

returns, via the intermediate steps

Cons (twice 1) (map twice (Cons 2 Nil))
Cons (* 2 1) (map twice (Cons 2 Nil))
Cons 2 (map twice (Cons 2 Nil))
Cons 2 (Cons (twice 2) (map twice Nil))
Cons 2 (Cons (* 2 2) (map twice Nil))
Cons 2 (Cons 4 (map twice Nil))

the list

Cons 2 (Cons 4 Nil)

The computational completeness of functional languages [Hin86] means that no functions need be built into the language, but any required function can instead be defined either by the user or provided by the DBA in a standard environment.

The extent of an entity type can be found by the built-in metalevel function 'all', which takes an entity type as argument and returns a list of all the entities of that type as its result. For example, the expression

map salary (all employee);

returns a list containing the salaries of all employees in the database. New entities may be created and deleted by the user at will.

4.2 Pattern Matching

When an expression (f e_1 e_2 ... e_n) is evaluated a *pattern-matching algorithm* selects the definition which is appropriate for its evaluation given the argument expressions e_1 to e_n. Often there are several definitions with which an expression can be matched and the pattern-matching algorithm must select from them. For example, the expression

factorial 0

matches both definitions (10) and (11) of Figure 4, although clearly we wish the former to be selected.

In functional programming languages, a *first-fit* matching strategy attempts to match the expression to be evaluated with each definition in turn in the order in which they appear in the program, and the expression is replaced by the right-hand side of the first definition which matches. Thus, if Figure 4 is the source code of a functional program, the evaluation of 'factorial 0' will match with (10), as intended. However, in the context of databases the term first fit becomes ill-defined. Does it mean (a) in the order that definitions are retrieved by the DBMS during pattern matching, (b) in the chronological order that definitions are inserted or updated, or (c) according to some other, user-specified, ordering? Interpretation (a) must be rejected outright since with it the pattern-matching semantics are beyond the control of the user. Interpretation (b) presents problems with respect to function updates; consider, for example, the function 'tax_code' consisting of the following definitions in chronological order:

```
1 tax_code 'carol' = '267L';
2 tax_code 'mir' = '242LX';
3 tax_code 'alex' = '293L';
4 taxcode x = '247L';
```

The deletion of any definition 1–4 presents no problem; similarly, the update of a tax code is also simple, provided the time attached to any definition is that of its original insertion rather than that of its latest update. However, the insertion of a definition with a new left-hand side, say

```
5 tax_code 'nigel' = '331L';
```

results in the function:

```
1 tax_code 'carol' = '267L';
2 tax_code 'mir' = '242LX';
3 tax_code 'alex' = '293L';
4 tax_code x = '247L';
5 tax_code 'nigel' = '331L';
```

whence (tax_code 'nigel') evaluates to the default case '247L' rather than to '331L' as intended. In order to obtain the semantics we require we have to delete equation 4 and re-insert it! Thus, we reject interpretation (b) as being impractical. The insertion problem could be overcome by adopting approach (c) above, but the explicit numbering of definitions, and the re-organisation which would have to precede certain updates, is not practical when functions consist of a large number of definitions. Thus, we reject first-fit pattern-matching altogether in the context of database and adopt a strategy which is not dependent on any ordering of definitions.

An alternative to a first-fit pattern-matching strategy is a *best-fit* one which uses the notion of pattern specialisation. Two patterns *overlap* if there is some expression which matches both patterns. One pattern, P_i, is a *specialisation* of another, P_j, if each expression which matches P_i also matches P_j but not vice versa. A set of patterns is *unambiguous* if for any overlapping patterns P_i and P_j, neither of which is a specialisation of the other, there is a pattern P_k which is a specialisation of both P_i and P_j such that any expression matching both P_i and P_j also matches P_k. Finally, if an expression matches two or more patterns then a best-fit strategy chooses the most specific, the existence of a unique most-specific pattern being guaranteed if the set of patterns is unambiguous.

For example, consider again Figure 4. The pattern of (10) is more specific than that of (11), and hence the expression 'factorial 0' will be matched with (10) as we intend. An example of two overlapping patterns, neither of which is a specialisation of the other is

P_1 Node v_1 Leaf v_2
P_2 Node v_1 v_2 Leaf

which may be made unambiguous by the addition of

P_3 Node v_1 Leaf Leaf

Any expression which matches both P_1 and P_2 will also match the more specific pattern P_3. Note that, in contrast to first-fit pattern matching, the order in which the data definition statements appear is always irrelevant.

A third pattern-matching strategy is *left-to-right best fit* [Pou90] which has the advantage that no update to a function can result in an ambiguous definition. Each data definition statement is formed into a *match tree*, by labelling the root of the tree with the name of the function, and labelling the arcs of the tree with the components of the formal parameters of the definition in the order in which they appear. For example, lines (12) and (13) of Figure 4 give rise to the trees:

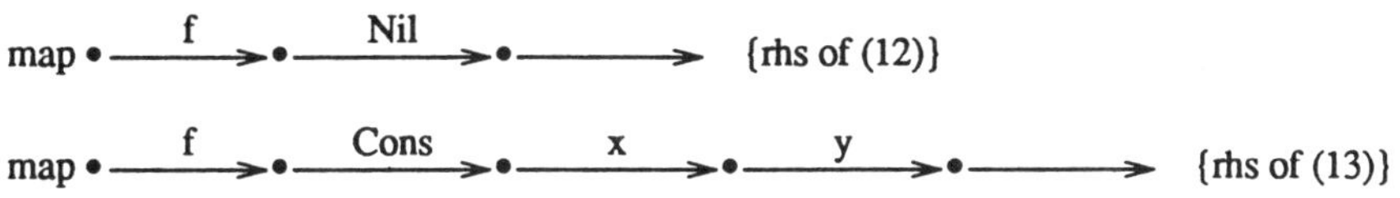

The match tree for an entire function is constructed in terms of the individual match trees of the data definition statements for that function. Firstly the variables in each data definition match tree are replaced by variables which reflect the position in which they appear in the tree, and the right-hand side of the data definition statement is accordingly adjusted to reflect this renaming. Thus, for example, the variable 'f' will be replaced by 'v_0' in both of the above match trees, whilst 'x' and 'y' will be replaced by 'v_1' and 'v_2' in the second. Then the match tree for the function is constructed by merging, from left to right, the match trees for the individual definitions. In the above case, this leads to the following match tree, which can clearly be stored directly as a set of triples by the repository manager.

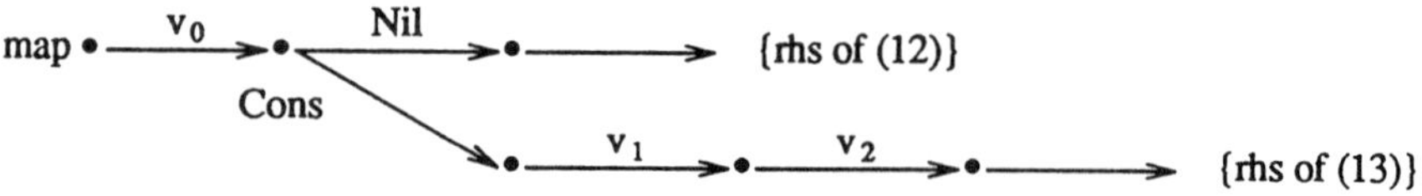

The process of pattern matching is that of finding a path through the match tree to a leaf node which identifies the appropriate right-hand side. Considering the arguments to a function as a list [H | T] (where H denotes the first argument and T the remaining arguments), then given a current node n_1 in the tree the following algorithm selects the next node. We note that in this algorithm, and henceforward throughout the paper, constants are regarded as constructor functions of arity 0.

1 If [H | T] is empty then n_1 identifies the right-hand side of the appropriate definition.
2 If H is currently unevaluated and there is only an arc labelled with a variable, v_i, emanating from n_1 to some node n_2, then match T from n_2, otherwise evaluate H to form H′ and apply rule (3) or (4) to [H′ | T].
3 If H is an n-ary constructor function together with n arguments, i.e. H is of the form $C_n t_1 \ldots t_n$, and there is an arc labelled C_n to some node n_2, then match $[t_1, \ldots, t_n \mid T]$ from n_2.
4 If there is an arc labelled with a variable, v_i (where v_i is the next variable expected in the match tree), from n_1 to some node n_2, then match T from n_2.
5 If none of rules 1 to 4 apply then the function does not match any branch of the tree and so the matching process fails.

Algorithm 1 The Pattern Matcher

Step 2 above indicates that a *lazy* evaluation of expressions has been adopted, meaning that the arguments to a function are left unevaluated for as long as possible (this is discussed in detail in Section 4.4). Using an eager strategy, this step would become

2′ if H is currently unevaluated then evaluate H to form H′ and apply rule (3) or (4) to [H′ | T].

It is clear that match trees can be represented naturally in the form of triples, and hence the repository manager described in Section 3 is well suited for their storage (all non-root nodes in these trees are unique system-generated identifiers). Given a current node n_1 in the tree and a list of arguments [H | T], the following retrieval requests are executed, corresponding to the first four cases of Algorithm 1:

1 The right-hand side of the definition identified by n_1 is retrieved as described in Section 4.3 below.
2 At most two triples – those matching $\langle n_1, ?, ? \rangle$ – need be retrieved. We note that since the match tree of some functions may have a very high branching factor (for example, the match trees for the functions 'works_in' and 'tax_code'), the adoption of a lazy retrieval strategy by the repository manager may result in considerable I/O savings.
3 At most a single triple identified by $\langle n_1, H, ? \rangle$ is retrieved.
4 At most a single triple identified by $\langle n_1, v_i, ? \rangle$ is retrieved.

An important observation is that all retrieval operations undertaken in traversing the match tree are of one of two forms:

$$\langle a, ?, ? \rangle$$
$$\langle a, b, ? \rangle$$

so the tuning facility provided through the splitting policy can be used to bias performance towards queries of this form.

4.3 Translation of Function Definitions

INTRODUCTION

The right-hand side of each data definition statement must be translated into a form suitable for evaluation by the inference engine. Possible forms include those of λ-abstractions, combinators, or super-combinators. Description of the translation process is far beyond the scope of this paper, although a lucid account can be found in [Fie88]. Here we give two examples of the translation of simple function definitions into combinator expressions, and show how the resulting expressions can be represented in a graphical form and evaluated by the process of graph reduction. Finally we consider how this graph can be stored and retrieved by the repository manager.

Expressions in combinatory logic [Hin86] take the following form:

$$\begin{aligned} \langle \text{expression} \rangle ::= \; & \langle \text{identifier} \rangle \mid \langle \text{expression} \rangle \langle \text{expression} \rangle \mid \\ & (\langle \text{expression} \rangle) \mid \langle \text{constant} \rangle \\ \langle \text{constant} \rangle ::= \; & \text{TRUE} \mid \text{FALSE} \mid 1 \mid 2 \mid \ldots \mid + \mid - \mid {}^{*} \mid \ldots \mid \text{S} \mid \text{K} \end{aligned}$$

where an ⟨identifier⟩ denotes another combinatory logic expression. The only method of combining expressions is that of function application, which is left associative. The combinators S (the 'distributor') and K (the 'cancellator') together with the other constants may be thought of as defining re-write rules as follows:

$+ \; e_1 \; e_2 \rightarrow e_3$ (where e_3 is the arithmetic sum of e_1 and e_2)
$- \; e_1 \; e_2 \rightarrow e_3$ (where e_3 is the arithmetic differences of e_1 and e_2)
:
$S \; e_1 \; e_2 \; e_3 \rightarrow e_1 \; e_3 \; (e_2 \; e_3)$
$K \; e_1 \; e_2 \rightarrow e_1$

with the boolean and integer constants re-writing to themselves. Theoretically S and K are sufficient to construct any computable function. However, in practice it is necessary for performance reasons to include a number of others, common ones being I (the 'identity'), B (the 'compositor') and C (the 'permutator'):

$I \; e_1 \rightarrow e_1$
$B \; e_1 \; e_2 \; e_3 \rightarrow e_1 \; (e_2 \; e_3)$
$C \; e_1 \; e_2 \; e_3 \rightarrow e_1 \; e_3 \; e_2$

For example, 'I' can be defined as 'SKK' since for any expression, e, SKKe = Ke(Ke) = e = Ie. As a simple example of the translation of functions into this fixed set of combinators, the definition for 'twice_successor':

twice_successor x = * 2 (+ 1 x);

gives rise to the intermediate lambda abstraction:

λx. *2(+ 1 x)

which is translated into the combinator expression:

B (*2) (C + 1)

See Field and Harrison [Fie88], chapter 12, for details of the translation process. As a further example, the right-hand side of the definition for head:

head (Cons x y) = x;

can be translated via the intermediate lambda expression

λx.λy.x

into the combinator expression

K

A number of optimisations can be carried out on translated function definitions [Tur79]. For example, for any commutative primitive function f the expression (C f) can be replaced by f, since for any arguments x and y, C f x y = f y x = f x y. Thus, the optimised version of 'twice_successor' is

B (*2) (+ 1)

Combinator expressions can be evaluated by a process termed *graph reduction*. Figure 5 shows (from left to right) the steps involved in the evaluation of 'twice_successor' when applied to the argument '3'. The root of the redex selected at each step in the evaluation is marked '†'. The only form of internal node is an application node (shown as '@') which denotes that the left child is to be applied to the right child. The root of the graph which represents the function 'twice_successor' is marked '‡'.

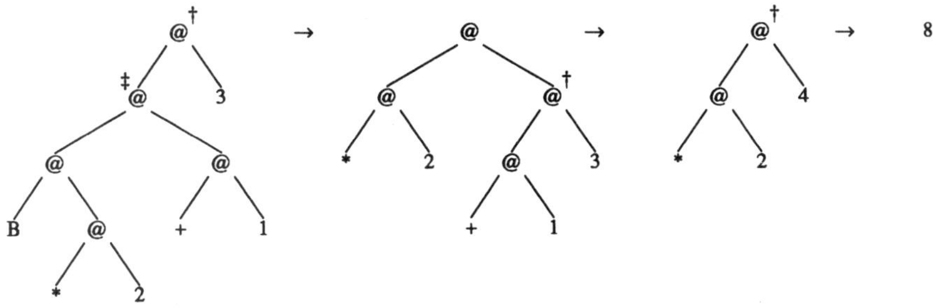

Figure 5

GRAPH STORAGE

The question which now must be addressed is that of how a graph, such as that for the function 'twice_successor', can be stored by the repository manager. Clearly we require that the graph should be simply and efficiently retrievable.

One solution is as follows. To each node of the graph an identifier is assigned: to the root of the graph is assigned the number 1; and if n is the identifier of a node, then 2n is assigned to its left child and (2n) + 1 to its right child. A unique identifier is then assigned to the graph as a whole. Finally, each node in the graph is stored as a triple of the form:

⟨graph_identifier, node_identifier, node_value⟩

Thus the graph of the function 'twice_successor' is expressed by the following triples, where g_n is the (unique) identifier assigned to the graph:

⟨g_n, 1, @⟩,	⟨g_n, 4, B⟩,	⟨g_n, 7, 1⟩,
⟨g_n, 2, @⟩,	⟨g_n, 5, @ ⟩,	⟨g_n, 10, *⟩,
⟨g_n, 3, @⟩,	⟨g_n, 6, + ⟩,	⟨g_n, 11, 2⟩

The set of triples into which a graph is decomposed contains all the information necessary for its reconstruction. Given a node n ($n \neq 1$), its parent is $\lfloor n/2 \rfloor$, and if n mod 2 = 0 then the node is a left child of its parent, otherwise it is a right child.

This method of storage accomplishes the first of our objectives, namely that the graph be retrieved simply, since all the above triples are identified by the operation:

open_virtual_file($\langle g_n$, ?, ?$\rangle$)

With regard to our second objective, namely that the graph be retrieved efficiently, there is no guarantee that all of these triples will lie within the same data page. Nevertheless, they will (by virtue of their common first field) lie in the same plane of the 3-dimensional data space. Furthermore, since the graph will only be retrieved in the above manner (viz. with the first field specified and the second and third fields unspecified), the splitting policy used for biasing performance towards the retrieval of match trees above will also be appropriate here.

GRAPH STORAGE OPTIMIZATION TECHNIQUES

Two important optimisation techniques for the storage of graphs are possible. The first technique involves simple function definitions – those with a right-hand side comprising a single node. For example, consider again the data definitions:

tax_code 'carol' = '267L';
tax_code 'mir' = '242LX';
:
tax_code x = '247L';

Using the technique outlined in Section 4.2 above, the match tree of the function 'tax_code' will be of the form:

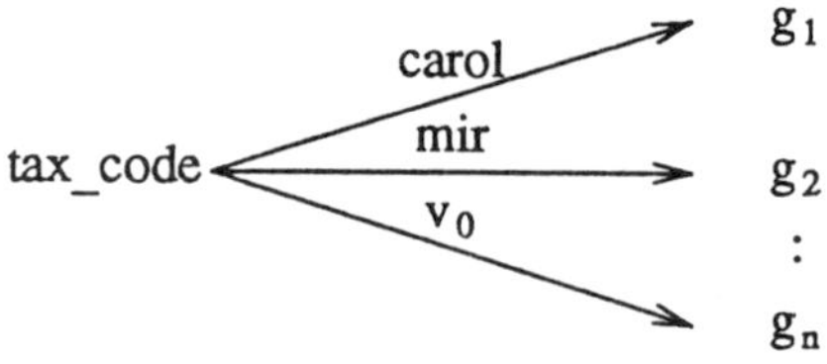

and the right-hand sides of the definitions will be stored as:

$\langle g_1, 1, \text{'267L'}\rangle, \langle g_2, 1, \text{'242LX'}\rangle, \ldots, \langle g_n, 1, \text{'247L'}\rangle$

To reduce a graph such as:

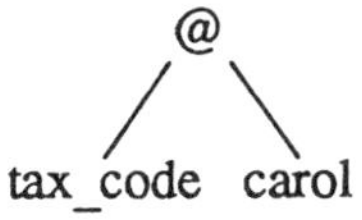

requires two retrieval requests to the repository manager: firstly to retrieve the (single) triple matching ⟨tax_code, carol, ?⟩ which contains g_1 as its third component, and secondly to retrieve the (single) triple matching $\langle g_1, ?, ?\rangle$. For simple definitions, such as these, we can obviate the need for the second retrieval request by storing the right-hand side directly in the leaf node of the match tree and tagging the value to identify the fact that it does not represent a graph identifier. Thus in the above instance the match tree becomes:

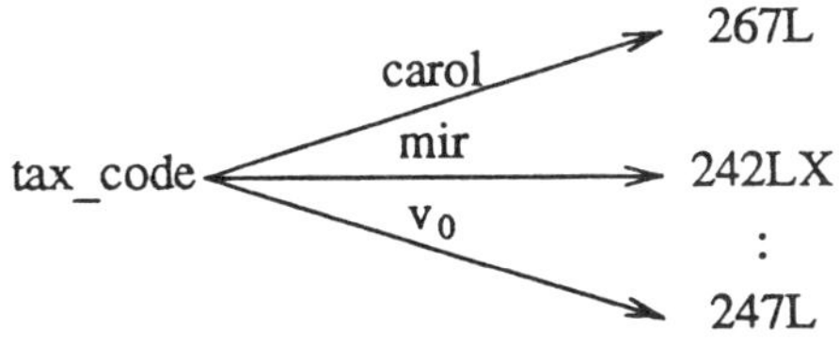

We note that this is simply the storage we would expect of a binary relation in a triple store. For many applications a large proportion of function definitions will be of this form, and consequently considerable savings can be made with respect to storage consumption and retrieval time.

A second area for optimisation is in the method of storage of the built-in function 'all'. Recall that 'all' takes as an argument an entity type and returns its extent. Thus in a database with two entity types, 'emp' (employee) and 'dept' (department), the match tree for 'all' would take the form

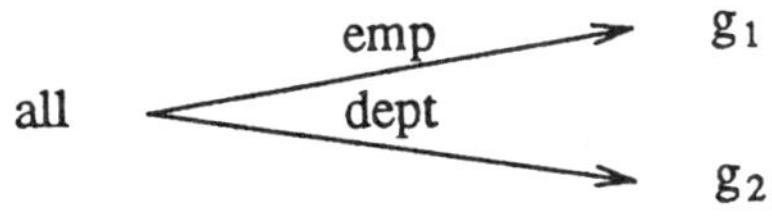

and the graph of g_1 would be of the form

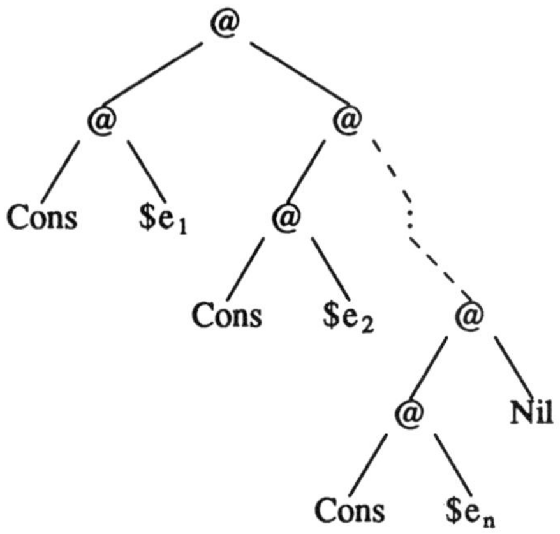

Each entity type may be associated with a large number of entities: envisage, for example, the number of entities of type 'department', 'employee' or 'order' for a medium-sized enterprise. Storage, in the form of a graph, of the list of entities associated with a given entity type is inefficient since given n entities there are 4n + 1 nodes in the graph. A more practical solution is to treat the function 'all' as a special case, and to store information relating entities to their types directly as triples of the form:

⟨all, department, d_1⟩, ⟨all, department, d_2⟩, ...,
⟨all, department, d_1⟩
⟨all, employee, e_1⟩, ⟨all, employee, e_2⟩, ..., ⟨all, employee, e_m⟩
⟨all, order, o_1⟩, ⟨all, order, o_2⟩, ..., ⟨all, order, o_n⟩

We note that this is the expected representation of 'isa' triples in a triple store. Using this technique, all the entities of a given type, t, are identified by the operation:

open_virtual_file(⟨all, t, ?⟩)

As well as reducing secondary storage requirements, this method brings additional advantages when evaluating expressions of the form 'all t'. In general there will be many entities of a given type, and consequently the complete evaluation of an expression of the form 'all t' will be very expensive. Frequently only a small subset of the entities will be required, especially in an interactive environment. It is therefore important for the system to construct lazily the list of entities belonging to a given type. This can be achieved by providing a subsidiary function, called next, which takes as a single argument a virtual file identifier, vf, and which returns:

- Nil, if vf is empty;
- Cons e (next vf), where the next record read from vf is ⟨all, type, e⟩, if vf is not empty;

Finally, the function all when applied to an entity type, t, simply applies next to the virtual file identifier returned by open_virtual_file(⟨all, t, ?⟩). Thus the evaluation of the expression

all order

will proceed as follows, where id_1 is a virtual file identifier returned by the operation open_virtual_file(⟨all,order,?⟩):

next id_1
Cons o_1 (next id_1)
Cons o_1 (Cons o_2 (next id_1))
Cons o_1 (Cons o_2 ... (Cons o_n (next id_1))...)
Cons o_1 (Cons o_2 ... (Cons o_n Nil)...)

A similar technique can be adopted to store any list of constants on the right-hand side of an equation for which the ordering is immaterial.

4.4 Evaluation Strategies

We recall that the evaluation of an expression proceeds by repeated selection and reduction of redexes. The evaluation process may continue until the expression contains no more redexes, when the expression is said to be in *normal form*. Clearly, at any point in the evaluation there may be more than one redex in the expression, and the selection of one particular redex over another may significantly affect the performance or even the termination of a computation. For example, consider the expression

K I (S I I (S I I)) x

which contains two redexes, (K I (...) x) and (S I I (S I I)); the following reduction order (where the redex selected at each step is marked by the superscript ′) gives:

K I (S′ I I (S I I)) x
→ K I (I′ (S I I) (I (S I I))) x
→ K I (S I I (I′ (S I I))) x
→ K I (S I I (S I I)) x

which is the original expression, whilst an alternative reduction order terminates with a normal form:

$$\begin{array}{ll} & K'\ I\ (S\ I\ I\ (S\ I\ I))\ x \\ \rightarrow & I'\ x \\ \rightarrow & x \end{array}$$

There are two principal strategies for selecting the next redex: *normal* order reduction selects the redex which is syntactically leftmost outermost in the expression, whilst *applicative* order reduction selects the redex which is leftmost innermost. Thus, in our example above, the first list of reduction steps uses applicative-order reduction whilst the second list uses normal-order reduction. Fortunately, the Church–Rosser Theorem states that if an expression can be reduced to two normal forms then these normal forms are identical; moreover, the Standardisation Theorem states that if an expression has a normal form then normal-order reduction is guaranteed to reach that normal form (see [Hin86]). Normal-order reduction may be thought of as delaying the reduction of redexes for as long as possible just in case the expressions they represent are later discarded (as in the above example), whilst applicative-order reduction always reduces the arguments of a redex before reducing the redex itself.

Instead of proceeding to normal form, the evaluation of expressions may continue only until there are no outer-level redexes, when the expression is said to be in *weak head-normal form* (WHNF). Normal-order reduction to WHNF is termed *lazy evaluation* whilst applicative-order reduction to WHNF is termed *eager evaluation*.

1. If the leftmost leaf is a *constructor function*, the graph is already in WHNF and the algorithm terminates.
2. If the leaf is a *built-in n-ary function*, f, and the n immediate ancestors of this node are application nodes identifying the arguments to f, then this sub-graph is replaced by the result of executing the built-in code for f for the given arguments.
3. If the leaf is a *user-defined n-ary function*, f, and the n immediate ancestors of this node are application nodes identifying the arguments to f, then Algorithm 1 is called for the function and its arguments, and this sub-graph is overwritten by a graph consisting of an application of the right-hand side of the definition returned by Algorithm 1 to the given arguments.
4. The only remaining possibility is that the leftmost leaf is an n-ary (built-in or user-defined) function which has only $m < n$ ancestors. In this case, the graph is already in WHNF.

Algorithm 2 Reduction to WHNF

An inference engine for a functional language typically comprises two recursive functions, Print and Eval. Given an expression, Print passes it to Eval for reduction to WHNF; upon return from Eval, the expression comprises an n-ary constructor function together with n (possibly unevaluated) arguments; the constructor function is then printed and Print is invoked recursively for each of the arguments. Eval is normally implemented by means of the repeated rewriting of the graph representing the expression to be evaluated. Eval examines the form of the leftmost leaf node of this graph and performs one of the actions listed inAlgorithm 2.

For example, as shown in Section 4.3, the definition of 'head' is simply the cancellator combinator, K; thus, the evaluation of

head (Cons 2 l)

(where l is a list of numbers) proceeds:

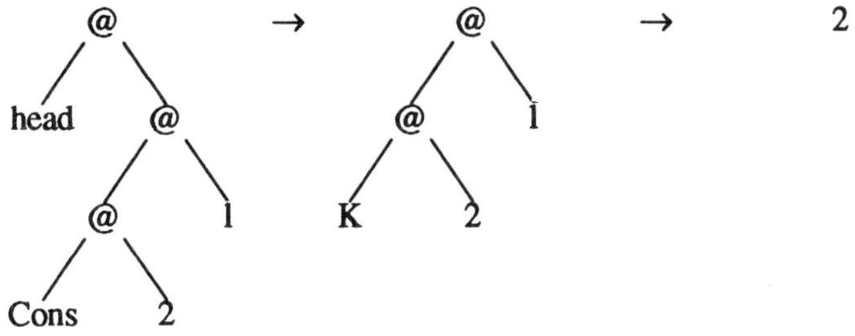

The first reduction is by case 3 of Algorithm 2, the second by case 2, and the final graph is irreducible (case 1).

Algorithm 2 defines a lazy Eval function ; a strict Eval function would invoke itself recursively for each of the arguments at step 3. The relative merits of these evaluation methods may be summarised as follows:

- The principal advantage of lazy evaluation over eager evaluation is that it ensures that arguments which are not used in the body of a function are never evaluated. As a simple example, consider the function 'and', defined as follows:

  and FALSE x = FALSE;
  and TRUE x = x;

  together with the query:

  and (equal 1 2) ⊥

  where ⊥ represents a non-terminating evaluation (such as the evaluation of the degenerate function definition f = f). An eager evaluation strategy will insist that both arguments to 'and' are fully evaluated before the function can be applied, and hence the evaluation will never terminate. In contrast, a lazy strategy will not itself evaluate either argument, but will call the pattern-matching algorithm (Algorithm 1) which will evaluate only the first argument in order to select the appropriate definition.

- A direct corollary of the above point is that lazy evaluation permits the evaluation of some expressions which would fail to terminate if eager evaluation were employed, as predicted theoretically by the Standardisation Theorem, and as demonstrated by the above example.
- Sub-graphs representing un-evaluated arguments are maintained for longer in main memory using lazy evaluation than would be the case with eager evaluation. These structures may be large and result in increased paging and garbage collection overheads.
- Pattern matching for lazy evaluation may require more retrieval requests. As noted in our discussion of Algorithm 1, the retrieval in step 2 is not required if an eager evaluation strategy is employed. Moreover, we observe that of all the retrieval requests issued by this algorithm, the request at step 2 is likely to be most expensive since it is a plane query of the form ⟨a, ?, ?⟩, all others being line queries of the form ⟨a, b, ?⟩.

5. CONCLUDING REMARKS AND FUTURE WORK

The work reported in this paper was undertaken in the context of the TriStarp project at Birkbeck College during the period 1984–1988. The repository manager described in Section 3 above was implemented [Der89] and used to support two deductive database systems, one based upon the logic paradigm (Exegesis [Sma88, Kin91]) and the other upon the functional (FDL [Pou 90, Pou 92]). Section 4 (with the exception of the introduction to 4.3) is based upon the implementation of FDL, described more fully in [Pou 92]. FDL continues to support research within the TriStarp project, while a language similar to FDL was used by the Imperial Cancer Research Fund in the analysis of protein sequences as part of the CARDS project [Add90].

More recently, as part of a separate project, a new deductive database language called PFL has been developed [Pou91, Sma91b] which combines a functional computational model with a relational data model. Functions are defined through the specification of equations and the type of a function is automatically inferred. Bulk data is stored in a special class of functions called selectors which incorporate a nested relation and allow associative retrieval of data from that relation. The implementation of PFL derives from that of FDL and PFPE [Sma91a]. The performance of PFL with respect to computationally intensive queries is comparable to that of contemporary functional programming languages ([Sma91a] gives performance figures). The performance of PFL with respect to data-intensive queries is currently being investigated using large volumes of road traffic accident data in an SERC-funded collaborative project (GR/G 19596).

Current research directions within the PFL project include the development of a functional meta-language, the declaration and automatic enforcement of integrity constraints over selectors, and the functional specification of user interfaces.

6. ACKNOWLEDGEMENTS

We would like to thank our friends and colleagues at Birkbeck College for their criticism and encouragement, and in particular Professor Peter King, co-ordinator of the TriStarp Project, and Dr Geoff Sharman and Norman Winterbottom of IBM U.K. Laboratories.

REFERENCES

[Add90] Addis, T. R. and Nowell, M. C. C. Scaling up Knowledge Systems: an Architecture for the Giga Knowledge Base, *Proceedings of Expert Systems '90*, Cambridge University Press,1990, pp. 238–251.

[Bat88] Batory, D. S., Leung, T. Y. and Wise, T. E. Implementation Concepts for an Extensible Data Model and Data Language, *A.C.M. Transactions on Database Systems*, Vol 13(3), September 1988.

[Bra76] Bracchi, G., Paolini, P. and Pelagatti, G. Binary Logical Associations in Data Modelling, in *Modelling in Data Base Management Systems*, North-Holland, 1976.

[Bun79] Buneman, P. and Frankel, R. E. FQL: A Functional Query Language, *A.C.M. SIGMOD Proceedings*, 1979, pp. 52–58.

[Cha78] Chang, C. L. DEDUCE 2 : Further Investigations of Deduction in Relational Data Bases, in [Gal78].

[Cha86] Chang, C. L. and Walker, A. PROSQL: A Prolog Programming Interface with SQL/DS, in [Ker86].

[Clo81] Clocksin, W. F. and Mellish, C. S. *Programming in Prolog*, Springer-Verlag, 1981.

[Dat85] Date, C. *An Introduction to Database Systems*, Volume II, Addison-Wesley, 1985.

[Der89] Derakhshan, M. *A Development of the Grid File for the Storage of Binary Relations*, Ph.D. Thesis, Birkbeck College, University of London, 1989.

[Fie88] Field, A. J. and Harrison, P. G. *Functional Programming*, Addison-Wesley, 1988.

[Fre87] Freeston, M. The BANG File: A New Kind of Grid File, *Proceedings of the A.C.M. SIGMOD Conference* 1987, pp. 260–277.

[Fro82] Frost, R. A. Binary Relational Storage Structures, *Computer Journal*, Vol 25, No 3, 1982.

[Gal78] Gallaire, H. and Minker, J. *Logic and Databases*, Plenum Press, 1978.

[Gal84] Gallaire, H., Minker, J. and Nicolas, J. M. Logic and Databases: A Deductive Approach, *A.C.M. Computing Surveys*, Vol 16, No 2, June 1984.

[Gra88a] Gray, P. M. D., Moffat, D. S. and Paton, N. W. A Prolog Interface to a Functional Data Model Database, *Proceedings of EDBT-88*, Springer-Verlag, LNCS 303, pp. 34–48, March 1988.

[Gra88b] Gray, P. M. D. and Lucas, R. *Prolog and Databases: Implementations and Applications*, Ellis Horwood, 1988.

[Hin85] Hinrichs, K. H. *The Grid File System: Implementation and Case Studies of Applications*, Swiss Federal Institute of Technology, Zurich, 1985.

[Hin86] Hindley, J. R. and Seldin, J. P. *Introduction to Combinators and λ-Calculus*, Cambridge University Press, 1986.

[Ker86] Kerschberg, L. (Ed) *Expert Database Systems*, Benjamin Cummings, 1986.

[Kin91] King, P. J. H. and Small, C. Default Databases and Incomplete Information, *Computer Journal*, Vol 34, No 3, 1991.

[Kul86] Kulkarni, K. G. and Atkinson, M. P. EFDM: Extended Functional Data Model, *Computer Journal*, Vol 29, No 1, 1986.

[Llo87] Lloyd, J. *Foundations of Logic Programming* (2nd Edition), Springer-Verlag, 1987.

[Mar84] Martin, N. The Construction of Interfaces to Triple Based Databases, *Proceedings of the 3rd BNCOD*, Cambridge University Press, 1984.

[Min78] Minker, J. An Experimental Relational Data Base System Based on Logic, in [Gal78].

[Nai83] Naish, L. and Thom, J. A. *The MU-Prolog Deductive Database System*, Technical Report 83/10, University of Melbourne, 1983.

[Nie84] Nievergelt, J., Hinterberger, H. and Sevcik, K. C. The Grid File: An Adaptable, Symmetric Multikey File Structure, *A.C.M. Transactions on Database Systems*, Vol 9, March 1984.

[Pey87] Peyton-Jones, S. *The Implementation of Functional Programming Languages*, Prentice-Hall, 1987.

[Pou90] Poulovassilis, A. and King P. Extending the Functional Data Model to Computational Completeness, *Proceedings of EDBT-90*, Springer-Verlag, LNCS 416, 1990, pp. 75–91.

[Pou91] Poulovassilis, A. and Small, C. A Functional Approach to Deductive Databases, *Proceedings of the 17th Int. Conf. on Very Large Databases*, 1991.

[Pou92] Poulovassilis, A. The Implementation of FDL, a Functional Database Language, *The Computer Journal*, Vol 35, No 2, 1992, pp. 119–128.

[Rei80] Reiter, R. A Logic for Default Reasoning, *Artificial Intelligence*, Vol 13, 1980.

[Riv76] Rivest, R. L. Partial-Match Retrieval Algorithms, *SIAM Journal of Computing*, Vol 5, No 1, March 1976, pp. 19–49.

[Sch82] Scheuermann, P. and Ouksel, M. Multidimensional B-trees for Associative Searching in Database Systems, *Information Systems*, Vol 7, No 2, 1982, pp. 123–137.

[Sha88] Sharman, G. C. H. and Winterbottom, N. The Universal Triple Machine: a Reduced Instruction Set Repository Manager, *Proceedings of the 6th British National Conference on Databases*, Cambridge University Press, June 1988.

[Shi81] Shipman, D. W. The Functional Data Model and the Data Language DAPLEX, *A.C.M. Transactions on Database Systems*, Vol 6, No 1, March 1981, pp. 140–173.

[Sma88] Small, C. Guarded Default Databases: A Prototype Implementation, in [Gra88b].

[Sma91a] Small, C. A Persistent Functional Programming Environment, *Proceedings of the 3rd PanHellenic Conference on Informatics*, 1991.

[Sma91b] Small, C. and Poulovassilis, A. An Overview of PFL, *Proceedings of the 3rd Int. Workshop on Database Programming Languages*, 1991.

[Tsu86] Tsur, S. and Zaniolo, C. LDL: A Logic-Based Data-Language, *Proceedings of the 12th Int. Conf. on Very Large Databases*, 1986.

[Tur79] Turner, D. A. A New Implementation Technique for Applicative Languages, *Software – Practice and Experience*, Vol 9, 1979.

[Tur86] Turner, D. A. An Overview of Miranda, *A.C.M. SIGPLAN Notices*, December 1986.

5
Object-Oriented Database Systems: State of the Art and Research Problems

RAINER UNLAND[1] AND GUNTER SCHLAGETER[2]

[1]*University of Münster, Institut für Wirtschaftsinformatik, Grevener Str. 91, 4400 Münster, Germany*
[2]*University of Hagen, Department of Computer Science, P.O. Box 940, D-5800 Hagen 1, Germany*

1. INTRODUCTION

One of today's most burning database issues is how to support adequately new classes of database applications that are not well served by conventional database systems. For example, CAD/CAM, CASE, large data-intensive AI applications or image and voice processing place demands on database systems that exceed the capabilities of conventional (relational) database systems by far. Examples of essential disadvantages are:

1 *Artificial representation of complex structured objects*
The relational data model fails to support the modelling of complex structured objects since it only allows the user to model objects by flat relations. Since relations are all at the same level, other meaningful relationships are either lost or have to be maintained entirely by the application.

2 *Properties of objects cannot be modelled in an appropriate way*
To allow the user to model the structure of complex objects naturally and efficiently additional data types should not only be provided by the data model of the database system but should also be definable by the user (extensibility).

3 *Operational semantics of complex structured objects is not expressible*
Relational data-modelling techniques fail to capture the operational semantics (i.e. set of operations applicable to an object) that are normally associated with complex structured objects. Instead, these

Expert Database Systems
ISBN 0-12-382255-6

semantics are completely specified by users within their application programs.

4 *Different levels of abstraction are not supported*
Objects are, in general, not static but correspond to a world that is evolving. Therefore, flexibility has to be provided. The system should allow the same object to be viewed at different levels of abstraction.

5 *Lack of trigger, constraint and event mechanisms*
Advanced database applications require powerful and efficient trigger, constraint and event mechanisms to be able to model the inherent complexity of such applications.

6 *Clumsy database access (impedance mismatch)*
The interface between programming and database languages is usually crude since each language provides a different type system as well as a different computational model. Moreover, interfaces are often designed as an afterthought. This causes the **impedance mismatch** because much of the meta-information (e.g. structures and operations) in either system is reflected at the interface rather than passing through it. Therefore, meta-information must be defined redundantly in both languages. Moreover, transformations must be defined whenever data or operations need to pass through the interface. Depending on the languages, such a transformation may withhold some semantics since, e.g. data structures are not supported adequately in both languages. Also, database systems permit us to handle sets of tuples at a time while programming languages act according to the record-at-a-time principle.

A database is supposed to represent the relevant semantics of an application as completely and accurately as possible. A data model defines general rules for the specification of the structures of the data and the operations allowed on it; i.e. it defines its miniworld semantics and ways in which it can be expressed. The relational data model is too simple to express the semantics of advanced database applications in an appropriate way. But if more semantics can be expressed in the database, the borderline between applications and database system has to be crossed less frequently, consistency can be maintained more readily, and efficient physical mechanisms can be provided. The overall objective of a main part of the database community, therefore, is to extend database technology to capture more meaning. The object-oriented world not only offers powerful modelling concepts but also provides a framework to represent and manage both program and data, thus, among other things, solving the impedance mismatch. At the same time, the object-oriented programming-language community feels the need to integrate some database functionality into object-oriented programming languages, for instance persistency and sharability of data.

In this paper we will concentrate on the question of what an object-oriented database system is and what problems are currently associated with this technology. Therefore, we will first discuss in Section 2 the object-oriented paradigm on a rather intuitive basis. Next we will discuss in Section 3 the roots and a first informal definition of object-oriented database systems. Section 4 concentrates on the special features of this technology by discussing its characteristics in more detail. Moreover, it will address a number of open questions which have to be resolved to make object-oriented technology a successful variant of database systems. In Section 5 a selection of five object-oriented database systems is presented. Some of these systems are commercially available while others are research prototypes. This section will show how differently the object-oriented paradigm is interpreted by different research groups. Finally, Section 6 concludes the paper.

2. THE OBJECT-ORIENTED PARADIGM

2.1. Introduction

Like human languages programming languages obey different paradigms. Currently the most common paradigm is the imperative paradigm in which a programmer tells a computer what it has to do with which item and when and how. The functional paradigm (at least in its purest form) eliminates variables and, thus, avoids the problem of side effects. Declarative or logic programming frees the programmer from the burden of declaring how a problem is to be solved. It allows him simply to describe precisely what the computer should produce and leaves it to the computer to determine how these results are to be achieved. But what is the essence of the object-oriented programming paradigm? Rentsch described the field of object-oriented programming languages as follows (/Rent82/): '... object-oriented programming will be in the 1980's what structured programming was in the 1970's. Everyone will be in favor of it. Every manufacturer will promote his products as supporting it. Every manager will pay lip service to it. Every programmer will practice it (differently). And no one will know what it is'. Although this statement seems to be a little bit overstated, it nevertheless describes the uncertainty which is partly associated with the term 'object-orientation'. One reason for this is that 'object-oriented' is currently a buzz-word which attracts a lot of people to mark their work or products by it. In the following we will, therefore, give a first intuitive specification of the characteristics we associate with the notion of object-orientation.

2.2. An Exemplary Scenario

Let us assume that we walk into a room. What we might see are some people, several chairs, a desk, etc. To the observer the interior of the room is a collection of objects: it is the nature of the human perception to dissect his environment into well-defined objects. But we not only recognize objects, mostly we also associate some functionality with them; i.e. we know to which messages (or activities) they may react in what way. For example, if we switch on a radio we know that we will, most probably, hear some music or some spoken words. Although in most cases we know what objects are good for we often don't know by which means their functionality is realized. For example, most people don't know how a radio transforms the signals it receives into music or spoken words.

After entering the room we notice a woman sitting at a typewriter. Although we haven't seen her before we know something about her, e.g. she has a name, she speaks a language, she is able to move, etc. We know this because she belongs to the class or category of human beings; more precisely, she is a woman and could well be our new secretary. Now let us assume that we entered the room to ask someone to take a letter to the post office. There are two more people in the room, our manager and a trainee. If we asked the trainee to do the job he would most probably react by answering: 'Yes, Sir'. If we, instead, asked our manager he would (in the best case) react by doubting our state of health. Although both people belong to the same category (men) they react differently to the same message.

This small exemplary scenario already allows us to deduce some general rules or characteristics about our environment:

1 Our environment exclusively consists of *objects*.
2 Together with the objects comes their *behaviour*; i.e. objects are described by their functionality.
3 Mostly we *know* the functionality of objects but we *don't know* how this functionality is realized.
4 Objects react to *messages*.
5 Only the objects *themselves* decide in which way they *react* to a message.
6 Different objects may *react* to the same message in *different ways*.
7 Objects *inherit characteristics* and *abilities* as a result of their membership of a special class or category.

2.3. Informal Discussion of Features

Although the above characteristics are rather intuitive, they, nevertheless, make up the main features of the object-oriented paradigm. More formally the features translate into the following characteristics: In an object-oriented system everything is an object. There is no distinction between user-defined objects and system-defined objects (uniform handling). Objects are **encapsulated** which means that there is no way to access an object except through the public interface (a set of operations) specified for it. Encapsulation is an especially important feature of object-oriented systems since it assures that an interface of an object is independent of its (internal) representation. Neither the implementation of its operations nor its structure are visible. To emphasize object independence, objects communicate by **message passing**. This paradigm for communication assumes that the user does not directly manipulate or view the (hidden) attributes of an object; instead, he sends a message to an object, and the object itself determines the method by which it will react.

An object belongs to a class and a class itself is treated as an object, too. A **class** is a template that special operations (like ***new***) can use to create new objects. Objects of the same class have common operations and, therefore, a uniform behaviour. Another important characteristic is inheritance. **Inheritance** makes it possible to declare a class as a specialization of another class, thus supporting the management of (hierarchical) relationships among classes as well as the reusability of software. The key idea of inheritance is to provide a simple and powerful mechanism for defining a new (sub)class that inherits the structure and the operations from an existing (super)class. New methods or new structure may be added while old methods and old structure may be overridden. In the above example the manager as well as the trainee may be modelled as belonging to different classes, each of which is realized as a specialization of the class *EMPLOYEE*. This allows the programmer to model different reactions to the same message (e.g. to the request to take the letter to the post office) while common behaviour is inherited, therefore, taken 'as is' from the (super)class (*EMPLOYEE*). While classes, such as *EMPLOYEE* and *FEMALES*, may overlap in the real world, object-oriented systems do not always allow such an overlapping; often the assumption is made that every object must belong to precisely one base class. The ability of different objects to respond differently to the same message is known as **polymorphism**.

The concepts of inheritance and polymorphism can best be exploited if the underlying system supports run-time type checking and **late binding** (operation names are translated into program addresses at run-time). While late binding clearly offers more flexibility it decreases efficiency and programming safety due to the necessity of performing run-time checks. Some people argue that a system has to support late binding to be object-oriented while others do not.

3. STATE OF THE ART OF THE OBJECT-ORIENTED DATABASE FIELD

3.1. Introduction

Although the quotation of Rentsch (see last section) is aimed at object-oriented programming languages its message is even more accurate for the situation in the object-oriented database field. The definition of an object-oriented database system is subject to considerable debate and it will probably be a long time before the community will agree on a common definition. The heated debate about what an object-oriented database system is can also be seen from the fact that there are a number of introductory papers to object-oriented databases, most of them defining an object-oriented database system in a different way (see, e.g. /ABDD89/, /Banc88/, /Beer89/, /BeMa91/, /BGHS91/, /Ditt87/, /KhAb90/, /Khos90/, /Kim90-1/, /Kim90-2/, /Kim90-3/, /Kim91/, /Maie89-2/, /Mano89/, /NeSt89/, /Nier89/, /PCKW89/, /Ston90/, /UnSc90/, /WeZd86/, /WiEK90/, /ZdHe90/, /ZdMa90/).

3.2. Historical Roots

Historical roots for object-oriented database technology are often described in terms of the development of semantic data models /HaML81/ and the development of abstraction-based languages within the discipline of programming languages. The knowledge representation ideas of AI technology (especially the frame model by Minsky (/Mins75/)) may also have influenced object-oriented database technology. However, AI is mainly regarded as an application area for object-oriented database systems and only rarely as a third discipline leading to this technology.

3.3. Top-down and Bottom-up Approach

According to these historical roots two major approaches can be observed. Especially researchers from the database community follow a **bottom-up approach**. They try to adjust conventional database technology to become object-oriented, first of all by supporting the concept of complex objects, (also called molecular, structured, or aggregate objects) on all levels of the system architecture. A **top-down approach** is followed mainly by programming language people. They try to adapt object-oriented programming languages to database technology by allowing objects to be persistent and sharable.

The bottom-up approach realizes at its lowest level an object server; i.e. a container which allows the system to handle adequately complex objects on the physical level. Access paths or indexing techniques for complex objects might be added to reflect the general and specific properties of the objects. On the interface level generic operations for both entire objects and components of objects are offered. In other words a database system is object-oriented if it provides a data model that allows the user to represent one miniworld entity (whatever its complexity and structure might be) by exactly one object in the database (in terms of the concepts of the data model), and that, additionally, offers appropriate operations to exploit the structure of the object (this corresponds to the notion **structurally object-oriented**, as introduced by Dittrich (/Ditt87/)). This (informal) definition concentrates on the notion of (complex) object as the central criterion to specify object-orientation. Concepts known from object-oriented programming languages such as inheritance or data abstraction are disregarded in this view of object-orientation, as is the problem of impedance mismatch. The data language of the database system and the corresponding programming language may still follow different programming paradigms.

The top-down approach takes as its basis an object-oriented programming language and enriches its functionality by concepts known from database systems, above all **persistence** (objects remain in existence even if the application program ends) and **object sharing** (independent applications may use the same data concurrently). A result of these activities might be a programming language in which there is a single model of data for both persistent and non-persistent data. In a broader sense such systems realize **behavioural object-orientation**, as defined by Dittrich (/Ditt88-2/). While the advantage of this approach is a unique language for both database access and application programming, its disadvantage is the rudimentary or missing realization of most other database concepts, such as indexing techniques, measures for concurrency control and reliability (recovery), or optimization strategies for queries on the database.

A major reason for the failure of nearly all programming languages to integrate database concepts is that the programming language environments and database systems are each designed within different cultures. They are usually built on different concepts for typing, computation and identity. Typing systems in (imperative) programming languages typically include arrays, lists, and atomic types, while typing systems in database languages typically include sets, records, and atomic types. Computational models in programming languages are typically rich in manipulation capabilities, while computational models in database languages typically include only search and simple update capabilities. The notion of identity in programming languages is typically weaker than that of database systems.

3.4. Basic Definition of the Object-Oriented Database System

If we take a closer look at both approaches above it seems reasonable to assume that both capture some aspects of a truly object-oriented database system while they neglect others. One may, therefore, argue that a true object-oriented database system is to be a symbiosis of the essential concepts of the two approaches. Accordingly, a first working definition is (see also (/Banc88/)):

> *Definition 3.1:* **object-oriented database system** (basic definition)
> An object-oriented database system should satisfy two criteria: it should be a database management system, and it should be an object-oriented system. The first criterion translates into six features: persistence; secondary storage management; data sharing (concurrency); data reliability (transaction management and recovery); ad hoc query facility; and schema modification. The second translates into eight features: types/classes; encapsulation/data abstraction; inheritance; polymorphism/late binding; computational completeness; object identity; complex objects; and extensibility.

4. FEATURES OF OBJECT-ORIENTED DATABASE SYSTEMS

In this section we will concentrate on the discussion of each feature which describes an object-oriented database system and how it can be interpreted. Moreover, we will discuss problems which may arise when these features are to be combined in an integral system. The discussion of database system concepts will lead to an extended definition of an object-oriented database system.

4.1. Types and Classes — Object and Values

TYPES AND CLASSES

In this section we will first introduce the conventional notion of type (class) as it is commonly used in imperative programming languages (object-oriented programming languages). Then we will concentrate on the notion of class in the context of object-oriented database systems.

Imperative programming and types

Modern (imperative) programming languages, like PASCAL or SIMULA, make distinctions between a type definition and a variable declaration to distinguish between the definition of a type and its use. A simple notion of **type** is that it includes a possibly infinite set of values (its domain) and a set of operations on those values. A **variable** of a specific type is constrained to assume values of that type. A type may be atomic or structured. An **atomic (basic** or **simple) data type** is a data type whose values are regarded as nondecomposable (from the user's point of view), like integer or character. A **structured (composite) data type (data structure, data aggregate)** is a data type whose values are composed of component elements that are related by some structure. This structure has to be considered by the user if he wants to access the data structure. Examples are array of integers or set of characters. Since a structured data type is a data type, it has a set of operations on its values and a set of operations that act on its component elements (/StWe85/). A structured data type is built using already existing data types and type constructors, like array, set, list, record; i.e. the **type constructor** lays down the structure of the structured data type.

In programming languages types are tools to increase correctness of programs and efficiency. By forcing the user to declare the structure of the objects he manipulates, the system checks that the user does not perform wrong assignments to, or manipulations on objects. Thus, types are used at compile-time to check the correctness of the programs, therefore eliminating the necessity of run-time checks. Another advantage is that procedures can be bound to the call at compile-time. By these means, expensive operations like context creation and procedure calling can be replaced by inexpensive operations like branching. Moreover, without a type-system, it is impossible for a compiler to optimize code. Since a compiler has no way to determine the procedure that implements an operation, it cannot find out whether the operation has side effects or affects control flow. Thus, common subexpression elimination, dead code removal, and other common optimizations are not generally applicable.

We can differentiate between two kinds of typing: static typing and strong typing (/Wegn89/). A programming language is said to be **statically typed** if the type of all expressions can be determined at compile-time (complete type checking at compile-time). If at compile-time the type compatibility of all expressions representing values can be determined from the static program representation the language is said to be **strongly typed** (may introduce the necessity of some run-time type checking). Every statically typed language is always strongly typed, but the converse is not necessarily true since a strongly typed language may allow the programmer to use, e.g. generic operations, such as sorting, that capture the structure of an algorithm uniformly applicable to a range of types.

Object-oriented programming and classes

Object-oriented programming is, first, what the name implies: writing programs that deal with objects; i.e. the object is the centre of attention. In object-oriented programming objects are usually treated as abstract data types (which will be discussed in more detail later). Rather than describing the individual structure of an object, one should concentrate on the behaviour that is common to a whole class of objects – the class of persons, of students, of teachers and so on; i.e. a class, first of all, describes the common behaviour of a (potentially infinite) set of objects. However, a class not only describes how an object must behave to belong to that class. It also serves as *the* (only) repository of all objects which currently belong to the class (these objects are often called **instances** of that class). This means that the notion of class is somewhat connected to run-time considerations or, to say it in the words of Bancilhon (/Banc88/), the notion of class covers two aspects: an object factory, and an object container. **Object factory** means that a class can be used to produce new objects (this is often called to **instantiate** an object) by performing an operation like ***new*** on the class. **Object container** means that *all* instances of a class are collected in *one* container which is, as such, accessible to the user. The user can manipulate the container by applying operations to objects of the class. The container is often called the **extension of the class**. The reason for the use of typing is increased programming safety due to the possibility of performing type checking at compile time. A type denotes the structure and the domain (of each subcomponent) of this structure. The (potentially infinite) set of entities of this structure which are in conformity with the domain specification(s) is called the **extension of the type**. From a slightly different point of view the extension of the type can be seen as the set of entities of a given structure which meet a given predicate (= domain specification). Since the extension of the type is related to and defined by the structure associated with the type, it is static. Classes primarily are to create, collect, and handle objects. The extension of a class is, therefore, the collection of all concrete objects which currently belong to that class; i.e. the extension of a class is dynamic. For example, in an imperative programming language the type integer denotes the well-defined and static set of values that are integers, but this set (extension) is not actually available to the programmer as a value. This especially means that the programmer cannot manipulate the extension of the type integer since the extension is the set of all potentially creatable entities of that type. If the programmer wants to collect a number of concrete entities of this set he has to define a specific data structure for holding sets of integer values, e.g. array of integer. If the concept of class is supported the programmer creates a new class and adds to this class all integers he wants to add. This means that the extension of a class does not describe the set of potential entities of a given structure but the set of concrete (instantiated) objects of this structure.

Classes revisited (part I)

Programming mostly does not concentrate on the maintenance of large volumes of objects of equal structure but on data processing. For this reason, usually a limited number of variables are defined which are used to process data at run-time (often most of them are of different type). However, data entities vanish at the end of the processing time of a program at the latest; i.e. it is not the container aspect of classes that programming concentrates on but the processing of data entities. Since access to main memory is fast there isn't the necessity to cluster data entities or to maintain a specific container for (the small number of entities of) each data type. Instead, main memory serves as *the* general container for all entities. Moreover, object-oriented programming languages typically fragment (complex) data entities; i.e. a complex data entity is recursively decomposed into a number of flat tuples of fixed size. Either the value of an attribute is atomic or the value of the attribute is represented by another tuple which is connected to the original tuple by a pointer (hierarchical decomposition). This results in a strong fragmentation of data entities in main memory. This strongly implies that the aspect that a class serves as a container is of minor interest with respect to object-oriented programming.

This stands in contrast to database applications. They usually concentrate on sets of objects of equal structure. This especially means that a class is often the starting point of any kind of data processing. However, as already mentioned, the nature of a class definition implies that it can be seen as a kind of type declaration and as the installation of the (only) container for all objects of that type. As a consequence we can't define a 'pure' type, say, *Address* and use it as a type declaration for a dependent attribute (an attribute (object) whose existence depends on the existence of another, more complex object). For example, if we want to define the attribute

ADDRESS_STUDENT for *STUDENT* and the attribute ADDRESS_RESEARCHER for *RESEARCHER* and want the values of both attributes to be of type *Address* such a definition is not possible: by defining the class *ADDRESS* we not only define a type but we also, implicitly, install a container for all instances of the type *Address*. As a consequence these instances have an existence of their own (they are independent); i.e. the address instance of a student object would not be deleted if the student object is removed. The above discussion strongly suggests that the mixing of class and type system is inadequate since types are orthogonal to classes (at least in the context of object-oriented database systems) (several other researchers agree with this position; see, e.g. the Panel on Inheritance, OOPSLA 1989 (/MJSS89/)). Instead, there should be a clear conceptual distinction between the definition of a type (type declaration) and the installation of a container for concrete entities of this type (class declaration). But, of course, both concepts have to be supported by a database system (a more comprehensive discussion can be found, e.g. in /AlCO85/, /AtBu87/, and /RiVe87/).

O_2 is one of the few object-oriented database systems that supports both types and classes; i.e. O_2 allows the programmer to define 'classes' *with* (corresponds to the notion of class) or *without* extension (corresponds to the notion of type). Note, however, that the term *extension* has a slightly different meaning here: *with extension* indicates that every newly created object of that type automatically becomes persistent while in the other case objects only become persistent if they are named; therefore, in both cases a kind of object container is maintained, in the first case the container is implicitly filled, in the other case explicitly.

GemStone does not differentiate between classes and types. However, in GemStone a class only serves to describe the common behaviour of objects of that class; i.e. GemStone does not install an object container (this has to be done explicitly; for more detail, see Section 5.1).

Classes revisited (part II)

The discussion in the previous section concentrated on the notion of class and type. In this section, we will discuss what 'kinds of typing' are provided by object-oriented systems. We will start by looking at the notions of type and class from a different point of view.

A type may be defined by a predicate for recognizing expressions of the type while a class may be defined by a template for object creation. In this sense, a class can be seen as a special kind of type, namely a type whose predicate is a template specification. For every class there is a type predicate that characterizes the set of all potential instances of the class, namely the predicate is an 'instance of the class' (/WeZd88/). Such a definition leaves some leeway for interpretation. It does not require instances of a class to rely on the same data structure, as in strongly typed object-oriented programming systems or in structural object-oriented database systems. Since a class commonly realizes the principle of data abstraction (a definition of this feature is given in the next section), its instances hide their internal representation. This means that a class definition must not necessarily determine the data structure of its instances. The question whether an object belongs to a specific class is determined by its functionality and behaviour and not by its structure. This understanding of the notion of class is quite common in a number of object-oriented systems. In these systems the internal representation of the instances of a class is defined by a fixed number of **instance variables** which are not bound to a specific type; that is, the structure of an instance of a class is only described by the number of its instance variables while the types of the instance variables are determined individually when the object is created or modified. In such an environment it is the concrete object, not the variable, that is typed (/Thom89/). An instance of a class is created by assigning instances of (other) classes to its instance variables. Due to the principle of data abstraction the concrete object which is referenced by an instance variable can be accessed by the operations which are associated with the instances of the class of that object. This not only allows the user to collect instances of different structure in one class but it also allows him to exploit extensively the feature of inheritance (which will be discussed later). However, on the other hand, it requires late (dynamic) binding since the concrete structure of an object (variable) is determined at run-time. While a lot of people argue that such an object world, which is based on 'run-time typing', is an essential feature for a programming language to be object-oriented (it provides more flexibility), others are convinced that the price to be paid (less efficiency and less run-time safety) is too high, therefore, demanding some form of early typing (static or strong typing). We will call a class **strongly (statically) typed (s-typed** or just **typed** for short) if its attributes are typed (which, of course implies that the system provides a kind of static or strong typing) (as, e.g. C++ (/Stro86/) or Eiffel (/Meye88/)) and **dynamically typed** (or **d-typed** for short) otherwise (as, e.g. SMALLTALK (/GoRo83/)). According to this definition two categories of object-oriented database systems can be distinguished, one category of systems that supports typed classes and another category that does not. Object-oriented database systems like O_2 (/VeBD89/), OOPS (/UnSc89-1/), OZ+ (/WeLo89/), and VBASE (/Andr91/) belong to the first category while GemStone (/MSOP86/), VISION (/CaSc87/), and ORION (/BCGK87/) are examples of the second.

There is no doubt about it, a system has to support the concept of class to be object-oriented. This seems to be a contradictory position to Bancilhon (/Banc88/) who claims that an object-oriented system has either to be class-based or type-based. But what Bancilhon probably means is that an object-oriented system has to support the notion of class but that it should be left to the designer of the system whether the data structure of a class is typed.

OBJECTS AND VALUES

A lot of people in the object-oriented field argue that everything is an object in an object-oriented system. However, with respect to object-oriented database systems (data models) there is a growing tendency to differentiate between objects and values (see, e.g. /Beer89/, /Deux90/,/HeSa90/, /HeSc91/). Since Beeri gives a nice description of the differences between an object and a value we want to follow his approach here (/Beer89/).

On a rather abstract level it can be stated that a *value* is used to describe *other things*, whereas *objects* are the *things being described*. However, if values can be used to describe other things they must carry their own meaning, i.e. they must permit a general, application-independent interpretation. This is the case with built-in data types like integer, real, character, etc. The structure and the elements (the domain) of data types are assumed to be given and, therefore, the elements are referred to as interpreted. On the other hand, the structure of objects is, first of all, uninterpreted. The meaning of objects is solely determined by their relationships to other elements in the database (e.g. membership in a class). In this sense, objects represent application abstractions (Beeri calls these objects **abstract objects**; we will use this term too). Throughout its lifetime, an abstract object is different from any other object, and is immutable, meaning that it does not ever change. In a database system, an abstract object represents an entity about which we want to record information; it is assigned a meaning by relating it to such information. The facility by which this is accomplished is the association of a state (description) with an abstract object. Since, therefore, the abstract object is distinct from its state, it is only the state that may change, not the object (for this reason object-oriented systems usually identify an abstract object by a unique object identifier). The state of an abstract object may be an atomic value, another abstract object, or a structured value. Structured values are obtained by (recursively) using constructors, such as set, list, tuple, etc. It is essential to understand that an abstract object cannot be structured; it is only its state that can be structured. And, as already mentioned, the state of an abstract object depends on the concrete context in which the abstract object is viewed. This especially means that the same object can be seen at different levels of abstraction (e.g. an object, John, can be seen as an employee or just as a person (generalization)). While generalization or specialization usually means that we view an object from a more generalized or more specialized point of view and, therefore, just add or remove properties, the above notion of abstract object even makes it possible to view an object in a totally different context (with a different state). For example, the abstract object John is associated with a specific state if we view John as an employee. However, in a different context, e.g. as a spectator of a football game, the same abstract object, John, may be associated with a different state. The possibility of multiple class membership (objects may be members of several classes at the same time; class membership can change dynamically) is an immediate consequence of the above understanding of the notion of abstract object.

4.2. Encapsulation and Data Abstraction

Encapsulation is the principle that a module can only be accessed via its external interface. It strictly distinguishes between the **implementation** of a module which is only visible to its implementor and therefore hidden, and its **interface** which describes the only way in which users can view the module.

In an object-oriented system the unit of modularity is the object, and thus, an object is the subject of encapsulation. Encapsulation on the level of objects (or data) is also called **data abstraction**. An **abstract data type** consists of two parts: the interface to the object, and the implementation of the object. The **interface** part is realized by a *set of operations* defined on the object and fully defines its *behaviour*. The user of an object does not need to understand how these operations are implemented or how the object is represented internally. The operations which come with an object define the only way in which an object can be accessed. The **implementation** part of the object describes the internal representation of the object (**data part**) and the implementation of each operation (**operation part**).

Since data abstraction allows the programmer to change the internal representation of a data structure of an object type without such a change influencing any program working on that object (type), a form of **data** or **implementation independence** is realized. Application programs are protected from implementation changes in lower levels of the system (/ABDD89/), at least, as long as such a change does not influence the interface or the semantics of an operation.

Most researchers feel that data abstraction is a mandatory feature in the context of object-oriented database systems (we agree with this position). Other researchers, however, do not take exactly this view (at least in the context of object-oriented programming languages). Wegner, for example, defines a language to be object-oriented if it supports objects as a language feature, if objects belong to classes, and if class hierarchies can be incrementally defined by an inheritance mechanism (/Wegn87-1 + 2/). However, according to Wegner, an object-based language requires objects to have a set of operations and a state that remembers the effect of the operations. Moreover, objects communicate by sending each other messages to perform operations. This definition is not far away from the definition of abstract data type (more precisely: it is a generalization). Therefore, in a little bit broader sense, the definition of Wegner conforms with the statement that '(something relatively close to) data abstraction' is a mandatory feature of object-oriented systems.

4.3. Inheritance

Inheritance is a technique that allows objects of different classes to share structure and behaviour related to their common part; i.e. it allows classes to be defined in terms of one or more other classes.

Let us consider the two classes *TEACHER* and *STUDENT*. Both classes have a common structure, e.g. name, address, marital status, faculty, and a common behaviour, e.g. they can change address or faculty and may get married. Additionally, each class has some specific structure and behaviour. A teacher has some income and the authorization to hold some examinations. Therefore, we need operations to change income and authorization for examinations. A student needs a set-of-grades attribute for which we also need a change operation. In an object-oriented system which offers the property of inheritance we can model such an environment by first modelling a (super)class *UNIVERSITY_MEMBER* which comprises the common properties and behaviours of *STUDENT* and *TEACHER*. Then, we can declare *TEACHER* as a subclass of *UNIVERSITY_MEMBER*. By these means, *TEACHER* inherits all attributes and operations of *UNIVERSITY_MEMBER*. Additionally, we add the special attributes *INCOME* and *AUTHORIZATION_FOR_EXAMINATIONS* and some operations to manipulate these attributes. Similarly, we can define *STUDENT* as a subclass of *UNIVERSITY_MEMBER*. Altogether, we have to implement six operations, three in *UNIVERSITY_MEMBER*, two in *TEACHER* and one in *STUDENT*. To model this scenario by means of a relational system, we have to design two independent relations, one for *TEACHER* and one for *STUDENT*. Moreover, we have to write code for each operation on the *Teacher* relation and on the *Student* relation, in all nine programs.

This simple example shows the main advantages of inheritance. It is a powerful organizational principle for concepts, because it can capture natural mechanisms, such as specialization, abstraction, approximation, and evolution. For example, *ELEPHANT*s specialize the properties of *MAMMAL*s; *MAMMAL* is an abstraction of the concept of *ELEPHANT*; the properties of *MAMMAL*s approximate those of *ELEPHANT*s; and *ELEPHANT*s evolved from early species of *MAMMAL*s (/Wegn89/). Furthermore, inheritance facilitates code reusability and supports programming safety, because every program is at the level at which the largest number of objects can share it.

The example above gives an intuitive definition of inheritance. But inheritance can be realized in different ways, depending on what we wish to inherit and when and how inheritance takes place. Mostly, inheritance is associated with a mechanism which allows a subclass to inherit structure (attributes) and behaviour (methods, operations) from its superclass. If a class is only allowed to inherit attributes and methods from *one* class, this is called **single** or **simple inheritance**. A natural extension of this basic form is **multiple inheritance** which allows a class to inherit from *multiple* superclasses. If single inheritance is provided, the classes form a hierarchy, called the **class hierarchy**. If multiple inheritance is supported, the classes form a **rooted directed** and **acyclic graph**, sometimes called a **class lattice**. Although multiple inheritance causes some more problems (e.g. resolution of name conflicts) its semantics are similar to single inheritance. For reasons of simplicity, we will concentrate on single inheritance in the following (a comprehensive discussion of multiple inheritance can be found, e.g. in /BrCK89/, /Card84/, /DuHa87/, /Hend86/, /Snyd86/). An excellent discussion of different forms of single inheritance can be found in /WeZd88/. They discuss inheritance as an incremental modification mechanism and identify four kinds of constraints on incremental modification, namely, behavioural, signature and name compatibility, and cancellation. The use of the first three types of inheritance strongly depends on the underlying systems. Behavioural compatibility normally needs to be used in statically (or strongly) typed systems, signature compatibility in strongly typed systems, while name compatibility is usually employed in dynamically typed systems; i.e. the number and forms of restrictions decrease from behavioural compatibility to name compatibility. Cancellation is a special form of inheritance which can be found rather seldom. A fifth and rather restrictive kind of inheritance can especially be found in statically typed systems. In such systems inheritance is often only used as a means for structuring data into more meaningful units; i.e. by inheritance a given set of objects is decomposed into a number of more meaningful but disjoint subsets. Only the leaf classes of an inheritance hierarchy are allowed to contain objects while inner classes must always be empty. With respect to our example scenario above this means that *UNIVERSITY_MEMBER* is the empty superclass of *TEACHER* and *STUDENT*. Moreover, the leaf classes have to form (disjoint) equivalence classes; i.e. a given university member can either be a student or a teacher but not both. In statically typed systems the system needs to decide the type of an object at compile-time and the above kind of inheritance is a means to make static type checking possible.

Inheritance in the presence of encapsulation produces some problems. Inheritance permits access to attributes defined by superclasses. Should a subclass, as a user of the superclass it inherits from, be allowed to see what is normally hidden from regular users? When a subclass adds a method that accesses inherited instance variables, it effectively violates encapsulation of that parent. Because attributes are supposed to be only accessible to implementors of the class, they are (implicitly) part of the contract between the designer of the superclass and the designer of the subclass. Thus, the freedom of the designer of the superclass to change the implementation of 'his' class is reduced if we neglect encapsulation. The designer can no longer safely rename, remove, or reinterpret an attribute without the risk of adversely affecting subclasses (/Snyd86/, /Nier89/). A similar problem is the visibility of inheritance. If we don't want to become dependent on the inheritance hierarchy the position of an object in the hierarchy has to be invisible to the users of the object; i.e. it should be possible to change the structure of an object without affecting users of the objects in the hierarchy.

This short discussion already indicates that the concepts of encapsulation and inheritance must be integrated very carefully in order not to remove the benefits of either. A more detailed discussion of these problems can be found in, e.g. /HaOB87/,/Mica88/, /Snyd86/ and /Zdon86-1/.

4.4. Polymorphism, Overloading, Late Binding

Polymorphism is defined to be the ability for operations (functions, methods) to operate on more than one type or class. **Polymorphic functions** are functions whose actual parameters can have more than one type. Cardelli and Wegner distinguish between two global categories of polymorphism, namely, universal polymorphism and ad-hoc polymorphism (/CaWe85/). **Universally polymorphic functions** (also called **generic functions**) work uniformly on a possibly infinite range of types as long as these types exhibit some common structure. A count function which counts the elements of a set irrespective of the type of the elements is an example of this kind of polymorphism. In contrast, **ad-hoc polymorphic functions** only work on a finite set of different and potentially unrelated types (which may not exhibit a common structure). Furthermore, the function may behave in unrelated ways for each type. With ad-hoc polymorphic functions, usually either the argument of the function is converted to the type expected by the function or there is a different function (body) for each type. Therefore, the only true forms of polymorphic functions are universally polymorphic functions since they execute the same code for arguments of any admissible type.

Universal polymorphism can be further subdivided into parametric and inclusion polymorphism. In **parametric polymorphism**, a polymorphic function has an implicit or explicit type parameter which determines the type of the argument for each application of that function; i.e. functions work uniformly on a range of types implementing the same behaviour irrespective of the object type. In **inclusion polymorphism** an object may be viewed as belonging to many different classes that need not be disjoint; that is, there may be inclusion of classes. Inclusion polymorphism is related to inheritance since inheritance allows an object belonging to a subclass to be used as if it belongs to (one of) its superclass(es).

Ad-hoc polymorphism can be further subdivided, too. In **overloading**, the same name is used to denote different functions and the context is used to decide which function is denoted by a particular instance of the name. Thus, the same function name can map to different code bodies. A **coercion** is a semantic operation that is needed to convert an argument to the type expected by a function, in a situation that would otherwise result in a type error. The distinction between overloading and coercion can be explained by the following example: An add-operation may be defined on two arguments of type real. But if one argument is of type integer this operation will no longer work. In the case of overloading the operation will be replaced by an operation which is defined, e.g. on integer and real. In the case of coercion the integer argument is coerced to a corresponding argument of type real.

In object-oriented systems we are mainly concerned with inclusion polymorphism, overloading, or parametric polymorphism.

If we want to exploit fully the advantages of inheritance and polymorphism we need some kind of dynamic type checking and dynamic (late) binding. In general, late binding makes type checking more complicated and in some cases impossible, but it still permits a good deal of compile-time type checking. The developers of VBASE recognized that 90% of all type checking and method binding can be done at compile-time (/AnHa87/). Researchers like Ralph Johnson take the view that it is possible to build systems with the flexibility of SMALLTALK or Lisp and with the safety of strong typing (/MJSS89/). Other researchers like Danforth and Tomlinson want to keep the advantages of dynamic typing (/DaTo88/). But, additionally, they want to offer the safety and efficiency of strong typing. They hold the opinion that flexibility in system description is closely related to the ability to control the time at which components are bound and the strength of such bindings. And a typing system can provide much of the information needed to effect binding decisions properly. Therefore, they suggest incorporating an explicit typing system that can support but does not require strong typing. For instance, GemStone (/MSOP86/) follows this approach by offering the facility (but not the need) to constrain the value of an attribute to a specific type.

For a more comprehensive discussion of this topic see, e.g. /Amer87/, /AtBu87/, /BrWe86/, /CaWe85/, /HaOB87/, and /Stro87/.

4.5. Computational Completeness

In sharp contrast to programming languages, database query languages usually impose severe restrictions on the kind of computations that can be performed. As a result application programs must be implemented in general-purpose languages while access to data is realized via declarative data sublanguages, like SQL. As a consequence data has to be passed between these two languages. Since both languages are usually semantically as well as structurally different such transformations may lead to a loss of information. This problem is known as **impedance mismatch**. Its avoidance is an essential motivation for the development of object-oriented database systems. Therefore, an object-oriented database system has to be computationally complete.

4.6. Object Identity

In advanced applications powerful data modelling concepts are needed. Of the utmost importance is the ability of the database system to support the modelling process of complex objects and versions. Especially, the modelling process of complex objects requires that objects can be distinguished. Let us, for example, consider a software engineering environment in which two software packages SP^1 and SP^2 share the same hash procedure P^h. The programmers of SP^1 and SP^2 are only interested in the functionality of P^h. Now, two situations may occur. The programmers of SP^1 and SP^2 both decide to use the same hash procedure P^h which means that P^h in SP^1 is identical to P^h in SP^2 (they are the same object). Whenever P^h is updated this update will be reflected in SP^1 as well as in SP^2. On the other hand, the programmer of SP^1 may want to use P^h as a first implementation which he wants to adapt to his special requirements at a later point of time. In this case SP^1 and SP^2 do not use the same procedure P^h. In case the programmer of SP^1 modifies his version of P^h this update is not meant to be reflected in SP^2.

What is needed is a handy concept which enables the user to distinguish an object from all other objects regardless of its contents, location or addressability. A common solution for this problem is identity. But, unfortunately, most programming and database languages do not support identity in an appropriate way since they mix addressability and identity (programming languages) or data value and identity (e.g. primary key in relational database systems). Object-oriented programming languages apply separate mechanisms for each concept. Each object has an identity regardless of where it is (physically) stored (**location independence**) or how it is modelled with descriptive data (**data independence**). /KhCo86/ and /KhAb90/ compare different implementation techniques for object identity using a taxonomy which is based on data and location independence. It turned out that the most robust technique for object identity is surrogates. **Surrogates** are system-generated, globally unique identifiers, completely independent of any physical location. They are associated with each object of any type at the instant the object is created. They cannot be changed; i.e. they represent the identity of the object throughout the lifetime of the object (for more detail, see, e.g. /Codd79/ or /Kent78/). However, surrogates only solve one facet of the problem. They allow the user to define objects irrespective of their content or location. But they seem to be an unsuitable concept to address the object; e.g. it is rather inconvenient for a user to be forced to use an identifier like 'E4356' to address a special supplier. This shows that surrogates or system-defined object identifiers do not make user-controlled keys obsolete. Quite the reverse; users will often need entity identifiers (such as part serial numbers) that are totally under their control or, even better, object identifiers which can be established by the users as, e.g. in O_2 where user-defined unique names can be attached not only to classes and attributes but to individual objects as well.

An object identifier has been introduced in nearly all object-oriented systems for the following reason. The state of an object is described by the values of its attributes, and the values may themselves be objects. Since in most object-oriented systems objects reside in a large virtual memory a natural representation for the state of an object is a set of pointers to the complex (sub)objects which represent the values of the attributes. This may lead to the assumption that an object identifier is only an implementation concept which cannot be claimed as mandatory since we discuss the features of an object-oriented database system from a conceptual point of view. On the other hand, we need a concept to distinguish an object from all other objects regardless of the content of the object. For such a purpose an object identifier seems to be the only reasonable concept. Thus, if we look at object identifiers as a concept to distinguish objects it is a mandatory feature of object-oriented systems.

4.7. Complex Objects

Complex objects (or, synonymously, composite objects, molecular objects, structured objects, aggregates) are built from other (complex) objects by applying object constructors. Subobjects or components can be objects in their own right. Unlike relational database systems, where the only constructors offered are the *set* and *tuple* constructors which can't be applied in a nested way, object-oriented database systems should permit the use of previously defined data types as building blocks for new data types and the nesting of data structures to arbitrary levels.

An object-oriented database system should allow us to describe dependencies or conditions which determine or restrict the viability of an object. For example, it should be possible to couple or decouple the existence of an object to the existence of another object. Or, it should be possible to specify whether an object can be shared by different objects. If possible, pointers should not be visible at the user interface. In /KiBG89/ an extended semantics of complex objects is defined which, among other things allows us to express constraints on persistence like the ones above.

We cannot discuss the subject of complex objects in more detail here; a comprehensive discussion of this topic is given, e.g. in /BaKh86/, /Ditt90/, /Hull87/, /Hull89/, /JhSt90/, /KiBG89/, and /VaKC86/.

4.8. Extensibility

Relational database systems rely on a simple data model. It offers a fixed number of predefined atomic data types and very few type constructors. Moreover, data types and data structures come with a fixed set of operations. It is not possible to integrate into the database system new operations that appear syntactically similar to the built-in operations. Moreover, complex data structures cannot be defined since an arbitrary nesting of type constructors is prohibited.

Of course, such limited data-modelling facilities restrict the possibilities of expressing application-specific semantics in the database system. Especially, when implementing a non-standard database application we always encounter the problem that the set of data types and operations does not support the application quite satisfactorily. Unfortunately, this statement is not confined to relational data models. It is valid for all data models. Consider, for example, a data type *Map*. Somewhat simplified a map can be viewed as a number of towns (nodes) connected by a number of roads (lines). Common data structures will fail to realize a map in a reasonable (efficient) way. Extensibility is the buzzword to solve this problem. It makes it possible to adapt the database system to the requirements of the application by allowing the programmer to embed new data types and functions which, from the programmer's point of view, cannot be distinguished from system-defined data types.

EXTENSIBILITY IN TERMS OF NEW DATA TYPES

In order to permit the integration of arbitrary data types into a data model, it must be possible to define new basic data types, to use previously defined data types as building blocks for other data types, or to nest data structures to arbitrary levels (e.g. list of sets of tuples). To get reasonable performance from such a system, we not only need a suitable collection of type constructors but we also need to implement them such that the mapping on external storage is efficient. This may lead to the assumption that all that is needed is to identify a fixed collection of basic type constructors and to implement the constructors in an appropriate way. But this will not always be sufficient, since the requirements of non-standard applications cannot be assessed in their entirety. Thus, if we want to provide a flexible data model we need extensibility even on the level of type constructors and basic data types; i.e. **externally defined data types (EDT**s) need to be integrated into deeper levels of the database system.

EXTENSIBILITY IN TERMS OF NEW FUNCTIONALITY

Since object-oriented database systems are meant to offer an interface which integrates a programming language and data management facilities they must allow the programmer to define and execute any kind of operations. Although the database system should maintain these operations too, they are executed on the level of the programming environment and not within the database. While this may be appropriate in most cases, it will be quite inefficient in other cases for the following reason. When an operation is called, the database has to prepare the call by transforming objects from their internal database representation into the representation chosen within the programming environment. Analogously, the results of an operation are again converted into the internal database representation. Unfortunately, such transformation can be rather time-consuming. Additionally, large amounts of data may have to be moved from the storage system to the application environment although only a small portion of them may be required by the operation. Such performance losses can only be avoided if operations can be integrated into the database system at appropriate levels of the architecture.

This short discussion already indicates that we do not only need extensibility on the level of the programming environment but also on the level of the storage or object manager.

While a lot of non-standard database systems provide extensibility in terms of an integration of new operations into the query language only very few of them also support the integration of new (polymorphic) data types and operations into deeper levels of the database system (e.g. EXODUS (/RiCa87/), OMS (/FrBo89/), and GENESIS (/BBGS88/)).

4.9. Persistence

Persistence is the ability of data to survive the execution of a process or an operation and to be reused later on in another process or operation. Programming languages neglected this feature for a long time. Data live as long as they are referenced, otherwise they may be removed, e.g. by the garbage collector. This simple rule is no longer applicable in the presence of persistence. Here, some data have to survive under any circumstances. In general, persistence should be orthogonal and some authors claim that it also should be implicit (/ABDD89/). **Orthogonal** means that each object, independent of its type, is allowed to become persistent as such. **Implicit** means that the user should not have explicitly to move or copy data to make it persistent. Especially, the last feature makes it necessary to define a criterion which determines the property of persistence. A first solution is to define the persistence property in the methods by using operations which make an object persistent. There is no need to say that this is not a satisfactory solution. Another straightforward solution, which is realized in some persistent languages, is to make everything persistent. The main drawback of this approach is that even intermediate results as well as dummy variables become persistent. A more appropriate approach is to let the system designer specify which classes are to be persistent or to store only data which is explicitly identified by a unique name. This approach was chosen in O_2 (/Banc89/). O_2 allows classes to be defined with (persistent) or without extension (non-persistent). Additionally, a new object which belongs to a non-persistent class can become persistent by giving it a unique name; e.g. '**add object** King: *TEACHER*' creates a persistent instance of class *TEACHER* with name King.

All three solutions have some drawbacks. It is a challenge to future research work to find more appropriate approaches.

4.10. Query Processing (Ad Hoc Query Facility)

A main characteristic of a (relational) database system is that it provides an interface that allows a user to define queries on the database in an ad hoc manner. For this purpose most conventional database systems offer an

SQL(-like) query language. We don't want to revive here the discussion whether SQL-like query languages are an adequate means to fulfil the desired task. However, the technical and economic availability of modern hardware (e.g. high-resolution, bit-mapped display screens and pointing devices) and software (window managers, graphics packages, browser) makes it strongly desirable to offer the service of querying the database in a user-friendly graphics-oriented way.

In the following, however, we will detach ourselves from the question of whether the query language should be graphics-oriented, or something else. Instead, we will discuss the demands imposed on such a language, though it is very doubtful if any approach will meet all of them in the near future.

Let us start with some rather general criteria (see also /Banc89/, /HeSc91/) which will be partly explained in more detail afterwards. A query language should be:

1 *application-independent*
The query language must not be designated to some application area. Instead, it has to be application-independent.

2 *high-level (descriptive)*
Although objects can be rather complex, simple (end-user understandable) facilities are needed to express non-trivial queries concisely. For this reason a query language should, of course, provide a collection of descriptive set-of-objects-at-a-time operators and not only a collection of navigational, one-object-at-a-time operators.

3 *optimizable*
The system has to be able to optimize the execution of queries. This requires that the set of operations be optimizable by algebraic or other conceptual strategies; e.g. the optimizer should be able to exploit the properties of commutativity and associativity of operations. Moreover, the optimizer should know the costs of different (alternative) access paths in order to be able to select the 'best' access strategy.

4 *closed*
The relational model is closed against the relational algebra since each operation yields a relation. The closure feature must also be fulfilled by a query language for object-oriented database systems. The result of a query must be usable as the input to a subsequent query. It is not sufficient to represent the result of a query as a table on the screen or by some other construct not used in the model itself.

5 *complete*
The query language needs to offer sufficient constructs to deal with all the modelling concepts provided by the underlying data model, e.g. constructs to handle complex objects, inheritance, data abstraction. This especially means that the query language has to provide possibilities for horizontal access (associative access) as well as vertical access (traversal of a complex object or class hierarchy (navigational access)). Moreover, operations should be applicable in any meaningful order; i.e. an arbitrary but meaningful nesting of operators should be possible (this is sometimes called **orthogonality** (see, e.g. /HeSc91/)). Again, the result of the application of any of these constructs must be represented in terms of the underlying data model (closure property).

6 *generic*
Generic operators, like selection, projection, set operators or comparison operators, are an essential ingredient of a descriptive query language. For an object-oriented query language a basic 'starter set' of generic operators seems also to be rather useful. They are the main difference between the built-in query language and the object-specific methods of the object-oriented programming environment.

7 *powerful*
The query language should remove the weakness of relational query languages, e.g. the inability to perform recursive traversal or transitive closure. As will be shown later, even the support of a join operation makes sense in an object-oriented environment (where implicit joins are already realized by the concept of complex objects).

8 *adequate*
Several recent approaches to query languages for object-oriented database systems always return sets of data values as the results of queries; i.e. they make relations a part of the data model and relations are the only possible results of queries. This, of course, is not what the user may expect to be the result. Mostly, it is the object the user is interested in. Other proposals do return objects as the result of a query. However, they generate new objects all the time. This especially means that the employee John is no longer the employee John, but a different object, if he is part of the result set of a query. This again may not be what the user expects. Moreover, such languages introduce semantic problems, such as equivalence of query expressions, and implementation overhead for massively generating new objects. What is needed is an **object-**

preserving semantics of query language operators; i.e. the result of a query should not only be a set of objects but the output set should consist of the same objects (or a subset) as the input set as long as the operations applied on the input set can be regarded as object-preserving (/HeSc91/).

9 *extensible*

Since the object-oriented data model usually permits the adding of new types (classes) and type constructors the query language should be able to deal with these new constructs and their operations in the same way as if they were built-in data types.

10 *efficient*

Each query operation should have an efficient implementation whose cost function should be understandable by the query optimizer. Moreover, it must be guaranteed that a finite result is evaluated in a finite amount of time.

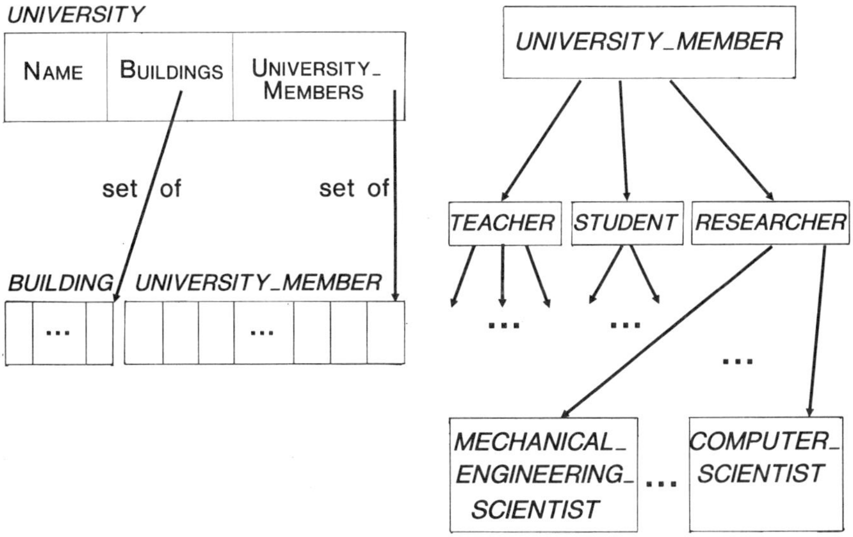

a) Complex object *UNIVERSITY*

b) Class hierarchy of *UNIVERSITY_MEMBER*

Figure 1 Simple application schema

In the remainder of this section, we will take a closer look at some of the above criteria. Our main objective is to address problems related to the definition of a sufficient object-oriented query language. For this reason, we will illustrate problems by example queries. These queries will be expressed in an SQL-like syntax. The statements are rather intuitive; they do not rely on any formal model nor will they suggest a way of how such queries can be formulated. Our language will operate on a simple schema (see Figure 1) which does not claim to be modelled in a meaningful manner. Classes (types) will appear in *UPPERCASE ITALIC*, attributes in SMALL CAPITALS.

We assume a class *UNIVERSITY* with the attributes NAME, BUILDINGS and UNIVERSITY_MEMBERS. The domain of BUILDINGS is a set of *BUILDING*s while the domain of UNIVERSITY_MEMBERS is a set of *UNIVERSITY_MEMBERS* (see Figure 1a). *UNIVERSITY_MEMBER* defines a subclass hierarchy in which *TEACHER, STUDENT* and *RESEARCHER* are subclasses of *UNIVERSITY_MEMBER* while *COMPUTER_SCIENTIST* and *MECHANICAL_ENGINEERING_ SCIENTIST* are subclasses of *RESEARCHER* (see Figure 1b).

The first and most important feature has been the subject of numerous heated debates (see, e.g. /Kim90-2/, /NeSt89/, /Ston90/). We do not want to repeat the discussion here. From our point of view, there is no question that a query language for an object-oriented database system must support horizontal as well as vertical access.

HORIZONTAL AND VERTICAL ACCESS

Horizontal (associative) access, of course, is nothing new, since it is provided by every common relational query language. The need for this kind of access in object-oriented database systems was not always clear. Especially, first prototypes of object-oriented database systems concentrated on vertical access only. However, in the meantime the support of associative access is more or less generally accepted. **Vertical (navigational) access** is known from hierarchical or network database systems and is needed to traverse complex objects or class hierarchies. Vertical access especially means that the query language has to contain a construct which allows a user to access not only the root of a complex object but also all its direct and indirect subobjects (transitive closure of a complex object). For reasons of efficiency most database systems only fetch the root of a complex object. Other components (especially shared subobjects) are fetched when needed. However, for reasons of concurrency control we need an operation which allows the user to access the complete complex object at once (or, more specifically, at least to lock the complete complex object; otherwise a shared subobject may be locked by a conflicting transaction in an incompatible mode which means that this subobject is no longer accessible).

JOIN

The ability to construct complex objects covers the possibility to model implicit joins. For instance, the complex attribute UNIVERSITY_MEMBERS of *UNIVERSITY* describes an implicit join between the class *UNIVERSITY* and the class *UNIVERSITY_MEMBER*. While these implicit joins are already a powerful modelling concept they do not remove the need for explicit joins. For example, if we want to find all students with the same address as a researcher we need explicitly to join the class *STUDENT* and the class *RESEARCHER* (with or without their subclasses) with ADDRESS being the shared attribute. Such explicit joins should be applicable to any two attributes (attribute sets) which are type-compatible.

ENCAPSULATION

The first issue we want to consider is the question whether the query language should be in a position to violate encapsulation (/Banc89/). Encapsulation enforces that objects can only be accessed via their methods. If the query language cannot violate encapsulation, then, basically, the only access to objects is through methods, and data values are invisible. This has two consequences. Firstly, a schema in the sense of a schema of a relational database system is not available since we don't know the structure of objects. Secondly, the user is restricted to the facilities of the methods defined. This changes the meaning of ad hoc to 'predefined ad hoc' since it does not allow the user to utilize data in all possible ways. As long as the query language can be seen as a pure query language (no integration of update facilities) this restriction seems to be artificial. Thus, there might be some good reasons for the query language to be able to violate encapsulation, but only in the ad hoc query mode (i.e. as long as it is not used as an embedded data-manipulation language or as a programming language). But, of course, the concepts of how object structure can be made visible have to be defined very carefully because the interface defined for an object may be different from the structure of the object. For instance, the object structure may contain attributes which are only needed to compute other attributes visible at the interface. Such attributes of the object structure will be called **private attributes** while attributes of the object structure which are visible at the interface (for which a method exists to get their value), will be called **public attributes**. But there is another category of attributes which does not belong to any of the above categories: namely, properties which do not correspond to any public or private attribute of the object structure, but which are computed by a method. Such attributes will be called **implicit attributes**. Private or public attributes belong to the class of **explicit attributes**. Let us assume that we need to know the number of successful tests of a student. There are good reasons (maintainability) not to define an explicit attribute for number of successful tests but to compute this attribute from the set of the student's tests each time the attribute is accessed. This is an example of an implicit attribute. If, for reasons of economy of storage, the domain of the attribute RELIGIOUS_COMMUNITY is designed to be of type *small integer* instead of *string* this is an example of a private attribute since the meaning of an integer value is not discernible to a user. Therefore, most probably, a method will exist which translates the value of the small integer into an appropriate string, e.g. 1 into Catholic, 2 into Protestant, etc.

Now, let us come back to the question of what the visible attributes of an object are to be. A first approximate definition may have this set as the union of the public and the implicit attributes. While this is a good definition in most cases, it may fail in others, e.g. if DATE_OF_BIRTH is modelled as a private attribute which is only used to compute AGE (there exists no method which allows the user to access the value of DATE_OF_BIRTH). In the ad hoc query mode, nevertheless, it may be desirable to read DATE_OF_BIRTH in a given situation. This leads to the need that the programmer of a class must have the opportunity to define public and private attributes explicitly instead of them being implicitly computed by the system. OOPS (/SUWZ88/) is an example of an object-oriented database system which supports such a distinction.

In the list of the requirements for an object-oriented query language which we stated at the beginning of this section genericity was mentioned as one criterion. This is not generally accepted since generic operations (defined on the level of the query language) are also suspected of violating the principle of encapsulation. However, as explained in /HeSc91/, neither generic operations nor the query language in general need to violate the principle of encapsulation if the object model or the schema definition language are modelled in an appropriate way. The query language does not need to access directly the structure of objects. It can, just as well, make use of the functions defined to access the structure. Let us again consider AGE. AGE can be the name of an attribute but also the name of a function which returns an integer as its return value. Then the query language can use ***age*** as an atomic type and, therefore, can compute a query like '**Select * From** *PERSON* **Where** *PERSON*.**age** < 65'. For the query language it is insignificant whether the value of age is obtained by just reading a concrete attribute value or by deriving (computing) the value from other attributes. And, of course, it is no problem to define a set of basic functions which simply (compute and) return the value of an attribute so that there exists a 1:1 relationship between the (public) attributes and these basic functions (for each attribute there exists an adequate function). While such an approach seems rather to conform with the intention of object-oriented query languages (and, of course with the object-oriented data model), nevertheless, most approaches to query processing do not follow this approach. Instead, they rely on the direct access of attribute values. We will call these approaches **attribute-oriented** in the following, while the other approach will be called **function-oriented**.

METHODS AND DATA

If we accept the violation of encapsulation by an attribute-oriented query language then the next question arises: What should we query, only attributes (data values) or, additionally, methods? Here, it seems to be quite reasonable to consider both, since this is the only way to exploit the power of object-oriented systems. Let us assume a query with a simple predicate like NAME = 'xy', where NAME is an attribute name, = an operator, and xy a value. In traditional database systems an attribute name is the name of an attribute of the given object, an operator is either a scalar comparison operator (e.g. =, >, <) or a set operator (contained-in, contains, set-equality, etc.), and a value is an instance of a simple data type (we don't consider a join operation here). In object-oriented systems, however, the programmer may define any kind of methods on a class. Such methods should be usable for any part of a predicate; that is, as the attribute name, the operator, or the value (see Example 4.1).

Example 4.1:

1 attribute name: Find all students with an average test result of at least 3.

> **Select** * **From** *STUDENT* **Where** ***STUDENT.average-test-result*** <3

where ***average-test-result*** is a (instance) method which computes the average test result of a student.

2 operator: Find all students whose name contains an 'A'.

> **Select** * **From** *STUDENT* **Where** *STUDENT*.NAME ***contains*** 'A'

where ***contains*** is a (instance) method which tests whether a given string contains an 'A'.

3 value: Find all students who are older than the average age of the students.

> **Select** * **From** *STUDENT* **Where** *STUDENT*.AGE > ***average-age***

where ***average-age*** is a (class) method which computes the average age of the students.

Although at first glance extremely powerful, the integration of methods into the query language causes some problems (even if we take the point of view that we do not deal directly with attributes but only with functions). We need to define the borderline between the (generic) operations of the query language and the methods of the programming environment. While an object-oriented system in its purest form is an empty system, (without any classes or methods; of course, all systems come with a predefined set of classes (types) and methods) a query language already provides a set of generic operators. In a query language, such operators have a fixed meaning. In the programming environment of an object-oriented system, however, such operators can be (re)defined with totally different semantics. For instance, the ***contains*** operator usually tests whether a set of objects is included in another set of objects. In Example 4.1 No. 2 the ***contains*** operator has a different meaning; it simply tests whether a string contains a given letter.

To summarize, query languages which allow the user to exploit methods are extremely powerful since methods may be rather complex. A method call may even realize a complex application program. This, of course, allows the programmer to provide a query interface which goes far beyond the scope of conventional query languages. On the other hand, we need a clear definition of how the query language and the programming environment have to interact.

Of course, a query language must be very powerful. But it also must be very handy. Therefore, it is unsatisfactory to offer just a wealth of methods to the user. Instead, he also needs a mechanism to handle them, e.g. to get their name, their meaning, and the number and types of the arguments. This implies that we need something like self-declarative method and object structure browsers as well as a clear concept of which methods should be visible to the user. One means to control the visibility of methods is to distinguish between private and public ones. **Private methods** are only accessible from the inside of a data type (e.g. as a means to implement public methods) while **public methods** realize the interface; i.e. public methods are visible to the user while private aren't.

INHERITANCE

At a first glance, the requirement for a query language to be complete and well-defined seems to be self-evident. But the realization of this feature causes some problems as the following discussion will show. Let us start with inheritance and with the query: 'Find all students who study at a given university'. In our schema, such a query is not easy to answer since students are not an explicit attribute of *UNIVERSITY*, but an integral part of the attribute UNIVERSITY_MEMBERS. Therefore, the fact that a university member is a student is not explicitly expressed but hidden in the fact that *STUDENT* is a subclass of *UNIVERSITY_MEMBER*s. This example shows that there is a need to allow the user to specify in a query a subclass of the domain of an attribute A as the 'relevant' domain of A; i.e. it has to be possible to define any direct or indirect subclass of the class which forms the domain of A (e.g. Students) as the target of a query which considers A in its predicate.

Example 4.2:

'Find all students who study at the University of Rome' could be formulated as:

> **Select** (UNIVERSITY_MEMBERS **Restricted to** *STUDENTS*) **From** *UNIVERSITY* **Where** *UNIVERSITY*.NAME = 'University of Rome'

A similar question is: What do we get if we query an attribute whose domain is an inner node of the class hierarchy (a class which is the root of a subclass hierarchy)?

Example 4.3:

'Find all researchers whose name is 'King'. This question translates into:

> **Select** * **From** *RESEARCHER* **Where** *RESEARCHER*.NAME = 'King'

What is the scope of such a query? Only all researchers who exactly belong to the class *RESEARCHER* or, additionally, all researchers who belong to any (direct or indirect) subclass of *RESEARCHER*, in our case *COMPUTER_SCIENTIST* and *MECHANICAL_ENGINEERING_SCIENTIST*. Both interpretations, i.e. to define the access scope of a query as only consisting of the instances of the given class or to extend it by the instances of all subclasses of the class, seem to be equally valid; i.e. the intention of a query depends on the given situation. For example, the above question clearly aims at the complete subclass hierarchy. Consider, however, this example: Given the class *CAR_RADIO* with its subclasses *CAR_RADIO_RECORDER* and *CAR_RADIO_WITH_CD_PLAYER*. If a customer wants to buy a 'pure' car radio which has a power of eight watts we only need to examine the class *CAR_RADIO*, which means that we are not interested in instances of subclasses.

Next, we want to consider briefly some constructs which should be part of a query language to enable a user to handle complex objects easily.

UNIQUENESS

Relational database systems determine the uniqueness of tuples by value equality. For object-oriented database systems, unlike relational systems, two different criteria exist for determining the uniqueness of an instance from a collection of instances (/Kim89/). One criterion is the equality of the object (identifiers) while another is the equality of the contents of the instances. Since both kinds of uniqueness seem to be useful we need features to handle both of them.

RECURSION

Another demand on a query language of an object-oriented database system are operations to handle cyclic branches in a class-composition hierarchy. A branch of a class-composition hierarchy is **cyclic**, if it contains a class C_i and a class C_j on the branch, such that (see also /Kim89/)

1 C_j is the (indirect) domain of an attribute of C_i, and C_i is the domain of an attribute of C_j, e.g. if *UNIVERSITY_MEMBER* contains an attribute whose domain is *UNIVERSITY* (see Figure 2a). A special case of this type of cycle is the single-node cycle where $C_i = C_j$.

2 C_j is the (indirect) domain of an attribute of C_i, and a superclass or a subclass of C_i is the domain of an attribute of C_j. Let us assume *PRIVATE_UNIVERSITY* is a subclass of *UNIVERSITY*. Then, an example of this type of cycle is obtained if *UNIVERSITY_MEMBER* contains an attribute whose domain is *PRIVATE_UNIVERSITY* (see Figure 2b).

3 C_j is a superclass or a subclass of C_i, and C_i is the domain of an attribute of C_j, e.g. if *RESEARCHER* contains an attribute whose domain is *UNIVERSITY_MEMBER* (see Figure 2c).

These different types of cycles need different types of operations to handle them.

ADEQUACY

Object-oriented systems require an object to belong to a class and a class to be positioned somewhere within the class hierarchy. Let us consider the result of a query. The objects of the result set can be, for instance, of

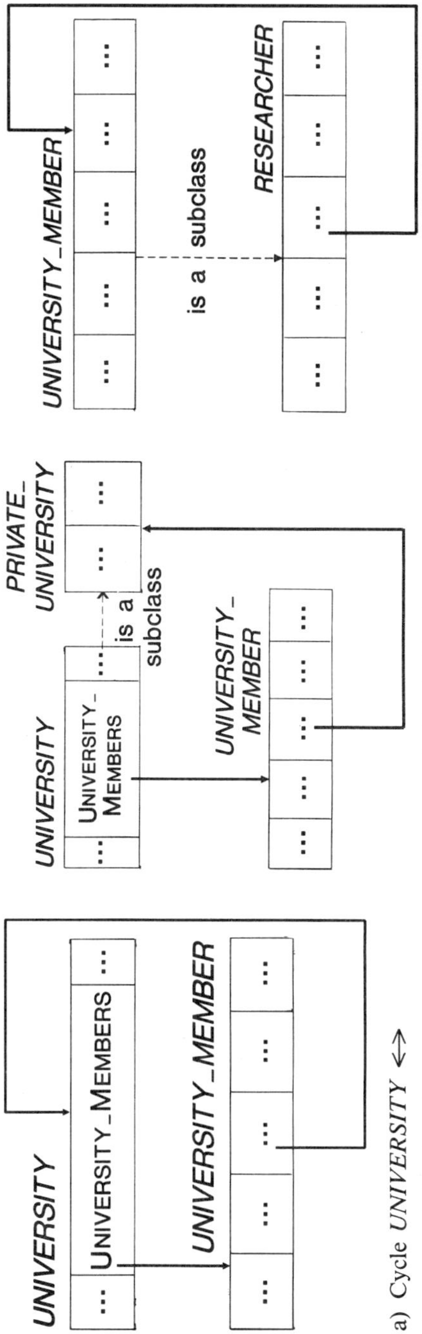

a) Cycle *UNIVERSITY* ⟷ *UNIVERSITY_MEMBER*

b) Cycle *UNIVERSITY* ⟷ *PRIVATE_UNIVERSITY*

c) Cycle *UNIVERSITY_MEMBER* ⟷ RESEARCHER

Figure 2 Different types of cycles

different structure (inhomogeneous set) or define a new class of objects. For instance, the query 'Find all researchers who live in Boston' is meant to return either a differently structured set of objects (objects of the class *RESEARCHER* and its subclass hierarchy (here: *COMPUTER_SCIENTIST* and *MECHANICAL_ENGINEERING_SCIENTIST*)), or a homogeneous set whose objects are (at least partly) an abstraction (generalization) of the original objects, e.g. computer scientists are no longer computer scientists but generalized to researchers. However, as we will see in a moment most query languages do not meet either of these intentions. In the case of an explicit join the resulting collection of objects will have a considerably different structure than the original objects. Usually, these objects will not fit in any of the already existing classes. This, of course, brings up the questions to which construct/class do the resulting objects belong, at which position in the class hierarchy can they be fitted in, and which operations can be applied to them? These questions are not easy to answer since the definition of a new class raises the problem of how to get methods for the new class. The higher a class is positioned in the class hierarchy the fewer are the operations which are inherited. Therefore, if the new class is inserted as a direct subclass of the root (an alternative sometimes used), the set of applicable operations is rather small. Since it is sometimes unavoidable to position newly created classes relatively high in the class hierarchy it seems to be inevitable that we provide a basic set of generic operators which can be applied to objects of each class regardless of the position of the classes in the class hierarchy (however, see also the section about genericity).

Another question is whether objects created during the execution of a query have to have their own object identity. On the one hand, these objects may look different from the original ones; on the other hand, they are, nevertheless, strongly connected to their originals (especially, in case of a projection: the student Smith is still the student Smith, even if his attributes are restricted to NAME and ADDRESS).

We do not want to beat about the bush: Most proposals for object-oriented query languages do not treat the above problems in an adequate way. The most simple proposal is just to extend the object-oriented database model by relations (set of data values) and only to provide **value-generating operators**; i.e. the result of a query is always a (set of) data value(s) (see, e.g. /AnHa87/, /WiLH90/). While this restriction, of course, means that the language is closed it is not adequate for the object model since the result of a query no longer contains objects but only data values. A special consequence of such an approach can be that the data model supports the notion of object, which especially means that there may be some objects that are described by identical data values. However, since the query language does not deal with objects but with sets of data values, the query language will delete duplicates.

Another approach is to introduce **object-generating operators** (most proposals follow this approach). In this case the result of a query may be a set of objects but all of these objects are new. In other words, the direct relationship (equality) between the objects of the input set of a query and the objects of the output set is lost. The 'new' object Smith is no longer the same object as the 'old' object Smith after an object-generating operator was applied to it. In such proposals the resulting set (class) of objects is usually positioned as a direct successor to the root class (often called *Object*) in the class hierarchy. Examples of query languages which provide object-generating operators are /AbKa89/, /AlSL89/, /Kim89/, /Maie86/, /ShZd89/. While almost all approaches to query languages only provide value-generating operators and/or object-generating operators the approaches of /HeSa90/, /ScSc90/ and /StÖz90/ depend on object-preserving operators. These operators, applied to a set of objects, always return the same set of objects (or a subset); i.e. the resulting objects of an object-preserving query are some of the existing objects from the database. In this sense these approaches realize the concept of abstract objects as introduced in Section 4.1. While object-preserving operators do preserve the identity of an object they, nevertheless, may create a different view on (the state of) the objects. For example, in the case of a selection the resulting objects are a specialization of the input class. The query '**Select** * **From** *RESEARCHER* **Where** *RESEARCHER*.HOMETOWN = New York' creates a class which is a subclass of *RESEARCHER* (e.g. *RESEARCHER_IN_NEW_YORK*). In contrast, a projection usually creates a superclass of the input class. The query '**Select** NAME, ADDRESS **From** *RESEARCHER*' results in a more generalized view on researchers. Of course, the existence of object-preserving operators raises the question of what the final position of the result class in the class hierarchy is. We do not want to discuss this issue here, especially since this question cannot always be answered easily. It is obvious that the determination of the 'right' position is not a trivial problem, especially if several operators are combined in a query, e.g. projection and selection (the interested reader is referred to the above literature). But it is also obvious that object-preserving operators are much closer to what the user often wants to express with his query. He does not always want to create new objects. He often wants to view an object in the sense of an abstract object which especially means that he wants to deal with the same objects, though in a different context.

While the object algebra of /ScSc90/ concentrates on object-preserving operators /HeSa90/ provide both kinds of operators. For this reason, they distinguish between object-generating operators and object-preserving operators; e.g. the object-preserving selection operator has an object-generating counterpart. It is left to the user to decide which kind of operator he wants to apply. In the case of object-generating operators the set of input objects is first transformed to a set of data values (duplicates are eliminated). In a second step, each data value is upgraded to an independent object by assigning it its own unique object identity.

As already mentioned, object-preserving operators will often cover the user's intention more accurately than object-generating operators. However, this is not the only advantage. They are also a rather useful concept if objects are to be modified or if views are to be created. If we want to create a view it is normally not our intention to create a class of new objects. For example, if we define a view to be a selection on the objects of an existing class we usually want the objects in the view to be the same objects as the objects of the base class. Moreover, if we want to update some objects of our view we want these updates to propagate to the base classes. For example, if our view contains all employees who do not earn more than a given amount of money it is usually our intention that an increase of the salary of these employees is not only visible in our view. Instead, such an update needs to propagate to the base class(es), too (here: to the class of all employees). Otherwise, our boss, if he is allowed to access all employee objects, would not see the increased salary.

GENERICITY

There are some strong arguments that an object-oriented query language should provide a basic set of generic operators. But there are also some severe problems with generic operators. One problem has already been mentioned and, therefore, will not be discussed here: in the case of attribute-oriented query languages the principle of encapsulation has to be violated. Another problem arises in the context of class-generating operators, like selection and projection. The question is which method can be applied to the objects of the newly created class? Since the attribute-oriented query languages do not usually preserve object-identity they create a class of new objects. In such an environment it is easy to decide which methods are still applicable. In the simplest case none except the generic operators of the query language. In such a case the problem is reduced to that of determining the semantics of a projection. Does a projection eliminate all private attributes and/or all public attributes which are not listed in the projection clause? Note that private as well as public attributes may be used to compute implicit attributes which, in turn, may still be an integral part of the resulting object class. This again is an indication that the query language should concentrate on functions and not on attributes. Although this procedure is clearly a solution it is most probably far from what the user expects and, therefore, does not convince. Therefore, we will discuss the problem in the context of a function-oriented and object-preserving query language (more specifically, we want to discuss it in the context of the approach of /ScSc90/). A pure selection operation does not usually create any problem. The new class can be regarded as a subclass of the old class and all methods of the old class can be applied to the objects of the new class. If some method does change the structure of an object in a way that it no longer fulfils the selection predicate, the object is simply no longer visible in the new class. For example, if the selection has created a class which contains all employees who earn less than a given amount of money the employee object is simply removed from the class if, after a raise in salary, the new salary exceeds the amount. A projection is a more complicated case. In a relational system a projection eliminates some attributes. For reasons of convenience let us assume that the objects of class can be described by a set of functions which correspond to the structure of the objects; i.e. for each attribute there is a function which returns the corresponding attribute value. Of course, in such a case the projection simply removes the functions which are to be eliminated by the projection. However, what happens to functions which access several attributes or which modify attributes (functions with side-effects)? One can argue that only those functions are included which do access attributes which were not eliminated by the projection. However, this cannot always be decided, since the interface of an object may contain functions which do not directly access an attribute but do derive its resulting value from other attributes of the object (e.g. AGE) or, even more complicated, from attributes from other objects in the database. A less convincing solution would be to enumerate explicitly in the projection each function which is to be applicable to the objects of the new class. This solution not only places much more burden on the user but it also makes the search for a right position of the new class in the class hierarchy more complicated since this proceeding is orthogonal to the principle of inheritance. Inheritance strictly regulates which functions must be part of a subclass.

A similar problem, which, however, is not restricted to object-preserving query languages, arises in the following example: Given a class *EMPLOYEE* with subclasses *HEAD_OF_DEPARTMENT*, *PROJECT_LEADER* and *OFFICE_WORKER*. Since each employee gets a salary a method exists which raises the salary (***raise-salary***). However, since the salary of objects from different (sub)classes is calculated differently a different method is defined for each class. Let us assume that the salary of all employees (including the employees of the subclasses) of the Computer-Science department are to be raised. The usual procedure is first to apply a selection on *EMPLOYEE*s and then to apply the ***raise-salary*** method on the resulting objects. However, in such a case it is absolutely necessary not to treat the objects of the subclasses as generalized objects on a higher level (maybe specialized afterwards due to the computation of the selection) since this would result in a wrong calculation of the respective salaries. Instead, the method body of the respective subclass has to be executed. However, such a procedure is only possible if the system supports dynamic binding. This, again, shows the inherent complexity which is bound up with the object-oriented approach and which is particularly present in the context of object-preserving query languages.

DYNAMICALLY TYPED SYSTEMS

Most of our discussion above concentrated on object-oriented systems in which classes are typed. This, particularly, has the pleasant consequence that objects of the same class have the same structure and, therefore, can be handled in the same way. If classes are dynamically typed, objects may have different structures. This, of course, aggravates the handling (of sets) of objects drastically; e.g. we need the instantiated structure of an object to be carried along with each object (or at least to be visible (accessible) to the user). Moreover, we need operations which allow the user to access objects of a given (sub)structure (or, more generally, of a given set of (sub)structures; e.g. all cars which have a catalyst (whose subcomponents which describe the catalyst are not empty (are instantiated))). This corresponds to an associative access but not with respect to the contents of objects of a class but the structure. We don't want to discuss this in more detail since its inherent complexity exceeds the scope of this paper.

QUERY OPTIMIZATION

Relational database systems provide an ad hoc query language which allows the user to perform associative retrieval which is optimized by the query optimizer. The ability to optimize queries derives largely from the fact that the relational model is very simple and uniform. In contrast to that, object-oriented languages are typically based on the message-passing paradigm; i.e. each message causes the execution of a method written in a computationally complete programming language. On the one hand, this gives the object-oriented model an expressive power that is significantly greater than the relational algebra. On the other hand, this results in severe restrictions for the optimization of object-oriented queries. Each user-defined type effectively introduces a new algebra. Moreover, the encapsulation of methods within objects makes it difficult to apply global query optimization. In general, it is impossible to achieve the same degree of optimization as in a relational language (/Kort88/). Critics of the object-oriented approach frequently point to the theoretical limits to optimization as a major drawback of the object-oriented approach (see, e.g. /Ullm87/) as compared with the relational approach. Nevertheless, a number of approaches to query optimization in object-oriented databases have been published. Most of these techniques try to identify and make use of similarities between the object-oriented model and the relational model. No doubt, however, query optimization remains a big challenge for research in object-oriented databases.

As the discussion above clearly indicates, query languages for object-oriented database systems have to consider various new aspects which lead to the need to integrate a large number of new constructs, operations, and methods, which result in a complex environment. It is an open issue how to offer an interface for an inexperienced user. We are convinced that such a language can only be graphics-oriented.

4.11. Schemas and Schema Modification

DATA ABSTRACTION

An essential reason for the use of database systems is that they provide **data-independence** which means that data are provided in a way which is independent of the applications which work on them. Data-independence can be seen from two points of view, namely, physical and logical data-independence. **Physical data-independence** implies that the physical representation of data is transparent to the applications; i.e. it should be possible to change the storage structures of or access strategies to data in response to changing requirements, without the necessity of modifying existing applications. **Logical data-independence** provides a distinction between an application-specific view of the data in the database and the logical view of the complete data stored in a database; i.e. it should be possible to change the logical view provided by the database without the necessity of modifying existing applications. The feature of data-independence is realized in most conventional database systems by an architecture which provides three levels of abstraction, namely, an internal (physical), a conceptual and an external schema. The **internal schema** is concerned with the way in which the data is actually stored on secondary storage and how it can be accessed. The **conceptual schema** describes in its entirety that part of the real world which is modelled in the database. Finally, the **external schema** is concerned with the way in which the data is viewed by individual applications. While these levels of abstraction are a commonly agreed quasi-standard for conventional database systems its realization in object-oriented database systems is not yet clear. Of course, current approaches to object-oriented database systems realize some kind of physical data-independence, especially with regard to the physical representation of data. However, access strategies are mostly only supported on a rather simple level, if at all. We will come back to this issue when we discuss secondary storage management. The question of what an external schema is supposed to be and how it can be established is currently seen as a field of research. There are only very few approaches which deal with this problem, e.g. /HeZd88/ or /TaYI88/. Views will be discussed in more detail at the end of this section.

CONCEPTUAL SCHEMAS

The conceptual model, as a representation of the entire information content of the database, is usually defined by means of the **conceptual schema** or **schema** for short. In the context of relational database systems a schema consists of the set of concrete relation types together with the description of the (uniform) structure of the tuples of each relation (the attributes). However, in the context of object-oriented database systems the notion of schema has a different, more complex, meaning. Similar to relational database systems a schema is, first of all, represented by the set of concrete class definitions. But unlike relational systems classes are, additionally, related to each other in several other ways. In the case of simple inheritance all classes are arranged in a class hierarchy (i.e. they form superclass/ subclass relationships). However, in general, such a class hierarchy does not correspond to an abstraction of the real world as it applies to the users of the database. The reason for this is that a class hierarchy normally also contains the definitions of constructs which are needed to represent and describe real-world entities within the database, like data types (character, number, string, etc.), data structures (bags, collections, arrays, etc.), control structures (whileTrue, untilTrue, etc.), and so on. Thus, an equivalent to the conceptual level in relational database systems cannot be identified in current approaches to object-oriented database systems.

Since object-oriented database systems typically provide some kind of data abstraction and, thereby, hide the internal representation of an object from the users, an application can only perform the operations which are associated with a given object. Therefore, the only parts of a class definition that have to be integral parts of the schema are the external interfaces associated with those classes of the class hierarchy which represent real-world entities. Thus, a schema modification is concerned with changes to the definition of the behaviour of a class and changes to the structure of the class hierarchy. Changes to the behaviour of a class include adding, deleting, modifying (the interface or semantics, not the implementation (at least as long as such a modification does not change the semantics of a method)), and renaming of a method (operation). Changes to the structure of a class hierarchy include creation, deletion, and renaming of a class, and alteration of the inheritance relationship between classes, that is, adding and deleting the superclass–subclass relationship between a pair of classes (including rearranging the class hierarchy). This definition stands in contrast to the definition of some researchers (e.g. /BKKK87/, /KiCh88/, /NgRi89/) who define the complete class definition as part of the schema; i.e. not only the interface part but also the implementation part (data part (representation or state of the object) as well as procedure part (implementation of each operation)). But since the implementation part of an object is assumed to be invisible to the users of the object (due to the principle of encapsulation) this definition moves part of the internal (physical) level of the database to the conceptual level. Moreover, /BMOP89/ defines the creation or deletion of an index on a class to be a schema modification. This results in a mixture of internal and conceptual levels, which database research originally tried carefully to avoid (for good reasons!).

It can be concluded that a generally accepted definition of the notion of schema in object-oriented database systems is not yet achieved. Especially, the three levels of abstraction of conventional database systems cannot be identified as such in current implementations of object-oriented database systems. It is a major challenge to future research on object-oriented database systems to develop concepts which support similar forms of data independence to those of conventional database systems.

SCHEMA MODIFICATION

Although the discussion above indicates that the use of the notion of schema may be misleading in the context of today's object-oriented database systems we will, nevertheless, carry on using this term because it is commonly used in the literature in this context.

With respect to the extended notion of schema, schema change operations fall into three categories (/NgRi89/):

1. changing class definitions, i.e. instance variables, constraints on them, or operations (methods)
2. adding, deleting, or renaming classes in the hierarchy
3. modifying the class hierarchy by changing the relationship between classes

In the following we will discuss these change operations only in brief. A more comprehensive discussion of these issues can be found, e.g. in /BKKK87/, /KiCh88/, /NgRi89/, /PeSt87/, /SkZd86/, and /SkZd87/.

1. Changing class definitions

Changing the structure of a class In principle, we can distinguish between different kinds of changes to the structure of a class. Adding or deleting an instance variable may or may not affect the external interface of the class. If, for example, a new attribute is added, this does not mean that the interface part of the class has to be changed too, since the new attribute may replace an old 'virtual attribute' (an attribute whose value is computed each time it is accessed). However, if the new attribute expresses some new property of the object this, of course, has to be reflected in the interface. Altogether, the adding of an attribute may only affect the internal level, e.g. if it only speeds up or reorganizes access to data (read value of concrete attribute instead of compute value of virtual attribute), or the conceptual level, if, e.g. some new property (attribute) is added, or both. Of course, the conceptual level is only affected, if, in addition to the change to the structure, the external interface is changed too, e.g. if a new operation is added which allows the user to access the newly created attribute. In principle, the change of the structure of a class does not correspond to a schema modification unless it is accompanied by the insertion, deletion or modification of the semantics of an operation.

With respect to the internal level any change of the structure of objects results in some implications to the representation of these objects on secondary storage. This is similar to a change of the structure of a relation in relational database systems. However, the situation is somewhat more complicated in object-oriented database systems due to the existence of the concept of inheritance. A change in the structure of a class also implies a change in the structure of all subclasses (for instance, name conflict resolution). Moreover, it is the responsibility of the programmer to recognize whether such a change in structure has to be considered in operations (interfaces) of the class or its subclasses. Changes in the implementation of an operation do not cause problems as long as they do not affect the semantics or the external interface of the operation.

Changing the operations of a class Adding a new operation does not cause any problems (with the exception of the simple problem of name conflicts which may arise if an operation with the same name already exists in some subclass). The deletion of an operation affects applications or other operations (also of subclasses) which make use of this operation. Adding and deleting operations are definitely schema modifications. The decision is more complicated if we consider the modification of an operation. If the type or number of parameters is changed, of course, this corresponds to a schema modification. If, however, the implementation part was changed the schema is only concerned if the modification influences the semantics of the operation; e.g. if the ***price*** operation of the class *ARTICLE* is modified in a way that it now shows the price inclusive of a local tax. In situations like this it is even impossible for the database system to decide on its own whether the schema is concerned. This again shows that the identification of different levels of abstraction in object-oriented database systems is far from being satisfactory or even solvable.

Note that the change of a class can be realized by modifying an existing class or by creating a new subclass. This, of course, may complicate the development of an accurate schema since an unrestricted insertion of new subclasses may lead to a rapidly growing class lattice which may contain numerous 'useless' classes or be totally confused.

2. *Adding, deleting, or renaming classes*

While the deletion of a class which is a leaf of the class hierarchy or the insertion of a class as a leaf seems to be straightforward, the deletion or insertion of an inner class may cause severe problems. In general, such a modification may cause extensive changes in the interface (withdrawal of inherited operations) as well as in the implementation part (withdrawal of inherited attributes and constraints) of subclasses. This may result in an extensive reconfiguration of the subclass hierarchy, both on the level of the interfaces and on the level of the internal representation of objects on secondary storage. Moreover, operations which were defined on the level of a subclass may no longer be applicable since they may use inherited but now removed attributes or operations.

3. *Modifying the class hierarchy*

The modification of the class hierarchy is similar to the deletion and insertion of a class. However, moving a class to another position in the class hierarchy does not only affect the subclass hierarchies but also the class itself. All attributes and methods which were inherited from the old superclass are removed and replaced by attributes and methods of the new superclass. This may result in a complete change of the information content (semantics) of a class.

Current approaches to schema modification are rather restricted. They mostly deal with the problem of how the implementation part of a class can be modified. Less attention is paid to the question of how such modifications may affect the interface part of the class and how a propagation of these changes into the applications can be controlled. In the following we will briefly discuss some approaches to the problem of how different versions of an object which originate from the fact that the structure of a class has changed can be handled.

Skarra and Zdonik proposed language constructs to filter objects between the database (representation on secondary storage) and the executing process (methods) (/SkZd86/). When a new version of an existing type is defined, the programmer (perhaps with automatic guidance) defines **filtering functions** which allow existing methods to deal with objects of the new version of the type and to allow new methods to deal with objects of the existing version of the type. The filter acts just like a database view. It gives the user of an object the illusion that the object is of the type expected. This approach presumes some form of version management of class definitions, or, at least, the ability of the system to manage several representations of a class definition. This approach is known as **object screening**, sometimes also called **object type versioning** (see, e.g. /BjHu89/).

An alternative to object screening is **object conversion**. In this case, all instances of a class are changed when the structure of the instances of a class is modified. Since, after such a change all instances of a class are in conformity with the new class definition the old definition can be dropped. While this approach is more efficient once the conversion has been performed, it produces high costs at the time when a class is modified.

The difference between object conversion and object screening is not only an implementation aspect. There is also a difference on the conceptual level. Object screening allows old object states still to be valid and accessible, while object conversion does not support such an evolutionary process. It allows only one class definition to be the basis for all instances of a class, namely, the currently valid class definition, regardless of whether older instances were defined under a different perspective. If, for example, an attribute is dropped the attribute is removed from all instances of the class, regardless of whether the attribute value is still valid for older instances. As an example let us consider class *INVOICE-FORM*. If a change is made to the invoice form, it would be desirable to be able to keep the old instances and at the same time create new instances according to the new invoice definition. Object screening is able to support such a coexistence of different types of instances, at least as long as it is possible to define appropriate filter functions. Hence, only object screening supports schema evolution as opposed to schema modification.

In ORION an approach to schema modification was pioneered in which guide-lines were defined which describe the way in which schema modification must take place (/BKKK87/). ORION does not support all kinds of schema modifications. To avoid improper modifications, a set of invariants was defined which determines what it means for a schema to be consistent; i.e. a number of rules were established which must be preserved across schema modifications. Moreover, the allowable schema change operations were defined and, for each change, the updates that must be performed in order to preserve the invariants. This approach was also pursued in GemStone (/PeSt87/). The major difference between the two is that the ORION approach supports object screening whereas the GemStone approach utilizes object conversion. However, in /BMOP89/ the GemStone people announce that they want to replace their concept of object conversion by a more flexible mechanism in which either screening or conversion may be used as appropriate.

In /Kim90-1/ it is stated that the database schema for an object-oriented database has two dimensions, the **class hierarchy**, which captures the generalization relationship between a class and its subclasses, and **a class-composition hierarchy** which represents the aggregation relationship between a class and its attributes and the domains of the attributes. Again it has to be noted that a class-composition hierarchy can only be visible, and therefore part of the schema, if the principle of data encapsulation is ignored (however, recall the discussion about encapsulation in the section about query processing (4.10)). While such a class-composition hierarchy exists in s-typed systems, like ORION, it does not exist in dynamically typed systems, like GemStone, since in such systems each object of a class may have its own structure.

VIEWS

The external schema is usually defined through the concept of view. A **view** is a virtual database whose schema and contents are derived from an existing database through a mapping process. A view may establish different names for attributes and relationships and may reflect a different structure of data, one that is more 'natural' or compatible with the user's perception. However, although a view allows the database designer to consider the special demands of a user, it is still a definition on a relatively neutral and low level, namely, on the level of 'pure' data. It is left to the application how it operates on the data, as long as the results of operations which are to be reflected in the database obey the restrictions imposed on the data by the schema and view mechanism of the database. Object-oriented database systems, however, provide an interface which is on a more specific level, namely on the level of operations on objects. Here a view must not define the data which are accessible to an application but the operations which an application needs to have at its disposal to perform its task accurately. Since these operations are the only way to access and manipulate data, a view definition may result in the need to define some 'view-specific' operations. While relational database systems make it possible to define a view on top of the conceptual schema, i.e. strictly to separate the definition of views from the definition of the general database content, object-oriented database systems only provide one common interface per class, the interface which consists of all operations which can be applied to the objects of the class. This implies that the interface of a class needs to provide not only the operations associated with the class but also operations which are only associated with a single view. The strict separation between conceptual and external schemas of a database system is blurred. There is just one common set of operations, and it is not clear which operations are application-independent (represent the conceptual schema) and which operations are strongly related to a special application (represent the external schema). In /ScLT90/ an approach is presented which permits us to assign methods explicitly to a specific view (by the extend operator). However, such an approach makes it rather complicated to position the by-the-view newly created class (type) in the class (type) hierarchy since the elimination or addition of a new method strongly affects the principle of inheritance. For example, if a new method is added and this method is meant only to be applicable to the class created by the view this class has to be a leaf class (otherwise its subclasses would inherit the added method).

A necessary condition for the creation of views is that the operators which can be applied to create a view are *object-preserving* (see Section 4.10 about query processing). Otherwise each view definition would create new objects (which is usually not the intention of the user).

For example, /ScLT90/ and /ScSc90/ allow arbitrary queries to serve as view definitions. Their query language provides a number of generic operators, like selection, difference, union, projection, join, etc. Since these operators are all object-preserving, views can be used as arguments of update operations. Briefly, all update operations have the same effect as if they were applied to the class(es) from which the view was derived. The main concepts of the query language have already been presented in Section 4.10 about query languages. Therefore, the interested reader is referred to that section.

4.12. Secondary Storage Management and Access Strategies

The success of database systems, of course, largely relies on their ability to provide fast access to objects of the database. Relational database systems are no slouches at associative retrieval. Their indexing routines are among the most sophisticated and highly tuned of any class of software systems although it took a long time for this goal to be reached. A major reason for this high standard of performance is that relational database systems are based on a rather limited set of type constructors (set and tuple) which, moreover, can't be applied in a nested way. Furthermore, attributes must be of an atomic type and access to data concentrates on associative retrieval. This rather restricted environment defines a solid basis for the development of efficient storage structures, sophisticated access strategies, and highly tuned optimization strategies.

Object-oriented database systems provide considerably extended data-modelling facilities. They, for instance, allow the programmer to use previously defined data types as building blocks for new data types or to nest data structures to arbitrary levels. This results in a considerably extended set of object types and data structures which have to be supported. Moreover, access to data can be subdivided into at least two different kinds, namely, access to data within a complex object (**vertical traversal**) and associative retrieval over a collection of (complex) objects (**horizontal traversal**). Access within a complex object includes direct access to attributes at arbitrary levels within a complex object as well as traversal of the logical object structure. In such an environment Maier, for example, defines an ideal database system as a database system in which attribute access is as fast for database items as for values in program memory (/Maie89-1/). Attribute access in program memory can take as few as one or two machine instructions. While Maier concludes that this speed may be unobtainable for database items, he assumes that coming within a factor of 10 is possible, rather than the factors of 1000 or 10,000 seen today. Zdonik wants navigation within complex objects at the speed of factor 3 of dereferencing virtual memory pointer (/ZdHe90/). These requirements, of course, place considerably extended demands on storage structures as well as on access strategies. In the following we will discuss some selected features with respect to secondary storage management and access strategies. Since storage structures for complex objects are intensively dealt with by researchers from the database community we want to refer the interested reader to the comprehensive literature in this field. Nevertheless, there is no question about it, a satisfactory solution for an efficient mapping of the data-modelling concepts of the object-oriented language front-end(s) of an object-oriented database system to secondary storage is not yet realized, and it can not be foreseen when such a rather desirable situation will be achieved. Moreover, it should not be concealed from the reader that most of the proposed techniques for storage management and access support run counter to the principle of encapsulation; i.e. they need to disregard the principle of encapsulation in this or that way. Another essential point is that most access strategies can only be applied if all objects of the set have the same structure. In particular, this means that most of the well-known and rather effective techniques cannot directly be applied to systems which do not require their classes to be typed (like GemStone). There seems to be a weak relationship between encapsulation and typing (at least with respect to access strategies). Techniques which need to violate the principle of encapsulation usually require the underlying system to be 'typed' while techniques which observe encapsulation can usually be employed in dynamically typed systems. This is caused by the fact that techniques which observe encapsulation cannot rely on knowledge about the structure of objects and, therefore, can be used in dynamically typed systems. On the other hand, a violation of encapsulation usually results from the fact that the technique exploits knowledge about the structure of the objects of a class. But, of course, a common structure is only existent if the system is typed.

NAVIGATION AND ATTRIBUTE ACCESS

Since objects in object-oriented database systems may be rather complex as well as extremely large it seems to be necessary to support access strategies within objects (e.g. indexes on attribute types which consist of collections of values or instances of other types). Moreover, a deferred loading of objects may be advantageous in which the root level of the object is provided to the user first and lower levels of the object hierarchy are put at the user's disposal on request. If further access patterns can be foreseen, prefetching of these parts of the object may improve access speed substantially. With respect to the representation of objects on secondary storage, clustering is a well-known strategy to speed up access. But since objects may be part of several objects (shared objects), either clustering can only be realized partially or it becomes necessary to replicate data.

INDEXING

In object-oriented database systems, there is a conflict between encapsulation and maintaining auxiliary access paths. Conventional database systems usually index on structure. In object-oriented database systems the question is whether, with respect to encapsulation, one should index on the structure of the objects of a class (neglects encapsulation) or on the results of operations (observes encapsulation).

Indexing on the structure of the objects of a class

If objects are to be indexed on their internal structure, one concern is how deep to index. Should it be only possible to index on the immediate instance variables of an object class or also on instance variables at deeper levels of the object hierarchy (subcomponents)? Moreover, if a subcomponent of an object is an instance of an independent class, how can we keep track of updates which were performed on such instances in other contexts? Another question is how indexes on non-atomic attribute types can be supported?

A further decision to be made is what to index: classes or collections or both. Let us, for example, assume that three classes are given, namely, *EMPLOYEE*, *SUPPLIER* and *ADDRESS*. *EMPLOYEE* and *SUPPLIER* may both use instances of *ADDRESS*. Should we define one single index for all instances of *ADDRESS* or two separate indexes, one for the instances used in *EMPLOYEE* and one for the instances used in *SUPPLIER*? A similar question arises if we consider inheritance. If, for example, a class hierarchy is given with *PERSON* as its root, *STUDENT* as a subclass, and *STUDENT-OF-COMPUTER-SCIENCE* as a subclass of *STUDENT*. Should an index on the attribute NAME be installed for each of these classes or should the index comprise all instances of the subclass hierarchy spanned by *PERSON*? Of course, such a decision mainly depends on the operations applied to the objects of the classes. If such operations mostly consider instances of one class, **single-class indexing** seems to be appropriate. On the other hand, if operations mostly consider all instances of a class hierarchy, **class-hierarchy indexing** seems to be superior. ORION, for example, supports both types of indexes (/KiKD89/).

Since operations may work on any collection of classes of a subclass hierarchy, index maintenance is an extremely sophisticated task. We have the classical conflicting goals here, with some complications added: indexes speed up data access in retrieval, but they slow down update operations. In the case of update, identification of the indexes to be modified is not a trivial task. Moreover, this situation complicates query evaluation. Should the optimizer use an index which only contains but does not match the search space of a predicate with the risk that the result consists of a superset of the expected set, or should the optimizer instead exploit several indexes which cover the search space completely or, at least, to a large extent?

Indexing on the results of an operation

Since object-oriented database systems compute data on a semantically higher level than conventional database systems (operations rather than data) one can think about installing indexes on the level of operations rather than on the level of data structures (see, e.g. /Maie89-1/ or /ZdHe90/). This approach seems to be more natural in the presence of encapsulation. If an index on the result of an operation is to be installed, we have first to apply the operation to all elements of a set; the results have to be organized into an index. Though this approach allows the operation to be executed efficiently, it causes several problems. One problem is to ensure that an arbitrary operation returns the same values when applied twice in a row; i.e. we need to know which other operations on an object can cause the result of the indexed operation to change. If we trust the implementor of a class to ensure that certain operations behave properly for indexing, this is contrary to what is provided in relational systems, where index maintenance is guaranteed no matter how a relation is defined (/Maie89-1/). Another problem is that the search space of several operations may be identical. For example, an operation that modifies instances of a given collection may use the same search predicate as an operation that retrieves instances of this collection. How can such similarities be recognized and how can we ensure that these operations use the same index?

Secondary storage management and optimization strategies in object-oriented database systems are still open issues. It is not yet clear what the internal model of an object-oriented database system may look like or how physical data independence can be achieved. There is, however, much work on the special aspect of storage management for complex objects; see, for instance, AIM-P (/DKAB86/), DASDBS (/PSSW87/), EXODUS (/CDRS89/), GENESIS (/BBGS88/), OMS (/FrBo89/), POSTGRES (/StRo87/, /JhSt90/), PRIMA (/HMMS87/), STARBURST (/SCFL86/).

4.13. Extended Definition of the Object-Oriented Database System

Up to now we have discussed the features of an object-oriented database system according to our first definition (3.1). However, a strong motivation for the varied and multilayered activities in object-oriented database research is the hope that these systems can serve non-conventional applications in a far better way than today's database systems. While some of the requirements of such application areas are well served by an object-oriented database system (e.g. rich modelling power through properties and behaviour, inheritance, complex objects), other requirements have not been considered so far, e.g. version management, long and nested transactions, cooperative work, and trigger and constraint mechanisms. This observation leads to a second, in a way extended, definition of an object-oriented database system.

First approaches to object-oriented database systems (e.g. GemStone) came closer to Definition 3.1 while many recent developments are more in line with Definition 4.1. ORION, for example, already provides version management and an extended transaction model.

It is still debatable exactly which features a database system has to provide to be called a non-conventional database system. Usually, besides

> Definition 4.1: **object-oriented database system** (*extended definition*)
>
> An object-oriented database system has to satisfy the criteria of definition 3.1 and, additionally, has to support the *features* which are required by the so-called *non-conventional application areas*.

the concept of complex objects, the following features are discussed in this context: version management, a considerably extended transaction management (which supports long and nested transactions and cooperative work, and offers appropriate recovery techniques), and trigger, constraint and event mechanisms. We will consider only some aspects of these features which are especially relevant to object-oriented systems.

4.14. Data Sharing and Reliability (Transaction Management, Concurrency Control, and Recovery)

Transaction management is concerned with supervising the way in which application programs share a common database. A transaction is usually viewed as both the unit of concurrency and the unit of recovery. More specifically, the notion of transaction is commonly associated with four properties (/HäRe83/), namely, atomicity, consistency, isolation, and durability (**ACID principle**). Concurrent transactions have to be controlled so that serializability is achieved, i.e. the results of an interleaved execution of the transactions have to be equivalent to the results of some serial execution of these transactions.

While this traditional concept of transaction processing works very well as long as transactions are rather short, it is no longer appropriate, if we consider non-conventional application areas. In such environments objects often need to be handled for a long period of time. Moreover, some application areas require work to be done in a cooperative manner. This requires a different interpretation of atomicity and isolation. Long transactions need a finer unit of recovery since it is unreasonable for a user to lose all his work (of days or weeks) in case of, e.g. a system malfunction. Moreover, cooperative work cannot be supported if the isolation of transactions is strictly required. These requirements led to an extension of the traditional theory of transactions in the way that the otherwise flat model of transactions is allowed to include transactions within transactions. This kind of transaction is called **nested transaction**. A nested transaction structure consists of a set of child transactions that execute atomically with respect to their parent and their siblings. This approach allows the user to structure and delegate his work, to define finer units of recovery, and to exploit parallel execution within his environment. Moreover, it allows the **operational integrity** (prevention of integrity violation which may result from the concurrent access of users to the data of the database) to be ensured entirely by the database system.

Especially in design environments this type of nesting is still too restrictive. In such application areas the support of cooperative work within groups of users is mandatory. Traditional concepts for transaction management start from the assumption that transactions are competitors rather than partners. In order to support cooperative work between users, the rigid measures of conventional transaction managers can be weakened, i.e. some responsibility for the operational integrity of data can be moved from the database system to the application environment. Of course, this has to be done in a controlled way and the database system should offer as much help as possible. There are some approaches which try to weaken the strict serializability criterion of transactions, e.g. by allowing transactions to exchange objects, to let other transactions see intermediate results, or to lend objects to other transactions (see, e.g. /KSUW85/). Moreover, some approaches introduce weaker lock modes which allow parallel transaction to work on the same objects, even if traditional lock modes do not allow such an interleaving (e.g. a concurrent read and update lock; see, e.g. /Unla90/). The interested reader is referred to, e.g. /HäRo86/, /HäRo87/, /Katz84/, /Kelt87/, /Kelt88/, /KoKB85/, /KSUW85/ , /Unla88/, /Unla90/, /UnSc89-2/, /UnSc91-1 + 2/. In the rest of this section we will concentrate on some aspects which are especially relevant in the context of object-oriented systems.

Data abstraction in object-oriented database systems might allow the applications programmer to realize a more adapted approach to concurrency control. The only way by which abstract data types can be accessed is via their operations. Since these operations are treated as part of the database system, their semantics can be exploited to achieve greater concurrency or to permit non-serializable behaviour in specific environments. This stands in contrast to conventional database systems. They define read and write operations as the level of abstraction at which application programs can interact with the database. As a consequence, serializability theory is completely based on primitive operations of the types read and write (/SkZd89/). Application semantics are not considered at all. Consider the example of a bank account. If two concurrent transactions each add an amount to the same account, this can be done in an interleaved way, since these operations are commutative. Nevertheless, conventional locking schemes will not permit such an interleaving, as the database system only sees the read and write operations required to perform the account modification. **Semantics-based concurrency-control protocols** permit the interleaving of such operations (apart from the fact that some kind of short lock is still needed for the pure modification process). Concurrency control is performed on the level of operations and, therefore, can consider the semantics of the types and their operations. Concurrent work on objects can be increased. The drawback of this approach is that it eliminates the common and neutral basis of conventional concurrency-control schemes. If, for instance, a new operation is to be integrated which displays all transactions on an account which took place in a given period of time, this operation can't just be mapped on the read operation of the database. Instead, all other operations on the type *Account* need to be considered to be able to decide what kind of concurrency-control measures are to be implemented. Due to the loss of the neutral basis concurrency-control measures have to be decided on a higher level. However, this level is not directly visible to the programmer but hidden in the implementation of the operations of the given type. Therefore, such an insertion is not only highly sophisticated but also error-prone. An operation like ***deposit*** of transaction T_1 will not conflict with a ***withdraw*** operation of a concurrent transaction T_2 as long as both operations are the only operations of the transactions on the database. But if T_1 also wants to perform a ***withdraw*** operation this operation may be rejected since it may violate a constraint (e.g. the balance must not be negative) which would not have been violated had the ***withdraw*** operation of T_2 not been permitted to execute in the meantime. The difficulty here comes from the fact that more than one operation is performed within one transaction (instead of treating an operation as an equivalent to a transaction).

To summarize, semantics-based concurrency control is useful, but it is hard to design and implement. For the time being, type-specific concurrency control may be applicable in special environments, but it is not sufficiently understood to be applied as a general approach to concurrency control. First approaches are presented in, e.g. /BaRa88/, /BaRa90/, /FLMW87/, /Herl87/, /HeWe88/, /SkZd89/, /SpSc84/ and /Weih88/.

Before we conclude this section let us just mention some other features which introduce a new dimension to the problems of concurrency control.

The existence of a class hierarchy and the fact that complex objects may contain other objects need to be considered especially by the concurrency-control mechanism for the following reasons:

1 If the scope of a query is not a single class but the complete subclass hierarchy (not only *UNIVERSITY_MEMBER* but also all direct and indirect subclasses of *UNIVERSITY_MEMBER*) the set of

objects of the subclass hierarchy must not be modified by a conflicting transaction.

2 If a complete composite object O is accessed by a transaction it has to be ensured that shared subobjects of O cannot be accessed in an incompatible way by concurrent transactions.

3 Since a subclass S inherits structure and behaviour from its superclasses it must be forbidden that a concurrent transaction modifies the definition of any of the superclasses of S while a transaction T accesses instances of S (otherwise inherited attributes or methods may be deleted from S or new attributes may be added to S while instances of S are accessed by T).

4.15. Versions

Conventional database systems work in terms of a single evolving logical state. As soon as an object is modified its previous state is discarded, the database system has no memory of prior states of objects. If the history of updates to an object is to be captured, an applications data structure must be introduced to record the evolving state of the object. People from the CAD/CAM, office automation, and software engineering communities especially show much interest in the incorporation of time, in one form or the other, as part of the explicit semantics of a database system. This interest has been fuelled by the inherent complexities in the development of complex application objects. Keeping track of the dependencies that exist between several versions of objects, which emerged from different periods of a complex design process, should be the job of the database system rather than the application. A version manager should be part of the database system.

There is no common concept of what versions are. Different application areas need different version concepts. Commercial application areas, for example, need some kind of **time-versioning** which means that versions are arranged in some linear order. Even this elementary time-versioning can be seen from different points of view, as different ordering relationships on the set of versions of an object can be distinguished:

- **time of realization**:
  defines the point of time at which the occurrence of an event is recognized in the real world. If, for example, the salary of an employee is to be increased on the first of July, this date defines the time of realization, regardless of when this event is reflected in the database.

- **time of storage**:
  defines the point of time at which an event is reflected in the database.
- **time of validity**:
  defines the time interval during which an event is valid in the real world.

In CAD/CAM versions are used for different purposes, e.g. to illustrate the life-cycle of a design object, to document the process of development (history), to represent different approaches to a problem (such versions are called **variants** or **alternatives**), or to express different views on an object (e.g. compiled code and source code of a module; such versions are called **representations**).

In literature a number of complex and sophisticated version models are proposed (see, e.g. /ChKi86/, /DaEn88/, /DiLo88/, /KaCB86/, /KaCh87/, /KaLe84/, /KlSW86/, /KSUW85/). Two main structures for relating versions can be distinguished (/KlSW86/):

1 Versions are ordered (not necessarily totally) by various relationships (e.g. time relations, development history). Version graphs or version sequences are used as a modelling tool.
2 Versions are classified according to specific properties (e.g. valid/invalid, transient/working/released). Partitioning is used as a modelling tool. Classes may determine the operations applicable to the versions in the various sets.

Current implementations of version management in object-oriented database systems only provide models which concentrate on time-versions or version graphs.

4.16. Active Objects, Trigger, Constraints, and Events

TRIGGER, CONSTRAINTS AND EVENTS

Non-standard database systems are supposed to support non-conventional application areas. For this purpose, besides a powerful management of complex objects, they should support the evolutionary process which characterizes the complex and time-consuming development of application objects. Consistency constraints must be maintained which are far more numerous and of higher complexity than in traditional business-oriented database applications. A good example is a design environment where consistency constraints must be met on different levels of the design process. In earlier phases constraints are to be considered on a more local and context-dependent basis (local consistency) while at the end of the entire design process global consistency has to be fulfilled. This indicates that a design process passes through a number of intermediate stages, each of which defines its own consistency constraints as well as checking or validating tools. The database management system, as the central repository for all data accumulated in a design process, must integrate mechanisms which allow the designer to formulate consistency constraints as well as general actions, to determine points of time or events at which these constraints are to be checked or at which the actions are to be performed, and to define reactions in case of a violation of a constraint or the failure of an action.

In the literature a number of concepts are proposed that allow the database management system to perform automatically some separately defined actions in response to certain events. These facilities are often referred to as **assertions**, **triggers**, or **rules**. However, most of the currently proposed strategies for executing triggered actions are rather restricted since triggers are associated with database operations (transactions) or with a simply determinable state of the database. But triggers have to be seen in a broader context. A general model for trigger and constraint mechanisms should be able to satisfy the following requirements (see also /DiKM86/):

1 A trigger should be executable, either explicitly by a user or automatically by the database system, at any point of time or as a response to any event.
2 It should support the definition of global consistency via various levels of local consistency.
3 A consistency constraint should not only be definable by a predicate but also by a checking or validating algorithm written in a programming language. Moreover, it should be possible to include complex checking or validating programs (tools) as part of a trigger.
4 It should be possible to define different reactions to consistency violations. This includes situations in which some consistency violation is accepted (switched off) or overridden by a more global consistency constraint.
5 It should be possible to define consistency constraints and reactions to violations at any point of time.
6 It should be possible to use a trigger to control a state or state transition of the database as well as to model the operational control of a process.

More specifically, a trigger can be seen as a rule which consists of three components (/HLMC88/):

Event: An event is an indicator that specifies when a trigger has to be executed. It can be bound to a database operation (or transaction), a clock event, or an externally defined event that is reported to the database system.

Condition: A condition is a predicate that is evaluated whenever the event occurs. If the predicate is true, then the action is executed. A condition can be omitted. Then the action is executed in any case.

Action: An action is a program to be executed in case an event occurs and the condition is satisfied. The action may include database operations as well as general-purpose language constructs. The action may be performed immediately or at a later point of time. Moreover, it may be executed as part of the process in which it was triggered (e.g. a transaction) or as a separate process which is independent of the triggering process.

There are a number of questions which arise in the context of triggers (/DiKM86/):

1 Can multiple independent triggers be defined for an event and which one is chosen if that event occurs? For such cases, e.g. POSTGRES (/StRo87/) defines a conflict resolution strategy which is based on trigger priorities. Note that it may sometimes be desirable to execute several triggers simultaneously.
2 How are nested triggers handled, i.e. triggers whose actions in turn raise events that are part of defined triggers (infinite loop, how to guarantee termination)?
3 How does the concept of trigger interact with concurrency control? What should be done in case the action of a trigger needs to access data which is currently locked (e.g. by a transaction) in an incompatible mode?

Although constraint mechanisms are considered essential for non-standard database systems, current object-oriented database systems mostly do not provide such facilities. One of the few exceptions is OOPS (/UnSc89-1/).

ACTIVE OBJECTS

A concept which is strongly related to trigger mechanisms is the concept of **active objects**. Though the concept is interpreted in different ways, it is generally accepted that active objects are objects with some inherent intelligence. They realize a high degree of autonomous responsibility and control; i.e. they can be considered as independent agents with their own source of knowledge and activity (/ElGi89/). Most object-oriented systems have objects that must receive messages before performing any action – these objects are passive. If objects can initiate actions asynchronously without receiving a message those objects are active. Consider a simple example. The object structure of a class *PERSON* may contain an attribute AGE. If AGE is computed each time the attribute is accessed (a message arrives), the object is passive. If AGE is automatically modified on each birthday of that person, the object is active. Active objects are rather advantageous in environments in which time constraints play a major role. Since the actual state of an object is always known the system does not need to compute it at the time the object is accessed. This, of course, allows the object to react faster to incoming messages. Database systems which incorporate the concept of active objects are sometimes called **active databases**. The first system was introduced by Morgenstern in 1983 (/Morg83/). Another large database project in this direction is HiPAC (**Hi**gh **P**erformance **AC**tive database system) (/Daya88/, /DBBC88/).

5. SOME EXEMPLARY OBJECT-ORIENTED DATABASE SYSTEMS

Currently, a number of systems can be identified which fit the list of requirements for object-oriented database systems, or come close to it. Examples of commercial systems are GemStone (/BMOP89/), VBASE (/Andr90/), ORION (/KBCG89/), IRIS (/FABC89/), and VISION (/CaSc88/, /CaSc90/). Some research prototypes are Alltalk (/RiMS88/), AVANCE (/BjBr88/), Cactis (/HuKi89/), ENCORE/OBSERVER (/WeZd86/), Extra/Excess (/CDWV88/), OOPS (/SUWZ88/), OZ+ (/WeLo89/), O_2 (/VeBD89/), Probe (/MaDa86/), TEDM (/ZhMa88/), VODAK (/DuKT88/), and ZEITGEIST (/FJLL88/).

Many of these systems have a two-layer architecture (see /Maie89-2/). The bottom layer supports a structural view of objects, whereas the top layer adds a behavioural view. Therefore, the bottom layer corresponds to a storage or object manager. It usually has a purely structural type system, and handles concurrency, recovery, associative access, authorization, and resource allocation. On top of the storage manager resides the execution layer which realizes the behavioural view. It implements a more sophisticated type system, enforces encapsulation and executes methods, making storage manager calls as needed. There is typically one instance of the storage manager in the database, but an instance of the execution layer for each active session. Some object-oriented database systems are able to distribute the layers, with the storage manager running on individual workstations. If the execution layer does sufficient buffering, such local distribution can be an enormous performance boost (/RuKC87/).

We will now discuss GemStone, IRIS, ORION, O2, and OOPS in more detail.

5.1. GemStone

GemStone is one of the few object-oriented database systems which are currently commercially available. Servio Logic Development Corporation, the manufacturer of this system, has been involved in research and development of object-oriented database systems since 1983. GemStone is a typical representative of the top-down approach. Starting point of the research work was an object-oriented language, called OPAL, which was extended by a disk-based storage manager. OPAL has much in common with SMALLTALK but it is especially geared toward database applications, i.e. OPAL can be used for data definition, data manipulation, and general computation. Moreover, it supports schema modification, conventional transaction management and recovery, and ad hoc query facility. Like SMALLTALK, OPAL provides the concepts of message passing, information hiding, data abstraction, polymorphism/late binding, complex objects management, object identity, simple inheritance, and extensibility in terms of new data types. Most parts of GemStone are implemented in C(+ +) with some programming environment implemented in SMALLTALK.

In the following we will briefly present some features of GemStone.

ARCHITECTURE

GemStone consists of two major components, Stone which corresponds to the storage manager and Gem, which realizes the execution layer. **Stone** provides secondary storage management, concurrency control, authorization, transactions, recovery, and support for associative access. Stone uses unique surrogates, called **object-oriented pointers (OOPs)** to refer to objects and an **object table** to map an OOP to a physical location. This level of indirection means that objects can easily be moved in memory. Stone is built upon the underlying VMS file system. The data model that Stone provides is simpler than the full GemStone model, and provides only operators for structural update and access. An object may be stored separately from its subobjects, but the OOPs for the values of an object's instance variables are grouped together.

Gem is located atop Stone, and elaborates Stone's storage model into the full GemStone model. Gem also adds the capabilities of compiling OPAL methods into bytecode and executing that code, user authentication, and session control. OPAL bytecodes are similar, but not identical, to the bytecodes used in SMALLTALK. Part of the Gem layer is the virtual image: the collection of OPAL classes, methods, and objects that are supplied with every GemStone system. For each user application, there is one Gem process. Each such process provides the full functionality of GemStone. Application interfaces exist for C, SMALLTALK-80 (Park Place Systems), and SMALLTALK/V (Digitalk). In addition there is a command line interface called TOPAZ that provides direct access to the full functionality of the system.

CLASSES/TYPES

In GemStone a class describes the structure and behaviour of its instances but does not serve, in general, to denote the collection of all its instances, its extension. Instead, collection objects – arrays, bags, sets – serve to group the instances of a class; i.e. a class only describes the structure and behaviour of its instances (this corresponds to a type definition) while the user explicitly assigns instances to one or more collections. The following is an example of a (simplified) structure definition of a class *ANIMAL*.

OBJECT **subclass**: *'ANIMAL'*
instVarNames: # ('NAME', 'FAVORITEFOOD', 'HABITAT')
constraints: # ()
isInvariant: false

The above class declaration defines a class *ANIMAL* as a subclass of *OBJECT* (GemStone does not support multiple inheritance). The attributes (**instVarNames**) are not typed; i.e. OPAL associates types with values, not the slots holding the values (which means that OPAL provides dynamic typing). Typing objects rather than attributes has some advantages during the development process of an application since it offers considerably more flexibility. However, OPAL allows attributes to be typed, e.g. when the application model has stabilized, for reasons of integrity and efficiency. This is done in the constraints section, e.g. **constraints**: # (#**Name**, *string*) restricts the value of attribute NAME to be of type *string* only. This facility, to type either objects or attributes, is a major difference between GemStone and other object-oriented database systems. Since classes in OPAL do not provide an object container, instances of classes are supposed to be collected in collection objects. Here again, OPAL allows us to type such collections. While, e.g. *BAG* subclass: '*BAG_OF_ANIMAL*' allows *BAG_OF_ ANIMAL* to contain any instance of any class, a constraint definition, like **constraints**: *ANIMAL*, restricts the instances of *BAG_OF_ ANIMAL* to be of type *ANIMAL*.

The **isInvariant** section allows the user to define whether instances of a class can be modified once they have been committed to the permanent GemStone database.

After the structure of a class is defined, the user can write the methods that establish the external interface of the class.

ASSOCIATIVE ACCESS

OPAL supports the use of indexes to speed up the evaluation of expressions. However, auxiliary storage structures are not automatically installed by the system but have to be integrated by the user. Moreover, proper typing has to exist for the path being indexed; i.e. it is only possible to install an index if all attributes along the path to the attribute to be indexed are typed. A central question in designing associative access was which to index, classes or collections? Many applications may use instances of the same class, and store them in different collections. Indexing on the class means that applications that do not use the index still bear the overhead for instances they use being in the index (index modification). Moreover, an index on a class, when applied, will return a superset of the instances of a collection (since a user-defined collection might not contain all instances of a class). On the other hand, indexing a collection allows the possibility that instances of subclasses be included, too, in a collection that is indexed. Therefore, and for several other reasons, OPAL only allows us to index collections.

SCHEMA MODIFICATION

As already mentioned, GemStone supports the concept of object conversion. For a further discussion of this topic see Section 4.11.

TRANSACTION MANAGEMENT AND RECOVERY

GemStone realizes the traditional transaction models; i.e. transactions are the unit of recovery and concurrency control follows the principle of serializability. The nesting of transactions is not supported.

Multiple concurrent users are served by providing each user session with a workspace. Whenever a session modifies an object, a shadow copy of that object is created. Aborting a transaction means throwing away objects shadowed in the workspace, and committing means replacing shared objects by their shadows.

GemStone provides both optimistic and pessimistic concurrency control. While the use of optimistic concurrency control is transparent to the user, he has to place locks on objects explicitly in case he wants to exploit pessimistic concurrency control. A transaction that uses locks is still governed by the optimistic control mechanism. The locks are simply a means to guarantee that, with regard to the locked objects, the transaction will pass the criteria for commitment under GemStone's optimistic mechanisms.

QUERY PROCESSING

GemStone provides associative access through a limited calculus sublanguage. The language is such that associative queries can be viewed as procedural OPAL code. This reduces the impedance mismatch between OPAL and the query language to a minimum. The query language supports selection on collections like set, bag, or array. Selection conditions are conjunctions of comparisons, where the comparisons are between path expressions and other path expressions or literals. Joins are mostly replaced by path-tracing. The following query is an example. *EMPS* is a collection of employees and the query finds all employees whose last name is Jones and who earn more than their manager.

EMPS **select:**
{anEmp | anEmp.NAME.LAST = 'Jones' **&**
anEmp.SALARY > anEmp.WORKSIN.MANAGER.SALARY}

VERSIONS

The current version of GemStone does not support any version mechanism.

LITERATURE

/BMOP89/, /CoMa84/, /MaOP85/, /MaSt86/, /MaSt87/, /MSOP86/, /PeSM87/, /PeSt87/, /PuMS87/.

5.2. ORION

ORION is a research prototype of an object-oriented database system which has been developed at MCC (Microelectronics and Computer Technology Corporation, Austin, Texas); it may be commercially available in the near future. It is designed for applications from the AI, multimedia documents, and computer-aided design domains. ORION is implemented in Common

LISP which also serves as the programming language of ORION. However, ORION extends Common LISP with object-oriented programming (message passing, information hiding, data abstraction, multiple inheritance, classification, complex objects management, object identity, extensibility in terms of new data types) and database capabilities (schema evolution, version control, ad hoc query facility, extended conventional transaction management and recovery, multimedia information management).

In the following we will briefly present some features of ORION.

ARCHITECTURE

The ORION architecture consists of four components: the message handler, the object subsystem, the storage subsystem, and the transaction subsystem. The **message handler** receives and handles all messages sent to the ORION system. These include messages for user-defined methods, access messages, and system-defined functions. A **user-defined method** is a method that the user defines and stores in ORION. An **access method** is one that retrieves or updates the value of an attribute of a class. **System-defined functions** include all ORION functions for schema definition, creation and deletion of instances, transaction management, and so on.

The **object subsystem** provides high-level functions, such as schema evolution, version control, query optimization, and multimedia information management. The message handler and object subsystem together correspond to the execution layer.

The **storage subsystem** provides access to objects on disk. It manages the allocation and deallocation of segments of pages on disk, finds and places objects on pages, and moves pages to and from disk. It also manages indexes on attributes of a class to speed up the evaluation of associative queries.

The **transaction subsystem** provides a concurrency control and recovery mechanism to protect database integrity while allowing the interleaved execution of multiple concurrent transactions.

CLASSES/TYPES

A class in ORION not only describes the structure and behaviour of its instances but also serves as an object container; i.e. ORION provides the usual notion of class (attached to a class is its extension). The following is a simplified example of a class definition.

(*make-class* *CLASSNAME*
    :superclass *LIST_OF_SUPERCLASSES*
    :attributes LIST_OF_ATTRIBUTES
    :methods ***List-of-Method-Specs***

CLASSNAME is the name of the new class. Since ORION supports multiple inheritance the *LIST_OF_SUPERCLASSES* may contain several superclasses. An attribute specification is a list consisting of an attribute name and the specification of the type of the attribute (see below). In contrast to GemStone, ORION types attributes and not objects (ORION is statically typed).

(ATTRIBUTENAME [**:domain** *DomainSpec*]
    [**:inherit-from** *SUPERCLASS*]

A *DomainSpec* has to be a LISP data type, a class, or a set of LISP data types or classes, and is used to specify the type(s) of the attribute. Since ORION supports multiple inheritance, name conflicts between attribute names of two distinct superclasses have to be resolved. This can be done by the user if the keyword **:inherit-from** is specified. In this case the attribute of which superclass is to be inherited can be specified. Otherwise, the attribute is inherited from the first superclass of the *LIST_OF_SUPERCLASSES*.

An instance can be created by sending a ***make*** message to the class to which the instance will belong:

(***make*** *CLASSNAME* :ATTRIBUTE1 value1
    ...
    :ATTRIBUTEN valueN

ORION explicitly supports the is-part-of relationship between objects. However, a composite object is defined as an object with a hierarchy of *exclusive* component objects. Thus, the first version of ORION does not support shared component objects. In /KiBG89/ this original approach was revised. The new approach was briefly discussed in Section 4.7. Here, we will concentrate on the currently valid approach. A constituent object of a composite object references an instance of its component class through a composite attribute. For this reason the attribute definition in the ***make*** *CLASSNAME* message is extended by the keyword **:composite**:

(ATTRIBUTENAME [**:composite** TrueOrNil])

In this case, the attribute type must not be specified. Instead, an instance of any class can be made part of a composite object but only at the time of creation of that instance. This is done by extending the ***make*** message with a parent argument:

```
(make CLASSNAME  :parent (ParentObject
                            PARENTATTRIBUTENAME)
                 :ATTRIBUTE1   value1
                      ...
                 :ATTRIBUTEN   valueN
```

This means that the composite object hierarchy is built up from the component object to its parent object, not, as one may assume, vice versa.

ASSOCIATE ACCESS

ORION supports indexes on classes and class hierarchies. Traditionally, an index has been maintained on an attribute of a single class. This means that to support the evaluation of a query whose access scope is a class hierarchy, the system must maintain one index on the attribute for each of the classes in the class hierarchy. However, it is clear that often it makes sense to maintain one index on the attribute for a class hierarchy, and use it to evaluate queries against any single class in the class hierarchy or any sub-hierarchy of the class hierarchy. Intuitively, it appears that a class-hierarchy index may in general be more effective in evaluating a query whose access scope spans a major subset of the classes in the indexed class hierarchy, while a single-class index should be more appropriate for a query against a single class.

SCHEMA MODIFICATION

As already mentioned in Section 4.11 ORION supports the concept of object screening. This concept is rather powerful and realizes one of the major contributions of ORION. For a further discussion see the section about schema modification (4.11).

TRANSACTION MANAGEMENT AND RECOVERY

ORION realizes the traditional transaction model; i.e. transactions are the unit of recovery and concurrency control follows the principle of serializability. The nesting of transactions is not supported. For concurrency control the locking technique was chosen. A transaction requires a read lock before reading an object, and a write lock before updating an object. This corresponds to the notion of level-3 consistency (/Gray79/) and protects transactions from such consistency anomalies as lost updates, dirty read, and unrepeatable read.

ORION supports two types of transactions: normal and hypothetical. A **hypothetical** transaction is a transaction that always aborts, and is important in application environments in which users often experiment with 'what-if' changes to the database.

Normal transactions can be combined in a session; i.e. a **session** encapsulates a sequence of transactions. Since the transactions within a session are strictly serial, that is, one transaction ends before the next one starts, there is only one active transaction per session. However, a session may have multiple windows, primarily as a short-term solution to the long-duration wait problem that arises in long-duration interactive transactions. Since ORION provides two-phase locking a transaction of a particular session S may be blocked if it cannot obtain a lock. In such a case, no more requests can be processed from the blocked window. If the user wishes to continue with S even while waiting for the lock, the user may do so by creating another window for S. Since all the windows of a session run the same transaction, they share the same locks.

QUERY PROCESSING

ORION supports associative access to instances of a class by a select message:

(select *CLASS* QueryExpression)

QueryExpression has to be a Boolean expression of predicates. It allows a query to restrict the instances of a class to be fetched by specifying predicates against any attributes of the class. An attribute may be one of two types: simple and complex. A **simple attribute** is one whose domain is a primitive class. A **complex attribute** is one whose domain is a class with one or more attributes, including other complex attributes. A predicate on a simple attribute is called a **simple predicate**; one on a complex attribute is called a **complex predicate**. A query with one complex predicate on a class requires the traversal of two classes: the class on which the predicate is applied, and the class that is the domain of the complex attribute. A query that involves one or more complex predicates and, therefore, involves a number of classes, brings out many of the same issues that complicate joins of relations in relational databases. It is important to consider all meaningful permutations of classes in the query graph representation of a query in object-oriented databases. However, the semantics of queries in object-oriented databases make it possible to eliminate many of the permutations of classes that may not be eliminated in relational queries. Given any permutation of n classes, there are two fundamental ways of traversing the classes in the permutation (which are both supported by ORION): forward and reverse traversal. In the **forward traversal**, the classes on a query graph are traversed in a depth-first order starting from the root of the query graph, and following through the successive domains of each complex attribute. In the **reverse traversal**, the leaf classes of a query graph are visited first, and then their parents, working toward the root class. Reverse traversal is usually mixed with forward traversal in case Boolean operators are present.

VERSIONS

In ORION a version mechanism is implemented which realizes the concept of version graphs. An object is either versioned or non-versioned. A versioned object is an instance of a class which the application declares to be versioned. This is done in the ***make-class*** message:

(***make-class*** *CLASSNAME* **:versionable** TrueOrNil)

The version model distinguishes **transient versions** (temporary versions) from **working versions** (stable versions). A transient version may be created from scratch or derived from an existing version. Any number of transient versions may be derived at any time from an existing version, giving rise to a **version-derivation hierarchy** for each versioned object. Each versioned object consists of a **generic instance** which refers to the abstract versioned object and **version instances** which form the version graph (see also Section 4.15).

LITERATURE

/BaKK88/, /BCGK87/, /BKKK87/, /ChKi88/, /GaKi88/, /KBBC88/, /KBCG87/, /KBCG89/, /KGBW90/, /KiBG89/, /KiCB87/, /KiCh88/, /KiKD89/, /Kim89/, /WoKi87/, /WoKL86/.

5.3. IRIS

IRIS is a research prototype of an object-oriented database system which has been developed at Hewlett-Packard Laboratories, Palo Alto, California. It is designed for new and emerging database application areas such as office information and knowledge-based systems, engineering test and measurement, and hardware and software design. The roots of the IRIS data model can be found in semantic data modelling, especially in previous work on DAPLEX (/Ship81/) and its extensions, and on the TAXIS language (/MBGW84/). The IRIS prototype is implemented in C.

IRIS provides the concepts of message passing, information hiding, data abstraction, multiple inheritance, classification, polymorphism in terms of overloading, complex objects management, object identity, extensibility in terms of new data types, schema modification, version control, ad hoc query facility, transaction management and recovery, and multimedia information management (it supports new data types like graphic images, voice, text, vectors, matrices).

In the following we will briefly present some features of IRIS.

ARCHITECTURE

The IRIS architecture consists of two major components: the object manager, which corresponds to the execution layer, and the storage manager.

The IRIS **Object Manager** implements the IRIS data model. Moreover, it provides the basis for a number of IRIS interfaces whose construction is made possible by a set of C language subroutines that defines the Object Manager interface. The Object Manager is responsible for the management of types, objects, functions, queries, updates, optimization and versions.

The IRIS **Storage Manager**, which is located beneath the Object Manager, is currently a conventional relational storage subsystem. It is very similar to the Relational Storage Subsystem (RSS) in System R (/ABCE76/). It is concerned with concurrency control, transaction management, recovery, indexing, buffer management, and secondary storage management. The Storage Manager distinguishes between structured and unstructured data (separate storage).

IRIS INTERFACES

IRIS supports several interactive and programmatic interfaces which are all based on the functionality provided by the Object Manager subroutine library. The most important interactive interfaces are Object SQL (OSQL for short), which is an object-oriented extension to SQL, and the Graphical Editor, which allows the user to explore interactively the IRIS type structure as well as the interobject relationship structures defined on a given IRIS database (see also the section about query processing below). The programmatic interfaces include a straightforward embedding of OSQL into various host languages (currently Common LISP and C) and an encapsulation of the IRIS DBMS as a programming language object whose methods correspond to the functions in the C subroutine interface to the IRIS Object Manager. That is, based on the functionality provided by the Object Manager library, this interface represents a collection of object types (classes) and their associated operations. Instances of these classes represent the entities required to access and manipulate an IRIS database. Typical classes might include DataBase, Function, Type, Scan, and Object. The class DataBase might support operations to start new database, connect to an existing database, commit or abort transaction, etc. Instances of the Function class might provide operations to create and/or update functions. A variety of programming languages may be used for such an interface (currently only LISP) and, depending on the constructs offered by the language, more or less of the implementation details may be hidden from programmers.

FUNCTIONS AND RULES

An IRIS **function** is a computation that may or may not return a result. Functions are defined on types and are applicable to the instances of the types. IRIS supports user-defined functions that are compiled, stored, and executed under the control of the database management system. The specification of an IRIS function, logically, consists of two parts: a declaration and an implementation. By separating the function declaration from its implementation, users are allowed to change the implementation without affecting application programs. A **function declaration** specifies the name of the operation and the number and types of its arguments and results. For example,

> **Create function marriage** (*Person* P) → [*Person* Spouse, *Charstring* Date] **forward;**

declares a function ***marriage***. The **forward** keyword declares that the function implementation will be specified later. Functions can be either single-valued or multi-valued, and they can return compound results. IRIS functions may be implemented as stored functions, derived functions, or foreign functions.

A **stored function** is implemented as a table that maps input values to corresponding result values. For example,

> **Store** *marriage*

causes a table to be created with three columns for the Person, Spouse, and Date. The mapping of several functions may be stored together in a single table. For example,

> **Store** NAME **on** *Person*, AGE **on** *Person*

would create a table storing all instances of Person with their Name and Age values.

A **derived function** is specified in terms of other functions. For example,

> **Create function** ***emp-manager*** (*Employee* E) → *Manager* **as**
> **select** M **for each** *Manager* M
> **where** M = ***department-manager***(***emp-department***(e));

specifies how the manager of an employee may be derived from other functions using a **select** statement. In general, function definitions may contain arbitrary queries and include calls to any implemented function. As a performance enhancement, IRIS supports **materialized derived functions.** This is similar to the notion of materialized views in relational database systems. IRIS can precompute a derived function and store the results in a table. Subsequent invocations of the functions are satisfied from the table. Updates invalidate the table. Currently, the table is not regenerated automatically.

A **foreign function** is a function that is implemented in a general-purpose programming language. This allows IRIS to extend its capabilities in unanticipated ways, e.g. to permit access to specialized storage managers, or to permit specialized operations that may be associated with new, user-defined data types. However, since IRIS does not understand the semantics of these functions, it cannot optimize them. But IRIS can optimize their usage. Since the query optimizer is rule-based, one may add rules appropriate to the particular foreign function of interest. Any language can be used to write foreign functions so long as the object code can be linked with the query processor.

IRIS supports the definition of simple views in a way similar to the approach of Zdonik (see views in Section 4.11). Views can be created by rules. For example,

> **Create function** ***grandparent*** (*Person* P) → *Person* **as**
> **select** GP **for each** *Person* GP **where** GP = ***parent***(***parent*** (P));

defines a ***grandparent*** function. Since IRIS supports the nesting of functions, a function can return multiple results, and a nested function call returns the concatenation of all the results obtained from calling the inner function.

CLASSES/TYPES

Objects in IRIS are classified by type (IRIS is statically typed). Types are named collections of objects, all of whose members share common properties. In this sense, the notion of type corresponds to the definition of class. Since the IRIS people use the term 'type' we will also use it in the following. Types are organized in a type structure that supports generalization and specialization. A type may be declared to be a subtype of another type. In that case, all instances of the subtype are also instances of the supertype (this stands in contrast to the definition in, e.g. ORION where instances of a subclass do not automatically belong to its superclasses). Since the IRIS type structure is a directed acyclic graph, IRIS supports multiple inheritance. Types are objects themselves, and their relationships to subtypes, supertypes, and instances are expressed as functions in the system. In the following example of a type definition in OSQL a type *Person* is declared with property functions NAME, ADDRESS, and PHONE. Each instance of *Person* must have a value for the NAME function:

Create type *Person* **subtype of** *Object*
(NAME *Charstring* **required,**
ADDRESS *Charstring*,
PHONE *Charstring*);

Such a creation of a type with properties is a syntactic shorthand for separately creating a type and each of the functions (e.g., **Create function** ***person-age***(*Person* P, *Integer* a) [function body]). Additional functions taking this type as an argument may be separately created and are semantically equivalent to properties created with the type. OSQL allows the programmer to define constraints on attributes, like **required, required unique**, **required many**, etc. To create instances of type *Person* a **Create function** can be used:

Create Person (NAME, ADDRESS, PHONE) **instances**
Smith ('Albert Smith', Oxford Street 24 London, 02345/6789)
Jones ('Isaac Jones', ..., ...)

This function binds the variables Smith, Jones, etc. to the objects created. If we want to bind a new type *Author* to Jones we can do that by using the **Add type** function:

Add type *Author* **to** Jones;

IRIS OSQL provides the functions Set, Add, and Remove to change the future behaviour of database functions. For example, the operation

set ***department-manager*** (Sales_dept) = John;

will cause future invocations of the ***department-manager*** function with the parameter Sales_dept to return the object currently bound to the variable John. IRIS also supports updates to multivalued functions. The following statements will add (remove) the employee bound to variable Sue to (from) the sales department:

Add (Remove) ***member*** (Sales_dept) = Sue;

ASSOCIATIVE ACCESS

Literature about IRIS doesn't give a hint as to whether associative access is supported within IRIS and, if so, in what way.

SCHEMA MODIFICATION

In order to support graceful database evolution, the Object Manager of IRIS allows the type graph to be changed dynamically. For example, new types may be created, existing types may be deleted, and objects may gain or lose types throughout their lifetime. However, the current version of IRIS does not support the change of a subtype/supertype relationship between existing types. Literature about IRIS does not indicate whether IRIS supports object conversion or object screening.

TRANSACTIONS AND RECOVERY

IRIS wants to support lengthy interactions with the database spanning minutes to many days. However, nothing is said in the literature about how this goal is to be achieved.

QUERY PROCESSING

The query processor of IRIS is a *rule-based* system that translates and optimizes IRIS queries and operations into an extended relational algebra format that is interpreted against the stored database. Queries are expressed in terms of functions and objects. IRIS supports two higher-level interfaces OSQL and Graphical Editor. These interfaces take the primitive notion of an atomic object and combine it with the set of property functions that the user considered to be intrinsic to the nature of the object. This is much like the treatment of entities and their attributes in the E-R model and is also close to the concept of an abstract data type in an object-oriented programming language. The functional emphasis in IRIS suggests the use of a functional style of interface for expressing the relationships between interconnected objects. However, because of the strong similarities of functional languages to a relational language, extensions to SQL were studied to accommodate the object model and a more functional style. As a result OSQL was developed to extend SQL in three ways:

1. Users manipulate types and functions rather than tables.
2. Objects may be referenced directly rather than indirectly, through their keys. Variables of the interface may be bound to objects on creation or retrieval (see, e.g. Smith and Jones in the example above) and may then be used to refer to the objects in subsequent statements.
3. User-defined functions and IRIS system functions may appear in where and select clauses to give concise and powerful retrieval.

All examples in the list above are formulated in OSQL.

The IRIS Graphical Editor provides a graphical interface that enables a user to browse and update an IRIS database. The type hierarchy is displayed as a directed, acyclic graph. Each type or instance of a type may be inspected to examine its properties, i.e. the functions defined on that type. The editor also supports updates to schemas. It is written in Objective-C.

VERSIONS

In IRIS a version mechanism is implemented which realizes the concept of version graphs. Like ORION, IRIS offers the possibility of indirect addressing, whereby objects can make generic references to other objects. The **generic instance** is an abstraction of the entity that may, itself, have properties (properties whose values are uniform over all versions). There is one generic instance for each version set (the set of all versions of an object). Information about the version set and the predecessor–successor relationships that hold between members of the set are maintained by functions on the generic instance and version objects.

Any reference to a versioned object can either be a **specific reference** to a particular version of the object, or a **generic reference** to the entity's generic instance. A generic instance can at any time be coerced to refer to a specific version of an object.

An object is either versioned or non-versioned. However, IRIS provides the ability to create versions of what were originally unversioned objects. The following example converts the unversioned object, mod_1, to a versioned object:

create version from mod_1 **instance** mod_1-vers_1

The new object, mod_1-vers_1, will be created with the same user types as the original, unversioned object. In addition, it will acquire the system type Version and it will be the first version of the version set. The original object, mod_1, will lose its system type *Unversioned* and acquire the system type *Generic*. Retaining its original object identifier, it will act as the generic instance of the newly created version set. Thus, the generic instance serves as a placeholder for existing references to the original, unversioned object. For a further discussion of the version mechanism of IRIS see Section 4.15.

LITERATURE

/Beec88/, /BeMa88/, /DeKL85/, /DFKL86/, /FABC89/, /FBCC87/, /Fish88/, /Kent90/, /LDFK87/, /LyKe86/, /LyVi87/, /LyVi88/, /WiLH90/.

5.4. O_2

O_2 is a research prototype of an object-oriented database system which has been developed at Altair in France. Altair is a consortium funded by IN2 (the computer subsidiary of the Intertechnique Group), INRIA (Institut National de Recherche en Informatique et Automatique; the French National Institute of Research in Computers and Control) and LRI (the research lab of the University of Paris XI, Orsay). It is designed to support traditional database applications, such as business applications, as well as new and emerging database application areas, especially office automation applications and management of spatial data. The O_2 prototype is implemented in C.

O_2 provides the concepts of message passing, information hiding, data abstraction, simple inheritance, classification, polymorphism in terms of overloading, static type checking, complex objects, object identity, extensibility in terms of new data types, ad hoc query facility and transaction management and recovery.

In the following we will briefly present some features of O_2.

ARCHITECTURE

Logically, the architecture of O_2 consists of four modules, the *Data (or Object)* Manager, the Method Manager, the Type Manager, and the Precompiler (/BBBD88/). The **Data** or **Object Manager** represents the storage layer and is responsible for the creation, storage, and maintenance of data (not really objects). It is implemented by the Wisconsin Storage System (WiSS; /CDKK85/). The **Type Manager** corresponds to a schema manager in a classical database system. It is responsible for the creation, storage, and maintenance of type structure descriptions. Moreover, it also manages the description of application programs (methods). The **Method Manager** creates, stores, and maintains source and object code of methods. Its data corresponds to the application programs in a conventional database system.

The O_2 system allows the user to define, access, and update complex objects. Complex objects are built using the atomic objects and the *set*, *list*, and *tuple* constructors. O_2 can be seen as an object-oriented layer running on top of C. This layer is in charge of the definition and the manipulation of objects whereas C deals with all computational aspects. Both features result in the programming language of O_2, called CO_2. Programming in CO_2 consists in writing C programs which contain special primitives for object manipulation. CO_2 follows the standard syntax of object-oriented languages. Thus, the basic construct of the O_2 layer is the message passing. The distinction between data definition language, by which the user can declare the type structure and hierarchy, and general-purpose programming language, by which the user can attach methods to types and to objects, makes it possible to replace the C language by another programming language. Currently, O_2 supports, as additional programming language, BASIC (results in BasicO_2). An integration of LISP is planned.

The **Precompiler** takes as input (when C is the programming language) CO_2 programs, calls the Type and Method managers to perform type checking, and generates C programs with calls to the Data and Method Managers. The Precompiler is called when a new type is inserted in the system, or when an existing type is being modified. It monitors compiling, dynamic linking, and loading of object code corresponding to methods. The Precompiler also translates every name into an internal representation: method names are replaced by internal code, type names are replaced by type identifiers, and attributes are replaced by an attribute number. Thus, the Data, Type, and Method Managers only deal with fixed-length representations and never see the actual names.

At run-time, the Data Manager is activated by message passing: it receives a message name and an object identifier. It first fetches the object to retrieve its actual type which is used to determine the actual method code to be applied. This binding is delayed until run-time (late binding) as it is permitted to redefine methods in subtypes of a given type. Finally, the selected method is executed.

CLASSES/TYPES

The O_2 data model relies on two kinds of concepts: values and objects. Values are not encapsulated, therefore, their structure is known by users. They are manipulated by a predefined set of primitives. Objects have identity and encapsulate values and user-defined methods. Values have types which specify their structure while objects have classes (O_2 is statically typed). Classes are created explicitly using commands and are parts of the inheritance hierarchy. Types are not created explicitly since they only appear as components of classes and do not appear in the inheritance hierarchy.

An **object** is a triple (oid,value, methods) consisting of an object identifier, a value and a set of methods. The **object identifier** uniquely identifies the object throughout the system. Classes identify the common structure of a set of objects. A **class** consists of a name, a type t, and a set of methods M. Every object in the class will have a value of type t and will have the same set of methods M. A value is either atomic or structured (of type tuple, set, or list; there is no restriction on the (recursive) use of these constructors). Since objects have identifiers, several objects can share a common component and objects can be cyclic. Values cannot be shared. A **named object** or value is an object or a value with a name.

The following is an example of a definition of the structural part of a class *MONUMENT*:

add class *MONUMENT*
type tuple (NAME: *String*
ADDRESS: **tuple** (STREET: *String*, CITY: *City*),
DESCRIPTION: *String*,
CLOSING-DAY: *list* (*String*),
ADMISSION_FEE: *Integer*)

O_2 allows the user to add special attributes or methods to special objects. For example, if an object Eiffel_tower is created as an instance of class *MONUMENT* the user may add an additional attribute HEIGHT to Eiffel_tower. One can also associate specific methods to named objects. These methods are used to characterize the exceptional behaviour of an object. One can also override an existing method in the class of the object with an exceptional method. The late binding process will associate the exceptional method to the object currently bound to a name.

PERSISTENCE

Persistence is defined in the model as follows: every *named object* or *value* is persistent. *Every component* of a *persistent object* or *value* is persistent, too. Nothing else is persistent.

The set of objects of a given class is the **extension** of that class. Note, however, that the objects of a class are not per se persistent (only if they have a name). Upon user request, the system offers automatic extension maintenance (persistence) as follows: given a class *C*, it creates a named value of type set(C) with name C and automatically inserts every newly created object of class C in it. Objects, of e.g. the class *MONUMENT*, are not persistent as long as they do not have a name. If we, however, add the keywords **with extension** in the class definition all objects of *MONUMENT* would be persistent.

METHODS

Objects are manipulated and accessed by methods. The user declares the **method** by giving its signature, that is, its name, the type or class of the arguments, and the type or class of the result if there is one:

add method ***increase-fee*** (amount: *Integer*) **in class** *MONUMENT*

Methods can be private or public. Private methods are only visible within their class, i.e. in the methods attached to that class. Public methods are visible by every class and can be freely used, i.e. they define the external interface of a class.

As already mentioned, the body of a method can be written in a general-purpose language, e.g. C. However, access to and manipulation of objects and values is done using O_2 features:

body increase-fee (amount: *Integer*) **in class** *MONUMENT*
CO_2 {(*self).admission_fee + = amount;}

The curly brackets delimit the CO_2 block of code as in pure C. The value of an object is obtained using the dereference method *, thus, 'self' is the object and '*self' is the associated value. This method is applied using a special syntax which follows the C '*' use. It illustrates the association between objects and values. As in standard programming languages, objects can be seen as pointers to values. In the above example, the value '*self' is tuple-structured, and the access to an attribute is done using the dot operator. The assignment is done as in C and increments the integer value representing the admission fee. Note that for the manipulation of O_2 values, such as dereferencing or extracting a tuple field, the C syntax is used. This way of manipulating objects is syntactically very close to what is done in C + +. In O_2, however, this similarity is purely syntactical, as objects and values are implemented and manipulated in a special way by the Object Manager and the CO_2 compiler generates calls to the Object Manager.

The dot operator also allows the user an easy manipulation of objects. For example,

'*Eiffel_tower.CLOSING_DAY [1] = "January 1st"'

modifies an entry of the CLOSING_DAY list of the object Eiffel_tower.

However, since the dot operator permits direct access to the value of an attribute it violates encapsulation.

INHERITANCE

O_2 supports multiple inheritance. In the case of name conflicts, the user has to redefine explicitly the attribute or method name. In O_2 inheritance is realized by set inclusion semantics. That is, a type is a subtype of another type if and only if every instance of this type is also an instance of its supertype. However, since O_2 allows the user to add new attributes, their definition of subtyping corresponds to our definition of subclassing (see Section 4.1). Every instance of a subclass is automatically considered as an instance of each of its superclasses. The following is an example of an inheritance definition:

> **add class** *HISTORICAL_HOTEL* **inherits** *Monument, Hotel*
> **type** *tuple* (YEAR_OF_CONSTRUCTION: *Integer*)

The effect of this declaration is the definition of a *HISTORICAL_HOTEL* class whose associated type is a subtype of the *Monument* and *Hotel* types. The user only has to give the extra attributes.

Since O_2 supports inheritance it also supports the redefinition of methods in subclasses. For this reason, late binding has to be provided. The actual code of a method to be executed is not selected at compile-time but at run-time depending on the actual type of the receiver object. If neither inheritance nor exceptional attributes are used, O_2 offers a static type-checking which detects the illegal manipulations of objects and values.

ASSOCIATIVE ACCESS

Literature about O_2 doesn't give a hint as to whether associative access is supported and, if so, in what way.

SCHEMA MODIFICATION

The support of schema modification is not yet clear in O_2.

TRANSACTIONS AND RECOVERY

The current version of O_2 provides a simple connection with transactions: any CO_2 program will be a transaction (two-phase locking is supported) and will be delimited by calling the begin-transaction and end-transaction primitives of the underlying (Pick) File System.

QUERY PROCESSING

The O_2 people are currently considering a query language for O_2. They are conducting three experiments on query languages; Lifoo (a functional language), Reloop (an SQL-like language), and another functional-oriented language which is strictly restricted to querying the database in the ad hoc query mode (no manipulation of data). We will briefly describe the main features of the last approach. The following are the design decisions for the query language:

1 The query language is a subset of the general-purpose programming language. Because of the specificity of the data model, values and objects are distinguished and there are some special primitives to access and manipulate the structured values. Since the programming language is the extension of an existing programming language, this set of primitives is clearly identified and simply taken to be the query language. According to this definition the query language can be used as an embedded part of the programming language or as a stand-alone ad hoc query facility. As an ad hoc query facility the language is allowed to violate encapsulation. Encapsulation is a mechanism to enforce a good structuring of the code and a good programming discipline. Because the query language is only used to query data in an interactive mode, there is less reason to enforce encapsulation. On the other hand, if the user is allowed to access the structure of objects directly this increases convenience. Thus, the query language allows the user to access data directly. Moreover, it allows him to make use of the methods defined for the objects.

2. The query language is functional in nature. Its syntax follows the syntax of CO_2 and is set-oriented.

3 The query language ignores types and the type hierarchy. Type checking is performed at run-time in the query mode and at compile-time in the programming mode. Since the schema contains type and data information, the only information needed while querying the database is that concerning the data and not the types.

Some example queries:

1 Where is the Eiffel Tower?
  Eiffel_tower.address

2 What is the description of the things I can do at the Eiffel Tower?
  set (x.DESCRIPTION: x **in** Eiffel_tower.THINGS_TO_DO)

THINGS_TO_DO is assumed to be an attribute of Eiffel_tower of type *set* (THINGS_TO_DO) and DESCRIPTION is an attribute of THINGS_TO_DO.

3 For each monument, list the name, the street and the admission fee.
set (**tuple** (name: x.NAME, street: x.ADDRESS.STREET, ad_fee: x.ADMISSION_FEE):
x **in** *MONUMENT*)

VERSIONS

Versioning will be taken into account for the next version of O_2.

LITERATURE

/AbKa89/, /Banc89/, /BBBD88/, /Benz90/, /CDLR89/, /Deux90/, /LeRi88/, /LeRi89-1/, /LeRi89-2/, /LeRV88/, /LeRV90/, /VeBD89/, /Zica90/.

5.5. OOPS

OOPS is a research prototype of an object-oriented database system which has been developed in a cooperative project between a large German office systems manufacturer (Triumph-Adler AG) and the departments of Computer Science of the Universities of Aachen and Hagen in Germany. Since the project started in 1983 it is one of the earliest projects in the field of object-oriented database system development.

OOPS is meant to support traditional database applications, such as business applications, as well as new and emerging database application areas, especially office automation applications and AI. Like GemStone, OOPS took as its basis a SMALLTALK-like programming language, called OOPL. But in contrast to SMALLTALK (and OPAL of GemStone) OOPL is statically typed.

OOPS provides the concepts of message passing, information hiding, data abstraction, meta-classes, simple inheritance, classification, polymorphism in terms of overloading, static type checking, complex objects management, object identity, extensibility in terms of new data types, ad hoc query facility, transaction management and recovery, and constraints and triggers. The development of the OOPS prototype took more than 25 man-years, the code comprises approximately 80,000 lines of code. It is implemented in C.

In the following we will briefly present some features of OOPS.

ARCHITECTURE

The OOPS architecture consists of two major components: the object-oriented system (OOS), which corresponds to the execution layer, and the storage manager.

The OOS realizes the features of OOPL (the programming environment which is provided by OOPS). Among other things, it is concerned with object management, message passing, and method execution. OOS consists of four components: an interpreter, a compiler, a system cache and an object cache.

The **interpreter** is the head of OOS. It is responsible for receiving, interpreting, executing and answering all messages. Moreover, the interpreter manages the object and the system caches.

Since OOPL supports strong typing a **compiler** is necessary to exploit this feature fully. Before a method is interpreted it is compiled first. Among other things, all context-sensitive checks are performed during compilation. The result of compilation is an intermediate code which is the basis for the interpreter.

The **system cache** and the **object cache** are buffers which realize the interface between the storage manager and OOS. By providing high traffic data objects in a cache, fewer disk accesses are needed.

Any entity or information OOS deals with is represented as an object. According to the intended use it can differentiate between data objects, needed by the applications, and methods, structure and system descriptions. Since the use of these two kinds of objects is different these objects are stored in different caches - data objects in the object cache, all other objects in the system cache. Since both caches are concerned with the management of objects they use the same set of operations. With the help of these operations the interpreter, among other things, is able to identify objects in a cache and to handle cache overflows. Every time the system is initialized a basic set of structure descriptions, system information and methods is loaded into the system cache. The object cache remains empty. Additionally needed system information, as well as all data objects, are loaded into the proper cache on request. To minimize access time to complex objects the interpreter only loads the requested parts of an object from disk. For example, if only fixed-length data are accessed, the variable-length parts of the object are not loaded.

If a cache overflow occurs, the interpreter decides which (part of an) object has to be removed. If this object has been modified, it is restored to the database. The logical unit of transfer between OOS and the database is an object (or a part of an object), and not a page.

The **storage manager**, which is located beneath OOS, is responsible for the maintenance of all permanent objects. Moreover, it is concerned with concurrency control, transaction management and recovery, indexing, and constraints and triggers. The storage manager distinguishes between structured and unstructured data (separate storage). Beside the storage of all (complex) data objects, the storage manager also maintains all information needed by the programming system in a **data dictionary**. Among other things, the dictionary maintains the descriptions of the logical structure and the physical representation of all objects of the programming system as well as the source and object codes of all methods of the system.

As modern hardware provides large main memory sizes OOPS took advantage of this feature and realizes a concept similar to the **database cache** method (/ElBa84/). This technique integrates buffer management and recovery techniques and, thus, leads to an essential performance enhancement.

CLASSES/TYPES

Figure 5.1 gives an example of a class definition in OOPL. In the example *PART* describes articles available for delivery by a commission agent. To keep the example brief only an extract of the class description of *PART* is presented (especially, only few instance methods are listed). Attributes are called **roles** in OOPL.

A class declaration in OOPL consists of four parts:

- class header
  - class name/kind of class (1)
  - superclass (2)
- instance components
  - nominator (6)
  - instance roles (5)
  - instance methods (7)
- class components
  - class roles (3)
  - class methods (4)
- constraints (8) and triggers (9)

The class components describe all features concerning the class itself while the instance components describe the property and behaviour of every single instance of the class. Therefore, class components realize a concept very similar to the concept of **metaclass** in TAXIS (/MBGW84/). A metaclass in TAXIS can be defined over a number of different classes while a metaclass in OOPL only describes the characteristics of *one* class.

OOPL distinguishes between objects and data values. An **object** is always **independent**. It has its own unique object identity and represents exactly one entity of the real world. Each object must belong to a class. A **class** not only describes the structure and behaviour of its instances but also serves as an object container; i.e. OOPL provides the usual notion of class (a class is a type declaration, and attached to a class is its extension). In contrast

```
------------------------------------------------------------------------ class header -------------------
1 class      permanent     PART
.........................................................................................................
2 superclass OBJECT
------------------------------------------------------------------------ class components ---------------
3 classRoles LASTPARTNO : Integer on creation <- 0;
.........................................................................................................
4 classMethods
a    (createPartNo) : Integer
        [LASTPARTNO <- LASTPARTNO + 1; ^LASTPARTNO];
------------------------------------------------------------------------ instance components ------------
5 roles
a    pub   PARTNO: Integer on creation <- Part createPartNo fixed;
     pub   PARTNAME: String [20];
b    pub   SELLPRICEUS: US$;
c    pub   SELLPRICEECU:  ECU    on  access  <-  FOREIGNMONEY  CurrentRate:(ECU)  *
             SELLPRICEUS;
d    pub   LISTOFDELIVERY: ListOf TermsOfDelivery;
e          MINIMUMSTOCKS: Integer;
     pub   STOCKS: Integer;
     pub   ONORDER: Integer;
           RESERVEDSTOCKS: Integer;
f    pub   LOCATION: SetOf Tuple (TOWN: String [20]; STREET: String [20] SHEDID: Integer)
.........................................................................................................
6 nominator  PARTNO
.........................................................................................................
7 methods
     reserved: (number : Integer)
        [RESERVEDSTOCKS <- RESERVEDSTOCKS + number];

     removeFromListDelivery: (delivery: TermsOfDelivery)
        [ self listOfDeliveryIncludes: (delivery);
         ifTrue: [self remove: (delivery) from: (LISTOFDELIVERY)]];
------------------------------------------------------------------------ constraints / trigger ----------
8 constraints                                                            /* constraint section */
a    sufficientStocks
b    on modification STOCKS, RESERVEDSTOCKS, ONORDER, MINIMUMSTOCKS
c       [(STOCKS - RESERVEDSTOCKS + ONORDER) > MINIMUMSTOCKS]
d    at EndOfTransaction
.........................................................................................................
9 rules                                                                  /* trigger section */
     violationSufficientStocks
a    on violation sufficientStocks                                            /* event */
b       [delivery: TermsOfDelivery; minimumPrice: US$; /* variable declaration */   /* action */
c       minimumPrice <- self minCurrentPrice          /* calculate cheapest price */
d       delivery <-                                   /* find first cheapest supplier */
           Select * From LISTOFDELIVERY Where
             [TermsOfDelivery.CURRENTPRICE = minimumPrice] first;
e       orderAt: (delivery.SUPPLIER)                  /* deliver order */
        article: (self)
        volume: (delivery.OPTDELIVERYQUANTITY);
f       ONORDER <- ONORDER + delivery.OPTDELIVERYQUANTITY];
------------------------------------------------------------------------ end class declaration ----------
```

bold type: reserved words
underlined: user-defined method filter
italics: user-defined objects (classes, attributes)

Figure 5.1 Class definition in OOPL

to SMALLTALK and GemStone, but like O_2, ORION and IRIS, OOPL supports strong typing.

Attributes of objects must always be typed in OOPL. The following data types are provided:

1 primitive
A primitive data type is irreducible in that it cannot be decomposed (e.g. 5e).

2 reference
A reference data type defines a typed relationship between independent objects of the database by the use of a pointer (e.g. 5d).

3 derived
The value of a derived data type is automatically computed from other information in the database every time the attribute is accessed (e.g. 5c). The result of such a computation can be of type primitive or reference. A derived data type emerges from a primitive or reference data type by adding the keyword **on access**. Derived attributes cannot be updated.

4 embedded
An embedded data type represents a complex property of an independent object (e.g. 5f). This means that they are not objects by themselves. They only exist in the context of other objects (their **father objects**). While independent objects can only be included via references into any other object embedded objects are physically included.

Attributes may automatically get initial values (default values) at creation time by using the **on creation** keyword. These initial values may be atomic values or they may be computed by sending messages to other objects or classes. For instance, to determine the value of PARTNo, the message ***createPartNo*** is sent to the class *PART* which starts the corresponding method (5a). The result of this method (a new part number) is assigned to the role PARTNo of the newly created object. The **fixed** keyword lays down that the attribute value cannot be updated.

Attributes can be marked as **public (pub)**. These attributes may be accessed and updated from outside the object via dot notation (object.attributeName, see, e.g. 9e, 9f) (there exists a system-defined method which returns the value of the attribute). All other attributes are **private** which means that they are hidden within the object. Hence, these attributes are not known outside the object; they can only be accessed by methods of *PART*.

OOPL provides a rich range of primitive and more sophisticated data types (and, of course, operations (methods) on these types), like *Time*, *Date* or *String*, and type constructors, like *graph*, *tree*, *list*, *stack*, *collection*, *set*, *tuple*, etc.

OOPL supports the concept of **object identifier** in two ways. On the one hand, any attribute combination of a complex object can be specified as a nominator. This corresponds to the notion of primary key in relational database systems. Additionally, the system provides a systemwide **unique identifier** which is also accessible to the user. The identifier can be used to express a relationship of an object to another object (e.g. object–subobject relationship). Moreover, the user may name objects explicitly.

The result of the execution of a method is either an object which is transferred to the sender of the activating message (*function method*), or a modification of the receiving object (*procedure method*). In the case of a function method the type of the result-object is defined after the method filter block (e.g. 4a).

PERSISTENCE

OOPL distinguishes between **permanent** and **temporary** objects. The distinction is made by the programmer who declares classes to be either **local** (to his program) or **permanent**. Only permanent objects are maintained in the database. Local objects are maintained in the local object memory. They live as long as a main memory reference to them exists; they are removed, at the latest, with the end of the application program.

INHERITANCE

OOPL realizes single inheritance. Inheritance is **strict**, which means that everything defined in a superclass must be satisfied by the instances of all subclasses, too. A subclass definition, however, may refine the domain of an object but it is forbidden to override a property.

CONSTRAINTS AND TRIGGERS

OOPL allows constraints and triggers (called **rules**) to be defined as part of the class declaration (see Figure 5.1, (8, 9)). Each constraint is given a name (8a). It is associated with an event which specifies the action which invokes the check of the constraint (8b) and it consists of a condition which evaluates to true or false (8c). Furthermore, it can be specified when the constraint has to be executed (8d). The execution can be triggered at the beginning or the end of the modifying method or transaction. By these means *preconditions* as well as *postconditions* for methods or transactions can be defined. If a condition is defined for a transaction and this condition is violated by executing a method outside a transaction the violation is ignored. The constraint and rule concept is very similar to the prerequisite/postcondition and exception concept of TAXIS (/MBGW84/).

In case an integrity violation is detected, the method (transaction) is not executed (precondition violated) or the modifications performed by the corresponding method (transaction) are undone (postcondition violated).

However, there is also the possibility to specify in the rule-section (9) which actions are to be performed in case of an integrity violation. If the constraint 'sufficientStocks' of the example is violated, a method is triggered which issues an appropriate order to restore the required number of parts (9a).

Triggers may not only be activated by integrity violations but also by other events:

- time
- arrival of a message
- execution of a transaction or method (before or after execution)
- date
- access to an attribute (before or after access)

ASSOCIATIVE ACCESS

OOPS only supports indexes on classes.

SCHEMA MODIFICATION

OOPS supports the concept of object conversion. However, if the structure of the instances of a class is modified the change of the instances is delayed until these objects are explicitly accessed (incremental modification). For this reason, OOPS maintains versions of class descriptions. By this version mechanism the conceptual schema can be modified on-line in a simple way without costly reorganization of the database at the same time.

TRANSACTION MANAGEMENT AND RECOVERY

OOPS realizes the traditional transaction model; i.e. transactions are the unit of recovery and concurrency control follows the principle of serializability. For concurrency control the two-phase locking technique was chosen. A transaction requires a read lock before reading an object, and a write lock before updating an object. This corresponds to the notion of level-3 consistency (/Gray79/) and protects transactions from such consistency anomalies as lost updates, dirty read, and unrepeatable read.

ORION, like OOPS, supports two types of transactions: normal and hypothetical. A **hypothetical transaction** is a transaction that always aborts, and is important in application environments in which users often experiment with 'what-if' changes to the database.

QUERY PROCESSING

It is intended to realize a QBE-like query interface. However, this interface is not yet implemented.

VERSIONS

The current prototype of OOPS does not support a version mechanism.

LITERATURE

/SUWZ87/, /SUWZ88/, /UnSc89-1/.

6. CONCLUSION

Object-oriented database systems are receiving a lot of attention from both industry and research. Due to the great complexity of this field it is no surprise that there has been considerable debate about what are to be the features of an object-oriented database system and how they are to be realized. On the one hand, a lot of experimental and theoretical work is under way. On the other hand, the field is currently characterized by the lack of a common data model as well as a formal foundation (/ABDD89/, /Nier89/). Whereas Codd's original paper gave a clear specification of what a data model for a relational database system is meant to be (/Codd70/), the community has not yet agreed on such a specification for an object-oriented database system.

A data model defines general rules for the specification of the structures of the data and the operations allowed on the data. In the relational world the data model is very simple, and the data structures automatically determine the operations permitted on the data. In contrast, object-oriented database systems allow us to define new data types. The types are not dictated by the data structures, but are defined explicitly.

Therefore, an important question is which features characterize the data model of an object-oriented database system (for an in-depth discussion of this topic see /Maie89-2/)? One possibility is to collect type constructors for forming the data structures in the representations. This choice is not very informative since it does not show how one perceives the data in the database. Another possibility is that the data model is the collection of types supplied with the system. However, object-oriented database systems allow the programmer to define new data types. Therefore, the collection of initial data types is very likely to be extended by a given application. Moreover, data models under this definition are hard to compare, as it is not always apparent if two data types are the same.

Probably the most useful alternative is to interpret a data model as the type definition system of an object-oriented database system. Such a definition might comprise the system-supplied (atomic) data types, the type constructors, and the encapsulation mechanism. But here the question arises whether the method language is part of the data model. Moreover, the current approaches to object-oriented database systems are based on the type systems of particular languages (SMALLTALK, C++, Common LISP, etc.). In such an environment, what can a general, language-independent standard for a data model for object-oriented database systems look like?

This short discussion already indicates why there is no general data model and why it will take a long time to achieve one, if this is possible at all (however, a first but incomplete suggestion was recently presented by Beeri (/Beer89/)). As long as we do not agree on a standard data model it remains open what features an object-oriented database system has to provide. Even if we agree on the features proposed in this paper or somewhere else the immense number of variants of these features makes it hard to derive any standard for an object-oriented database system (see, e.g. the different realizations of features in the object-oriented database systems discussed in Section 5).

At the time relational database systems attracted people's attention, a common underlying model was mostly worked out and people were mainly developing implementation technology. With object-oriented database systems we are simultaneously choosing the specification of the system and producing the technology to support its implementation. We may hope that, out of the set of experimental prototypes being built, a suitable model and an appropriate implementation technology will emerge. We should, however, be aware of the risk that a system might emerge as *the* system, not because it is the best, but because it is the first one to provide a significant subset of the functionality demanded by the market. This situation can certainly be avoided if we manage to agree on a workable definition of an object-oriented database system in the near future (/ABDD89/). To conclude, the development and implementation of object-oriented database systems still requires solutions in many dimensions. The effort is characterized by the need to integrate widely different concepts from various fields.

REFERENCES

/ABCE76/Astrahan. M.; Blasgen, M.; Chamberlin, D.; Eswaran, K.; Gray, J.; Griffiths, P.; King, W.; Lorie, R.; McJones, P.; Mehl, J.; Putzolu, G.; Traiger, G.; Wade, B.; Watson, V.: System R: A relational data base management system; *ACM Transactions on Database Systems (TODS)*, Vol. 1, No. 2; June 1976

/ABDD89/Atkinson, M.; Bancilhon, F.; DeWitt, D.; Dittrich, K.; Maier, D.; Zdonik, S.: The Object-Oriented Database System Manifesto; *Proc. The 1st Int. Conf. on Deductive and Object-Oriented Databases (DOOD89); Kyoto, Japan; Dec. 1989.*

/AbKa89/Abiteoul, S.; Kanellakis, P.: Object Identity as a Query Language Primitive; *Proc. ACM-SIGMOD Int. Conf. on Management of Data; Portland, Oregon; May 1989.*

/AlCO85/Albano, A.; Cardelli, L.; Orsini, R.: Galileo: A Strongly-Typed, Interactive Conceptual Language; *ACM Transactions on Database Systems*; Vol. 10, No. 2; June 1985.

/AlSL89/Alashqur, A. M.; Su, S. Y. W.; Lam, H.: OQL: A Query for Manipulating Object-Oriented Databases; *Proc. 15th Int. Conf. on Very Large Data Bases (VLDB); Amsterdam, Netherlands; August 1989.*

/Amer87/America, P.: Inheritance and Subtyping in a Parallel Object-Oriented Programming Language; *Proc. of the European Conf. on Object-Oriented Programming, Paris, France; June 1987.*

/Andr90/Andrews, T.: The VBASE Object Database Environment; in:/CaML90/.

/Andr91/Andrews, T.: Programming with VBASE; in: /GuHo91/.

/AnHa87/Andrews, T.; Harris, C.: Combining Language and Database Advances in an Object-Oriented Development Environment; *Proc. ACM 2nd Int. Conf. on Object-Oriented Programming Languages, Systems and Applications (OOPSLA); Orlando, Florida; Oct. 1987.*

/ArKa88/Arapis, C.; Kappel, G.: Organizing Objects in an Object Software Base; in: *Active Object Environments*; D. Tsichritzis (Editor); University of Geneva; 1988.

/AtBu87/Atkinson, M.; Buneman, P.: Types and Persistence in Database Programming Languages; *ACM Computing Surveys*, Vol. 19, No. 2; June 1987.

/BaBu90/Bancilhon, F.; Buneman, P. (Editors): *Advances in Database Programming Languages*; Addison-Wesley; 1990

/BaKh86/Bancilhon, F.; Khoshafian, S.: A Calculus for Complex Objects; *Proc..ACM SIGACT/SIGMOD/SIGART Symposium on Principles of Database Systems (PODS), Boston; 1986.*

/BaKi90/Bancilhon, F.; Kim, W.: Object-Oriented Database Systems: In Transition; *ACM SIGMOD RECORD*; Vol 19, No. 4; Dec. 1990.

/BaKK88/Banerjee, J.; Kim, W.; Kim, H.-J.: Queries in Object-Oriented Databases; *Proc. of the 4th Int. Conf. on Data Engineering; Los Angeles, California; Feb. 1988.*

/BaMa88/Bancilhon, F.; Maier, D.: Multilanguage Object-Oriented Systems: New Answers to Old Database Problems; in: *Programming of Future Generation Computers II*; K. Fuchi, L. Kott (Editors); Elsevier Science Publishers B. V. (North-Holland); 1988.

/Banc88/Bancilhon, F.: Object-Oriented Database Systems; *Proc. 7th ACM SIGART/SIGMOD/SIGACT Symposium on Principles of Database Systems (PODS), Austin, Texas; 1988.*

/Banc89/Bancilhon, F.: Query Languages for Object-Oriented Database Systems: Analysis and a Proposal; *Proc. GI/SI Conf. on Database Systems for Office Automation, Engineering, and Scientific Applications*; Springer, IFB 204; Zurich, Switzerland; March 1989.

/BaRa88/Badrinath, B. R.; Ramamrithan, K.: Synchronizing Transactions on Objects; *IEEE Transactions on Computers*; Vol. 37, No. 5; May 1988.

/BaRa90/Badrinath, B. R.; Ramamrithan, K.: Performance Evaluation of Semantics-Based Multilevel Concurrency Control Protocols; *Proc. ACM-SIGMOD Int. Conf. on Management of Data; Atlantic City, NJ; May 1990.*

/BBBD88/Bancilhon, F.; Barbedette, G.; Benzaken, V.; Delobel, C.; Gamerman, S.; Lècluse, C; Pfeffer, P.; Richard, P.; Velez, F.: The Design and Implementation of O_2, an Object-Oriented Database System in Ditt88-1; 1988.

/BBGS88/Batory, D.; Barnett, J.; Garza, K.; Smith, K.; Tsukuda, K.; Twichell, B.; Wise, T.: GENESIS: An Extensible DBMS; *IEEE Transactions on Software Engineering*; Vol. 14, No. 11; Nov. 1988.

/BCGK87/Banerjee, J.; Chou, H. T.; Garza, J. F.; Kim, W.; Woelk, D.; Ballou, N.: Data Model Issues for Object-Oriented Applications; *ACM Transactions on Office Information Systems (TOIS)*; Vol. 5, No. 1; Jan. 1987.

/Beec88/Beech, D.: A Foundation for Evolution from Relational to Object Databases; *Proc. Int. Conf. Extending Data Base Technology (EDBT)*; Lecture Notes in Computer Science 303, J. W. Schmidt, S. Ceri, M. Missikoff (Editors); Springer; 1988.

/Beer89/Beeri, C.: Formal Models for Object-Oriented Databases; *Proc. 1st Int. Conf. on Deductive and Object-Oriented Databases (DOOD); Kyoto, Japan; Dec. 1989* and (similar version): A Formal Approach to Object-Oriented Databases; *Data and Knowledge Engineering*, No. 5; Elsevier Science Publishers; North-Holland; 1990.

/BeGo83/Bernstein, P. A.; Goodman, N.: Multiversion Concurrency Control – Theory and Algorithms; *ACM Transactions on Database Systems*; Vol. 8, No. 4; Dec. 1983.

/BeMa88/Beech, D.; Mahbod, B.: Generalized Version Control in an Object-Oriented Database; *Proc. of the 4th Int. Conf. on Data Engineering; Los Angeles, California; Feb. 1988.*

/BeMa91/Bertino, E.; Martino, L.: Object-Oriented Database Management Systems: Concepts and Issues; *IEEE Computer*; Vol. 24, No. 4; April 1991.

/Benz90/Benzaken, V.: An Evaluation Model for Clustering Strategies in the O_2 Object-Oriented Database System; *3rd Int. Conf. on Database Theory (ICDT); Paris, France; Dec. 1990.*

/BGHS91/Blair, G.; Gallagher, J.; Hutchison, D.; Shepherd, D.: *Object-Oriented Languages, Systems and Applications*; Pitman; 1991.

/BHJL87/Black, A.; Hutchinson, N.; Jul, E.; Levy, H.; Carter, L.: Distribution and Abstract Types in Emerald; *IEEE Transactions on Software Engineering*, SE-13 (1); Jan. 1987.

/BjBr88/Björnerstedt, A.; Britts, S.: AVANCE: An ObjectManagement System; *Proc. ACM 3rd Int. Conf. on Object-Oriented Programming Languages, Systems and Applications (OOPSLA); Orlando, Florida; Sept. 1988.*

/BjHu89/Björnerstedt, A.; Hulten, C.: Version Control in an Object-Oriented Architecture; in: /KiLo89/.

/BKKK87/Banerjee, J.; Kim, W.; Kim, H.-J.; Korth, H.: Semantics and Implementation of Schema Evolution in Object-Oriented Databases; *Proc. ACM-SIGMOD Int. Conf. on Management of Data; San Francisco, California; May 1987.*

/BlGM89/Blair, G.; Gallagher, J.; Malik, J.: Genericity vs Inheritance vs Delegation vs Conformance vs ...; *Journal of Object-Oriented Programming*; Sept./Oct. 1989.

/BMOP89/Bretl, R.; Maier, D.; Otis, A; Penney, J.; Schuchardt, B.; Stein, J.; Williams, H.; Williams, M.: The GemStone Data Management System; in: /KiLo89/.

/BrCK89/Bretthauer, H.; Christaller, T.; Kopp, J.: Multiple vs. Single Inheritance in Object-Oriented Programming Languages:. What do we really want?; Research Report GMD 415; Schloss Birlinghoven, P.O. Box 12 40, D-5205 Sankt Augustin 1, West Germany; Nov. 1989.

/BrWe86/Bruce, K.; Wegner, P.: An Algebraic Model for Subtypes in Object-Oriented Languages; *SIGPLAN Notices*, Vol. 21, No. 10; Oct. 1986.

/CaML90/Cárdenas, A.; McLeod, D. (Eds.): *Research Foundations in Object-Oriented and Semantic Database Systems*; Prentice-Hall Series in 'Data and and Knowledge Base Systems'; 1990.

/Card84/Cardelli, L.: A Semantics of Multiple Inheritance; in: *Semantics of Data Types*, Lecture Notes in Computer Science; Vol. 173; G. Kahn, D. MacQueen, G. Plotkin (Editors); Springer, New York; 1984

/CaSc87/Caruso, M.; Sciore, E.: The VISION Object-Oriented Database System; *Proc. of Workshop on Database Programming Languages; Roscoff, France; Sept. 1987*

/CaSc88/Caruso, M.; Sciore, E.: Meta-Functions and Contexts in an Object-Oriented Database System; *Proc. ACM-SIGMOD Int. Conf. on Management of Data; Chicago, Illinois; June 1988*

/CaSc90/Caruso, M.; Sciore, E.: The VISION Object-Oriented Database System; in: /BaBu90/

/CaWe85/Cardelli, L.; Wegner, P.: On Understanding Types, Data Abstraction, and Polymorphism; *ACM Computing Surveys*, Vol. 17, No. 4; Dec. 1985

/CDFG86/Carey, M.; DeWitt, D.; Frank, D.; Graefe, G.; Richardson, J.; Shekita, E.; Muralikrishna, M.: The Architecture of the EXODUS Extensible DBMS; *Proc. of the ACM-IEEE Int. Workshop on Object-Oriented Database Systems; Pacific Grove, CA*; IEEE Computer Society Press No. 734; Sept. 1986

/CDKK85/ Chou, H.T.; DeWitt, D.; Katz, R.; Klug, A.: Design and Implementation of the Wisconsin Storage System; *Software – Practice and Experience*; Vol. 15, No. 10,; Oct. 1985

/CDLR89/Cluet, S.; Delobel,C.; Lécluse, C.; Richard, P.: Reloop, an Algebra Based Query Language for an Object-Oriented Database System; *Proc. 1st Int. Conf. on Deductive and Object-Oriented Databases (DOOD); Kyoto, Japan; Dec. 1989*

/CDRS89/Carey, M.; DeWitt, D.; Richardson, J.; Shekita, E.: Storage Management for Objects in EXODUS; in: /KiLo89/

/CDWV88/Carey, M.; DeWitt, D.; Vandenberg,S.: A Data Model and Query Language for EXODUS; *Proc. ACM-SIGMOD Int. Conf. on Management of Data; Chicago, Illinois; June 1988*

/ChKi86/Chou, H.T.; Kim, W.: A Unifying Framework for Version Control in a CAD Environment; *Proc. 12th Int. Conf. on Very Large Data Bases (VLDB); Kyoto, Japan; August 1986*

/ChKi88/Chou, H.T.; Kim, W.: Versions and Change Notification in an Object-Oriented Database System; *Proc. of the 25th Design Automation Conf.; June 1988*

/Codd70/Codd, E. F.: A relational model for large shared data banks; *Communications of the ACM*; Vol. 13, No. 6; June 1970

/Codd79/Codd, E. F.: Extending the Database Relational Model to Capture More Meaning; *ACM Transactions on Database Systems*; Vol. 4, No. 4; Dec.1979

/CoMa84/Copeland, G.; Maier, D.: Making SMALLTALK a Database System; *Proc. ACM SIGMOD Int. Conf. on Management of Data; Boston, MA; June 1984*

/DaEn88/*IEEE Database Engineering*; Special Issue on Temporal Databases; Vol. 11, No. 4; Dec. 1988

/DaTo88/Danforth, S.; Tomlinson, C.: Type Theories and Object-Oriented Programming; *ACM Computing Surveys*, Vol. 20, No. 1; March 1988

/Daya88/Dayal,U.: Active Database Management Systems; *Proc. 3rd Int. Conf. on Data and Knowledge Bases: Improving Usability and Responsiveness; Jerusalem, Israel; 1988*

/DBBC88/Dayal, U.; Blaustein, B.; Buchmann, A.; Chakravarthy, U.; Hsu, M.; Ledin, R.; McCarthy, D.; Rosenthal, A.; Sarin, S.: The HiPAC Project: Combining Active Databases and Timing Constraints; *SIGMOD RECORD*; Vol. 17, No.1; March 1988

/DeKL85/Derrett, N.; Kent, W.; Lyngbaek, P.: Some Aspects of Operations in an Object-Oriented Database; *IEEE Database Engineering*; Vol. 8, No. 4; Dec.1985

/Deux90/Deux, O. *et al*: The Story of O_2; *IEEE Transactions on Knowledge and Data Engineering*; Vol. 2, No.1; March 1990

/DFKL86/Derrett, N.; Fishman, D. N.; Kent, W.; Lyngbaek, P.; Ryan, T.: An Object-Oriented Approach to Data Management; *Proc. of Compcon 31st IEEE Computer Society Int. Conf.; San Francisco, CA; March 1986*

/DiKM86/Dittrich, K.; Kotz, A.; Mülle, J.: An Event/Trigger Mechanism to Enforce Complex Consistency Constraints in Design Database; *ACM SIGMOD RECORD*, Vol. 15, No.3; Sept. 1986

/DiLo88/Dittrich, K.; Lorie, R.: Version Support for Engineering Database Systems; *IEEE Transactions on Software Engineering*; Vol. 14, No. 4; 1988

/Ditt87/Dittrich, K.: Object-Oriented Database Systems (A Workshop Report); in: *Entity-Relationship Approach*, S. Spacapietra (Editor), Elsevier Science Publisher B. V. (North-Holland), 1987

/Ditt88-1/Klaus Dittrich (Editor):Advances in Object-Oriented Database Systems; *2nd Int. Workshop on Object-Oriented Database Systems; Bad Münster, FRG*; 'Lecture Notes in Computer Science', Vol. 334, Springer; 1988

/Ditt88-2/Dittrich, K.: Preface; in:/Ditt88-1/

/Ditt90/Dittrich , K.: Object-Oriented Database Systems: The Next Miles of the Marathon; *Information Systems*; Vol. 15, No. 1; 1990

/DKAB86/Dadam, P.; Kuespert, K.; Andersen, F:; Blanken, H.; Erbe, R.; Guenauer, J.; Lum, V.; Pistor, P.; Walch, G.: A DBMS Prototype to Support NF^2-Relations: An Integrated View on Flat Tables and Hierarchies; *Proc. ACM-SIGMOD Int. Conf. on Management of Data; Washington, D.C.; May 1986*

/DuHa87/Ducournau, R.; Habib, M.: On Some Algorithms for Multiple Inheritance in Object Oriented Programming; *Proc. of the 1st European Conf. on Object-Oriented Programming (ECOOP); Paris, France; June 1987*

/DuKT88/Duchene, H.; Kaul, M.; Turau, V.: Vodak Kernel Data Model; in: /Ditt88-1/

/ElBa84/Elhardt, K.; Bayer, R.: A Database Cache for High Performance and Fast Restart in Database Systems; *ACM Transactions on Database Systems (TODS)*; Vol. 9, No 4; Dec. 1984

/ElGi89/Ellis, C.; Gibbs, S.: Active Objects: Realities and Possibilities; in: /KiLo89/

/FABC89/Fishman, D.H.; Annevelink, J.; Beech, D.; Chow, E.C.; Connors, T .; Davis, J.W.; Hasan, W.; Hoch, C.G.; Kent, W.; Leichner, S.; Lyngbaek, P.; Mahbod, B.; Neimat, M.A.; Risch, T.; Shan, M.C.; Wilkinson, W. K.: Overview of the Iris DBMS; in: /KiLo89/ and in: /CaML90/

/FBCC87/Fishman, D.H.; Beech, D.; Cate, H.P.; Chow, E.C.; Connors, T.; Davis, J.W.; Derrett, N.; Hoch, C.G.; Kent, W.; Lyngbaek, P.; Mahbod, B.; Neimat, M.A.; Ryan, T.A.; Shan, M.C.: Iris: An Object-Oriented Database Management System; *ACM Transactions on Office Information Systems*; Vol. 5, No. 1; Jan. 1987.

/Fish88/Fishman, D.H.: An Overview of the Iris Object-Oriented Database Management System; *Proc. of Compcon 33rd IEEE Computer Society Int. Conf.; San Francisco, CA; March 1988*

/FJLL88/Ford, S.; Joseph, J.; Langworthy, D.; Lively, D.; Pathak, G.; Perez, E.; Peterson, R.; Sparacin, D.; Thatte, S.; Wells, D.; Agarwala, S.: ZEITGEIST: Database Support for Object-Oriented Programming; in:/Ditt88-1/

/FLMW87/Fekete, A.; Lynch, N.; Merritt, M.; Weihl, W.: *Nested Transactions, Conflict-Based Locking, and Dynamic Atomicity*; Technical Report MIT/LCS/TM-340; Laboratory for Computer Science, Massachusetts Institute for Technology, Sept. 1988

/FrBo89/Freitag, J.; Bode, T.: *A General Manager for Storage Objects as the Basis for the Implementation of Complex Objects in an Object Management System*; Technical Report, University of Dortmund, P.O. Box 500, D-4600 Dortmund, West-Germany; and (in German) *Proc. GI Conf. on Database Systems for Office Automation, Engineering, and Scientific Applications, Zurich, Switzerland, 1989*

/GaKi88/Garza, J.; Kim, W.: Transaction Management in an Object-Oriented Database Systems; *Proc. ACM-SIGMOD Int. Conf. on Management of Data; Chicago, Illinois; June 1988*

/GoRo83/Goldberg, A.; Robson, D.: *SMALLTALK-80: The Language and its implementation*; Addison-Wesley; 1983

/Gray79/Gray, J.: Notes on Data Base Operating Sytems; in: *Operating Systems: An Advanced Course*, Bayer, R.; Graham, R.M.; Seegmüller, G. (Editors); Springer; 1979

/GrMa88/Graefe, G.; Maier, D.: Query Optimization in Object-Oriented Database Systems: A Prospectus; in: /Ditt88-1/

/GuHo91/Gupta, R.; Horowitz, E. (Editors): *Object-Oriented Databases with Applications to CASE, Networks, and VLSI CAD*; Prentice-Hall; 1991

/HaML81/Hammer, M.; McLeod, D.: Data Description with SDM: a Semantic Database Model; *ACM Transactions on Database Systems* (TODS); Vol. 6, No. 3; Sept. 1981

/HaOB87/Halbert, D.; O'Brien, P.: Using Types and Inheritance in Object-Oriented Programming; *Proc. of the 1st European Conf. on Object-Oriented Programming (ECOOP); Paris, France; June 1987*

/HäRe83/Härder, T.; Reuter, A.: Principles of Transaction Oriented Database Recovery; *ACM Computing Surveys*, Vol. 15, No. 2; June 1983

/HäRo86/Härder, Th.; Rothermel, K.: *Concurrency Control Issues in Nested Transactions*; IBM Almaden Research Report, San Jose; 1986

/HäRo87/Härder, Th.; Rothermel, K.: Concepts for Transaction Recovery in Nested Transactions; *Proc. ACM-SIGMOD Int. Conf. on Management of Data; San Francisco, California; May 1987*

/Hend86/Hendler, J.: Enhancement for Multiple-Inheritance; *SIGPLAN Notices*; Vol. 21, No. 10; Oct. 1986

/Herl87/Herlihy, M.: Optimistic Concurrency Control for Abstract Data Types; *Operating Systems Review*; Vol. 21, No. 2; April 1987

/HeSa90/Heuer, A.; Sander, P.: *Preserving and Generating Objects in a Rule Language*; Technical Report, University of Clausthal, Erzstr. 1, D-3392 Clausthal-Zellerfeld, Germany; 1990

/HeSc91/Heuer, A.; Scholl, M.: Principles of Object-Oriented Query Languages; *Proc. GI Conf. on Database Systems for Office Automation, Engineering, and Scientific Applications*; Springer; Kaiserslautern, Germany; March 1991

/HeWe88/Herlihy, M.; Weihl, W.: Hybrid Concurrency Control for Abstract Data Types; *Proc. ACM Symposium on Principles of Database Systems, 1988*

/HeZd88/Heiler, S.; Zdonik, S.: Views, Data Abstraction, and Inheritance in the FUGUE Data Model; in: /Ditt88-1/

/HLMC88/Hsu, M.; Ladin, R.; McCarthy D.: An Execution Model for Active Data Base Management Systems; *Proc. 3rd Int. Conf. on Data and Knowledge Bases: Improving Usability and Responsiveness; Jerusalem, Israel; 1988*

/HMMS87/Härder, T.; Meyer-Wegener, K.; Mitschang, B.; Sikeler, A.: PRIMA – a DBMS Prototype Supporting Engineering Applications; *Proc. 13th Int. Conf. on Very Large Data Bases (VLDB); Brighton, England; 1987*

/HuKi89/Hudson, S.; King, R.: A Self-Adaptive, Concurrent Implementation of an Object-Oriented Database Management System; *ACM Transactions on Database Systems (TODS)*; Vol. 14, No. 3; Sept. 1989

/Hull87/Hull, R.: A Survey of Theoretical Research on Typed Complex Database Objects; in: *Databases*, J. Paradaens (Editor); Academic Press (London); 1987

/Hull89/Hull, R.: Four Views of Complex Objects: A Sophisticate's Introduction; *Proc. of the 3rd Int. Conf. Foundations of Data Organization and Algorithms (FODO); Paris, France; June 1989*

/JhSt90/Jhingran, A.; Stonebraker, M.: Alternatives in Complex Object Representation: A Performance Perspective; *Proc. of the 6th Int. Conf. on Data Engineering; Los Angeles, California; Feb. 1990*

/KaCB86/Katz, R.H.; Chang, E.; Bhateja, R.: Version Modelling Concepts for Computer-Aided Design Databases; *Proc. ACM-SIGMOD Int. Conf. on Management of Data; Washington, D.C.; May 1986*

/KaCh87/Katz, R.H.; Lehmann, T.J.: Managing Change in a Computer Aided Design Database; *Proc. 13th Int. Conf. on Very Large Data Bases (VLDB); Brighton, England; 1987*

/KaLe84/Katz, R.H.; Lehmann, T.J.: Database Support for Versions and Alternatives of Large Design Files; *IEEE Transactions on Software Engineering*; Vol. 10, No. 2; 1984

/Katz84/Katz, R.H.: Transaction Management in the Design Environment; in: *New Applications of Data Bases*; G. Gardarin, E. Gelenbe (Editors); Academic Press; 1984

/KBBC88/Kim, W.; Ballou, N.; Banerjee, J.; Chou, H.-T.; Garza, J.; Woelk, D. : Integrating an Object-Oriented Programming System with a Database System; *Proc. ACM 3rd Int. Conf. on Object-Oriented Programming Languages, Systems and Applications (OOPSLA); Orlando, Florida; Sept. 1988* and in: /CaML90/

/KBCG87/Kim, W.; Banerjee, J.; Chou, H.-T.; Garza, J.; Woelk, D.: Composite Object Support in an Object-Oriented Database System; *Proc. ACM 2nd Int. Conf. on Object-Oriented Programming Languages, Systems and Applications (OOPSLA); Orlando, Florida; Oct. 1987*

/KBCG89/Kim, W.; Ballou, N.; Chou, H.-T.; Garza, J.; Woelk, D.: Features of the ORION Object-Oriented Database System; in: /KiLo89/

/Kelt87/Kelter,U.: Concurrency Control for Design Objects with Versions in CAD Databases; *Information Systems*; Vol. 12, No. 2; 1987

/Kelt88/Kelter, U.: Concepts for Transactions in Non-Standard Database Systems; (in German); *Informationstechnik it*; Vol. 30, No. 1; 1988

/Kent78/Kent, W.: *Data and Reliability*; North-Holland, New York; 1978

/Kent90/Kent, W.: The Iris Object-Oriented Database System; *Proc. of the 8th British National Conf. on Databases; University of York; July 1990*

/KGBW90/Kim, W.; Garza, J.; Ballou, N.; Woelk, D.: Architecture of the ORION Next-Generation Database System; *IEEE Transactions on Knowledge and Data Engineering*; Vol. 2, No.1; March 1990

/KhAb90/Khoshafian, S.; Abnous, R.: *Object-Orientation Concepts, Languages, Databases, User Interfaces*; Wiley; 1990

/KhCo86/Khoshafian, S.; Copeland, G.: Object Identity; *Proc. ACM 1st Int. Conf. on Object-Oriented Programming Languages, Systems and Applications (OOPSLA); Portland, Oregon; Sept. 1986*

/Khos90/Khoshafian, S.: Insight into Object-Oriented Databases; *Information and Software Technology*; Vol. 32, No. 4; May 1990

/KiCB87/Kim, W.; Chou, H.T.; Banerjee, J.: Operations and Implementation of Complex Objects; *Proc. 3rd Int. Conf. on Data Engineering; Los Angeles, California; 1987*

/KiBG89/Kim, W.; Bertino, E.; Garza, J.: Composite Objects Revisited; *Proc. ACM-SIGMOD Int. Conf. on Management of Data; Portland, Oregon; May 1989*

/KiCh88/Kim, W.; Chou, H.T.: Versions of Schema for Object-Oriented Databases; *Proc. 14th Int. Conf. on Very Large Data Bases (VLDB); Los Angeles, California; August 1988*

/KiKD89/Kim, W.; Kim, K.-C.; Dale, A.: Indexing Techniques for Object-Oriented Databases; in: /KiLo89/

/KiLo89/Kim, W.; Lochovsky, F. (Editors): *Object-Oriented Concepts, Databases, and Applications*; Addison-Wesley; 1989

/Kim89/Kim, W.: A Model of Queries for Object-Oriented Databases; *Proc. 15th Int. Conf. on Very Large Data Bases (VLDB); Amsterdam, Netherlands; August 1989*

/Kim90-1/Kim, W.: Object-Oriented Databases: Definition and Research Directions; *IEEE Transactions on Knowledge and Data Engineering*; Vol. 2, No.3; Sept. 1990

/Kim90-2/Kim, W.: Research Directions in Object-Oriented Database Systems; *Proc. 9th ACM SIGART/SIGMOD/SIGACT Symposium on Principles of Database Systems (PODS); Nashville, Tennessee; April 1990*

/Kim90-3/Kim, W.: *Introduction to Object-Oriented Databases*; MIT Press; May 1990

/Kim91/ Kim, W.: Object-Oriented Database Systems: Strengths and Weaknesses; *Journal of Object-Oriented Programming*, Vol. 4, No. 4, July/Aug. 1991

/KlSW86/Klahold, P.; Schlageter, G.; Wilkes, W.: A General Model for Version Management in Databases; *Proc. 12th Int. Conf. on Very Large Data Bases (VLDB); Kyoto, Japan; August 1986*

/KoKB85/Korth, H. F.; Kim, W.; Bancilhon, F.: A Model of CAD Transactions; *Proc. Int. Conf. on Very Large Data Bases (VLDB); Stockholm, Sweden; 1985*

/Kort88/Korth, H. F.: Optimization of Object-Retrieval Queries; in: /Ditt88-1/

/KSUW85/Klahold, P.; Schlageter, G.; Unland, R.; Wilkes, W.: A Transaction Model Supporting Complex Applications in Integrated Information Systems; *Proc. ACM-SIGMOD Int. Conf. on Management of Data; Austin, Texas; May 1985*

/LDFK87/Lyngbaek, P.; Derrett, N.; Fishman, D.H.; Kent, W.; Ryan, T.A.: Design and Implementation of the IRIS Object Manager; *Proc. of a Workshop on Persistent Object Systems: Their Design, Implementation and Use; Scotland; Aug. 1987*

/LeRi88/Lècluse, C; Richard, P.: Modeling Inheritance and Genericity in Object-Oriented Databases; *Proc. of the 2nd Int. Conf. on Database Theory (ICDT); Brugge, Belgium; August 1988*

/LeRi89-1/Lècluse, C; Richard, P.: Modeling Complex Structures in Object-Oriented Databases; *Proc. 7th ACM SIGART/SIGMOD/SIGACT Symposium on Principles of Database Systems (PODS); Philadelphia; March 1989*

/LeRi89-2/Lècluse, C; Richard, P.: The O_2 Database Programming Language; *Proc. 15th Int. Conf. on Very Large Data Bases (VLDB); Amsterdam, Netherlands; 1989*

/LeRV88/Lècluse, C; Richard, P.; Velez, F.: O_2, an Object-Oriented Data Model; *Proc. ACM-SIGMOD Int. Conf. on Management of Data; Chicago, Illinois; June 1988*

/LeRV90/Lècluse, C; Richard, P.; Velez, F.: O_2, an Object-Oriented Data Model; in: /BaBu90/

/Lieb86-1/Lieberman, H.: Delegation and Inheritance: Two Mechanisms for Sharing Knowledge in Object-Oriented Systems; *3ème Journées d'Etudes Langages Orientés Objets*; J. Bezivin, Cointe, P. (Editors); AFCET, Paris, France; 1986

/Lieb86-2/Lieberman, H.: Using Prototypical Objects to Implement Shared Behaviour in Object-Oriented Systems; *Proc. ACM 1st Int. Conf. on Object-Oriented Programming Languages, Systems and Applications (OOPSLA); Portland, Oregon; Sept. 1986*

/LyKe86/Lyngbaek, P.; Kent, W.: A Data Modeling Methodology for the Design and Implementation of Information Systems; *Proc. of the ACM-IEEE Int. Workshop on Object-Oriented Database Systems; Pacific Grove, CA*; IEEE Computer Society Press No. 734; Sept. 1986

/LyVi87/Lyngbaek, P.; Vianu, V.: Relational Translations of Semantic Models: A Case Study Based on Iris; *Proc. ACM-SIGMOD Int. Conf. on Management of Data; San Francisco, California; May 1987*

/LyVi88/Lyngbaek, P.; Vianu, V.: Mapping a Semantic Database Model to the Relational Model; *Database Engineering*; Vol. 11, No. 2; June 1988

/MaDa86/Manola, F.; Dayal, U.: PDM: An Object-Oriented Data Model; *Proc. of the ACM-IEEE Int. Workshop on Object-Oriented Database Systems; Pacific Grove, CA*; IEEE Computer Society Press No. 734; Sept. 1986

/Maie86/Maier, D.: *A Logic for Objects*; Technical Report No. CS/E©012; Oregon Graduate Center, 19600 S. W. von Neumann Drive, Beaverton, Oregon 97006-1999; Nov. 1986

/Maie89-1/Maier, D.: Making Database Systems Fast enough for CAD Applications; in: /KiLo89/

/Maie89-2/Maier, D.: Why isn't there an Object-Oriented Data Model?; *Proc. IFIP 11th World Computer Conf.; San Francisco, CA; Aug. 1989*

/Mano89/Manola, F.: *An Evaluation of Object-Oriented DBMS Develop-*

ment; Technical Report; GTE Laboratories Inc.; 40 Sylvan Road, Waltham, MA 02254; Oct. 1989

/MaOP85/Maier, D.; Otis, A.; Purdy, A.: Object-Oriented Database Development at Servio Logic; *IEEE Database Engineering*; Vol. 8, No. 4; Dec. 1985

/MaSt86/Maier, D.; Stein, J.: Indexing in an Object-Oriented DBMS; *Proc. of the ACM-IEEE Int. Workshop on Object-Oriented Database Systems; Pacific Grove, CA*; IEEE Computer Society Press No. 734; Sept. 1986

/MaSt87/Maier, D.; Stein, J.: Development and Implementation of an Object-Oriented DBMS; in: /ShWe87/

/MBGW84/Mylopoulos, J.; Borgida, A.; Greenspan, S.; Wong, H.: Information System Design at the Conceptual Level – The TAXIS Project; *IEEE Database Engineering*; Vol. 7, No. 4; Dec. 1984

/Meye86/Meyer, B.: Genericity versus Inheritance; *Proc. ACM 1st Int. Conf. on Object-Oriented Programming Languages, Systems and Applications (OOPSLA); Portland, Oregon; Sept. 1986*

/Meye88/Meyer, B.: *Object-Oriented Software Construction*; Prentice-Hall; International Series in Computer Science; 1988

/Mica88/Micallef, J.: Encapsulation, Reusability and Extensibility in Object-Oriented Programming Languages; *Journal of Object-Oriented Programming*; April/May 1988

/Mins75/Minsky, M.: *A Framework for Representing Knowledge*; *Psychology of Computer Vision*, MIT Press, Cambridge MA, 1975

/MJSS89/Moss, E.; Johnson, R.; Snyder, A.; Stemple, D.; Ungar, D.: Inheritance: Can we have our cake and eat it too?; Panel, *Proc. ACM 4th Int. Conf. on Object-Oriented Programming Languages, Systems and Applications (OOPSLA); Portland, Oregon*; pp. 485–490; Oct. 1989

/MMNM87/Morris, J.; Meyer, B.; Nerson, J.-M.; Matsuo, M.: Eiffel: Object-Oriented Design for Software Engineering; *Proc. of 1st European Software Engineering Conf., Strasbourg, France; Sept. 1987*

/Morg83/Morgenstern, M.: Active Databases as a Paradigm for Enhanced Computing Environments; *Proc. 9th Int. Conf. on Very Large Data Bases (VLDB), Florence, Italy; 1983*

/Moss86/Moss, J.E.B.: *An Introduction to Nested Transactions*; COINS Technical Report 86-41; University of Massachusetts at Amherst; Sept.1986

/MSOP86/Maier, D.; Stein, J; Otis, A.; Purdy, A.: Development of an Object-Oriented DBMS; *Proc. ACM 1st Int. Conf. on Object-Oriented Programming Languages, Systems and Applications (OOPSLA); Portland, Oregon; Sept. 1986* and in: /CaML90/

/NeSt89/Neuhold, E.; Stonebraker, M.: Future Directions in DBMS Research (Laguna Beach Report); *SIGMOD Record*; Vol. 18, No.2; July 1989

/NgRi89/Nguyen,G.; Rieu, D.: Schema Evolution in Object-Oriented Database Systems; *Data and Knowledge Engineering*; Vol. 4, No. 1; July 1989

/Nier89/Nierstrasz, O.: A Survey of Object-Oriented Concepts; in: /KiLo89/

/Osbo88/Osborn, S. L.: Identity, Equality and Query Optimization; in: /Ditt88-1/

/PCKW89/Parsaye, K.; Chignell, M.; Khoshafian, S.; Wong, H.: *Intelligent Databases: Object-Oriented, Deductive Hypermedia Technologies*; Wiley; 1989

/PeSM87/Penny, D.; Stein, J; Maier, D.: Is the Disk Half Full or Half Empty?: Combining Optimistic and Pessimistic Concurrency Mechanisms in a Shared, Persistent Object Base; *Proc. of the Workshop on Persistent Object Stores; Appin, Scotland, Aug. 1987*

/PeSt87/Penny, D.; Stein, J: Class Modification in the GemStone Object-Oriented DBMS; *Proc. ACM 2nd Int. Conf. on Object-Oriented Programming Languages, Systems and Applications (OOPSLA); Orlando, Florida; Oct. 1987*

/PSSW87/Paul, H.B.; Schek, H.J.; Scholl, M; Weikum, G.: Architecture and Implementation of the Darmstadt Database Kernel System; *Proc. ACM-SIGMOD Int. Conf. on Management of Data; San Francisco, California; May 1987*

/PuMS87/Purdy A.; Maier, D.; Schuchardt, B.: Integrating an Object Server with Other Worlds; *ACM Transactions on Office Information Systems*; Vol. 5, No. 1; Jan. 1987 and in: /GuHo91/

/Rent82/Rentsch, T.: Object Oriented Programming; *SIGPLAN Notices*, Vol. 17, No. 9, pp. 51–57; 1982

/RiCa87/Richardson, J.; Carey, M.: Programming Constructs for Database System Implementation in EXODUS; *Proc. ACM-SIGMOD Int. Conf. on Management of Data; San Francisco, California; May 1987*

/RiCa89/Richardson, J.; Carey, M.: Persistence in the E Language: Issues and Implementation; *Software – Practice and Experience*; Vol. 19, No. 12; Dec. 1989

/RiMS88/Riegel, S.; Mellender, F.; Straw, A.: Integration of Database Management with an Object-Oriented Programming Language; in: /Ditt88-1/

/RiVe87/Richard, P.; Velez, F.: An Object-Oriented Formal Data Model; *Proc. of Workshop on Database Programming Languages; Roscoff, France; Sept. 1987*

/RuKC87/Rubenstein, W.; Kubicar, M.; Cattell, R.: Benchmarking Simple Database Operations; *Proc. ACM-SIGMOD Int. Conf. on Management of Data; San Francisco, California; May 1987*

/Salt78/Saltzer, J.: *Naming and Binding of Objects*; 'Lecture Notes in Computer Science', Goos and Hartman (Editors); Springer, 1978

/SCFL86/Schwarz, P.; Chang, W.; Freytag, J.; Lohman, G.; McPherson, J.; Mohan, C.; Pirahesh, H.: Extensibility in the Starburst Database System; *Proc. of the ACM-IEEE Int. Workshop on Object-Oriented*

Database Systems; Pacific Grove, CA; IEEE Computer Society Press No. 734; Sept. 1986

/ScLT90/Scholl, M.; Laasch,C.; Tresch, M.: *Updatable Views in Object-Oriented Databases*; Technical Report No. 150, ETH Zurich, Department of Computer Science, CH-8092 Zurich, Switzerland; Dec. 1990

/ScSc90/Schek, H.J.; Scholl, M.: A Relational Object Model; *3rd Int. Conf. on Database Theory (ICDT); Paris, France; Dec. 1990*

/Ship81/Shipman, D.: The Functional Data Model and the Data Language DAPLEX; *ACM Transactions on Database Systems (TODS)*; Vol. 6, No. 1; March 1981

/ShWe87/Shriver, B.; Wegner, P. (Editors): *Research Directions in Object-Oriented Programming*; Computer Science Series, MIT Press, Cambridge, Massachusetts; 1987

/ShZd89/Shaw, G.; Zdonik, S.: Object-Oriented Queries: Equivalence and Optimization; *Proc. 1st Int. Conf. on Deductive and Object-Oriented Databases (DOOD); Kyoto, Japan; Dec. 1989*

/SkZd86/Skarra, A.; Zdonik, S.: The Management of Changing Types in an Object-Oriented Database; *Proc. ACM 1st Int. Conf. on Object-Oriented Programming Languages, Systems and Applications (OOPSLA); Portland, Oregon; Sept. 1986*

/SkZd87/Skarra, A.; Zdonik, S.: Type Evolution in an Object-Oriented Database; in: /ShWe87/ and in: /CaML90/

/SkZd89/Skarra, A; Zdonik, S: Concurrency Control and Object-Oriented Databases; in: /KiLo89/

/Snyd86/Snyder, A.: Encapsulation and Inheritance in Object-Oriented Programming Languages; *Proc. ACM 1st Int. Conf. on Object-Oriented Programming Languages, Systems and Applications (OOPSLA); Portland, Oregon; Sept. 1986*

/SpSc84/Spector, A.; Schwarz, P.: Synchronizing Shared Abstract Types; *ACM Transactions on Database Systems (TODS)*; Vol. 2, No. 3, August 1984

/Stei87/Stein, L.: Delegation is Inheritance; *Proc. ACM 2nd Int. Conf. on Object-Oriented Programming Languages, Systems and Applications (OOPSLA); Orlando, Florida; Oct. 1987*

/Ston90/Stonebraker, M. *et al.*: *Third-Generation Data Base System Manifesto*; The Committee for Advanced DBMS Functions; Technical Report; GTE Laboratories Inc., 40 Sylvan Road, MS 62, Waltham, MA 02254; 1990

/StÖz90/Straube, D.; Özsu, M.: Type Consistency of Queries in an Object-Oriented Database System; *Proc. ACM 5th Int. Conf. on Object-Oriented Programming Languages, Systems and Applications, together with European Conf. on Object-Oriented Programming (OOPSLA/ECOOP); Ottawa, Canada; Oct. 1990*

/Stro86/Stroustrup, B.: The C++ Programming Language; Addison-Wesley; 1986

/Stro87/Stroustrup, B.: What is 'Object-Oriented Programming'?; *Proc. of the European Conf. on Object-Oriented Programming (ECOOP); Paris, France; June 1987*

/StRo87/Stonebraker, M.; Rowe, L.A.: *The POSTGRES Papers: (The Design of POSTGRES; The POSTGRES Data Model; A Rule Manager for Relational Database Systems; The Design of the POSTGRES Storage System; A Shared Object Hierarchy)*; Electronics Research Laboratory; College of Engineering, University of California Berkeley, Memorandum No. UCB/ERL M86/85; June 1987; additionally *Proc. ACM-SIGMOD; Washington, D.C.; May 1986; Proc. ACM SIGMOD; San Francisco, California; May 1987, Proc. 13th Int. Conf. on Very Large Data Bases (VLDB); Brighton, England; 1987; Proc. 3rd Int. Conf. on Data Engineering; Los Angeles, California; 1987; Proc. ACM-IEEE Int. Workshop on Object-Oriented Database Systems; Pacific Grove, CA; Sept. 1986*

/StWe85/Stubbs, D.; Webre, N.: *Data Structures with Abstract Data Types and Pascal*; Brooks/Cole; Monterey, California; 1985

/SUWZ87/Schlageter, G.; Unland, R.; Wilkes, W.; Zieschang, R.; Maul, G.; Nagl, M.; Meyer, R.: OOPS – An Object-Oriented Programming System with Integrated Data Management Facility; (in German) *Proc. GI 2nd Conf. on Database Systems for Office Automation, Engineering, and Scientific Applications; Darmstadt, West Germany; 1987*

/SUWZ88/Schlageter, G.; Unland, R.; Wilkes, W.; Zieschang, R.; Maul, G.; Nagl, M.; Meyer, R.: OOPS – An Object-Oriented Programming System with Integrated Data Management Facility; *Proc. of the 4th Int.Conf. on Data Engineering; Los Angeles, California; Feb. 1988*

/TaYI88/Tanaka,K.; Yoshikawa, M.; Ishihara, K.: Schema Virtualization in Object-Oriented Databases; *Proc. of the 4th Int. Conf. on Data Engineering; Los Angeles, California; Feb. 1988*

/Thom89/Thomas, D.: What's in an Object?; *BYTE*; March 1989

/ToSK89/Tomlinson, C.; Scheevel, M.; Kim, W.: Sharing and Organization Protocols in Object-Oriented Systems; *Journal of Object-Oriented Programming*; Nov./Dec. 1989

/Ullm87/Ullman, J.: Database Theory – Past and Future; *Proc. 6th ACM SIGART/SIGMOD/SIGACT Symposium on Principles of Database Systems (PODS); 1987*

/Unla88/Unland, R.: A General Model for Locking in Non-Standard Database Systems; Research Report; University of Hagen, Department of Computer Science; 1988; and (in German), *Proc. GI 3rd Conf. on Database Systems for Office Automation, Engineering, and Scientific Applications; Zurich, Switzerland; 1989*

/Unla90/Unland, R.: A Flexible and Adaptable Tool-Kit Approach for Concurrency Control in Non-Standard Database Systems; *3rd Int. Conf. on Database Theory (ICDT); Paris, France; Dec. 1990*

/UnSc89-1/Unland, R.; Schlageter, G.: An Object-Oriented Programming

Environment for Advanced Database Applications; *Journal of Object-Oriented Programming*; Vol. 2, No. 1,; May/June 1989

/UnSc89-2/Unland, R.; Schlageter, G.: A Multi-Level Transaction Model for Engineering Applications; *Proc. 1st Int. Symposium on Database Systems for Advanced Applications; Seoul, South Korea; April 1989*

/UnSc90/Unland, R.; Schlageter, G.: Object-Oriented Database Systems: Concepts and Perspectives; *Proc. Int. Symposium "Database Systems of the 90s"; Müggelsee, Berlin, Germany*; Lecture Notes in Computer Science 466, A. Blaser (Editor); Springer, Nov. 1990

/UnSc91-1/Unland, R.; Schlageter, G.: A Flexible and Adaptable Tool Kit Approach for Transaction Management in Non Standard Database Systems; *IEEE Database Engineering Bulletin*; Special Issue on 'Transaction Models for Advanced Database Applications'; March 1991

/UnSc91-2/Unland, R.; Schlageter, G.: A Transaction Manager Development Facility for Non Standard Database Systems; in: *Transaction Models for Advanced Database Applications*; A. Elmargarmid (Editor); Morgan Kaufmann; 1991

/VaKC86/Valduriez, P.; Khoshafian, S.; Copeland, G.: Implementation Techniques of Complex Objects; *Proc. 12th Int. Conf. on Very Large Data Bases (VLDB); Kyoto, Japan; August 1986*

/VeBD89/Velez, F.; Bernard, G.; Darnis, V.: The O_2 Object Manager: an Overview; *Proc. 15th Int. Conf. on Very Large Data Bases (VLDB); Amsterdam, Netherlands; August 1989*

/Wegn87-1/Wegner, P.: Dimensions of Object-Based Language Design; *Proc. ACM 2nd Int. Conf. on Object-Oriented Programming Languages, Systems and Applications (OOPSLA); Orlando, Florida; Oct. 1987*

/Wegn87-2/Wegner, P.: The Object-Oriented Classification Paradigm; in: /ShWe87/

/Wegn89/Wegner, P.: Learning the Language; *BYTE*; March 1989

/Weih88/Weihl,W.: Commutativity-Based Concurrency Control for Abstract Data Types; *Proc. IEEE 21st Annual Hawaii Int. Conf. on System Sciences (HICSS); Hawaii; Jan. 1988*

/WeLo89/Weiser, S.; Lochovsky, F.: OZ+: An Object-Oriented Database System; in: /KiLo89/

/WeZd86/Wegner, P.; Zdonik, S.: Language and Methodology for Object-Oriented Database Environments; *Proc. IEEE 19th Annual Hawaii Int. Conf. on System Sciences (HICSS); Hawaii; Jan. 1986*

/WeZd88/Wegner, P.; Zdonik, S.: Inheritance as an Incremental Modification Mechanism or What Like Is and Isn't Like; *Proc. of the 2nd European Conf. on Object-Oriented Programming (ECOOP); Oslo, Norway; Aug. 1988*

/WiEK90/Winblad, A.; Edwards, S.; King, D.: *Object-Oriented Software*; Addison-Wesley; 1990

/WiLH90/Wilkinson, K.; Lyngbaek, P.; Hasan, W.: The Iris Architecture and Implementation; *IEEE Transactions on Knowledge and Data Engineering*; Vol. 2, No.1; March 1990

/Wilk88/Wilkes, W.: Instance Inheritance Mechanisms for Object-Oriented Databases; in: /Ditt88-1/

/WoKi87/Woelk, D.; Kim, W.: Multimedia Information Management in an Object-Oriented Database System; *Proc. 13th Int. Conf. on Very Large Data Bases (VLDB); Brighton, England; 1987*

/WoKL86/Woelk, D.; Kim, W.; Luther W.: An Object-Oriented Approach to Multimedia Databases; *Proc. ACM-SIGMOD Int. Conf. on Management of Data; Washington, D.C.; May 1986*

/ZdHe90/Zdonik, S.; Heiler, S.: Object-Oriented Database Management Systems; Tutorial No. 1; *Proc. 6th Data Engineering; Los Angeles, California; Feb. 1990*

/ZdMa90/Zdonik, S.; Maier, D. (Editors): *Readings in Object-Oriented Database Systems*; Morgan Kaufmann; San Mateo, California; 1990

/Zdon86-1/Zdonik, S.: Why Properties are Objects or Some Refinements of 'is-a'; *Proc. ACM/IEEE Fall Joint Computer Conf., Austin, Texas; Nov. 1986*

/Zdon86-2/Zdonik, S.: Version Management in an Object-Oriented Database; *Proc. IFIP 24th Workshop on Advanced Programming Environments; Trondheim, Norway; 1986*

/Zdon88/Zdonik, S.: Data Abstraction and Query Optimization; in: /Ditt88-1/

/ZhMa88/Zhu, J.; Maier, D.: Abstract Objects in an Object-Oriented Data Model; *Proc. of the 2nd Int. Conf. on Expert Database Systems; Tyson Corner, Virginia; April 1988*

/Zica90/Zicari, R.: *A Framework for Schema Updates in an Object-Oriented DataBase System*; Technical Report No. 90-025; Politecnico Di Milano, Dipartimento Di Elettronica, Piazza Leonardo Da Vinci 32, 20133 Milano, Italia; Feb. 1990

6
Database Machines

V. A. J. MALLER

Department of Computer Studies, Loughborough University of Technology, Loughborough, Leics., LE11 3TU.

1. BACKGROUND

The concept of a database machine had its origins in the early research on non-numeric processing and associative storage carried out in the 1960s. In particular, it was recognised that rotating magnetic storage, in which the data was being continuously scanned, could be converted into a form of associative memory if appropriate matching logic were to be inserted in the data channels. Some studies were carried out by research groups in Europe and North America but, although the concept appeared promising, the prevailing electronic technology made the building of such a machine impractical.

Nevertheless, the concept of constructing a storage system which could be accessed directly by using the intrinsic properties of the data items themselves, as keys rather than relying on some explicit referencing structure, was seen as extremely useful. Indeed, the requirement for such devices arose quite naturally from the observations that, in the minds of users, information was always identified by meaning and much automated data processing was concerned with extracting the relevant information from files, using complex criteria involving multiple key matching.

The rapid technological growth of high-capacity disk storage throughout the 1960s not only made interactive computing practical but also led inevitably to files of steadily increasing size being stored and accessed on-line. The growth in the size of such stored files was accompanied by demands from users for increasingly flexible access, which, in practice, meant the use of multiple data items as keys. This situation became most extreme in the case of information retrieval from very large text files in which every significant word could be used as a search term.

Expert Database Systems
ISBN 0-12-382255-6

To cope with this situation in a conventional processing environment, the only practical approach, if a serial search were to be avoided, was to generate an index list for each word. The search then became an exercise in index manipulation (Bird, 1978). Indexes, however, cannot alone satisfy the totality of required search functions and, indeed, the utility of indexes is more often assumed than proved. Index maintenance, moreover, can present a very significant processing overhead, particularly if the data set is at all volatile. Recognising this, several research groups started to investigate various ways in which special hardware could be used to achieve high-speed serial search (Slotnik, 1970; Coulouris *et al.*, 1972). Such an approach was not seen as replacing indexes but complementing them, since much could always be gained by some form of data-set partitioning. The view was held that substantial performance improvements would be achieved from a better engineering balance being struck between the granularity of the index and serial search (Bird, 1982).

By 1970, the concept of a database had emerged, which, for a given application, contained a model expressing the logical structure of the information related to the application, together with an associated set of data files. Such a system offered its users logical integrity and consistency, irrespective of their view of the data. Although the database approach offered many advantages, the software overhead associated with the implementation tended to be very high. This frequently forced system builders to forgo generality in the interests of run-time efficiency. This, in turn, led to systems being built which were often inflexible and difficult to adapt to evolving requirements.

The development of relational techniques in the early 1970s introduced the beginnings of mathematical rigour which had hitherto been largely absent, into the database field, and established a recognised set of basic database operations. Early implementations of relational databases, however, whilst demonstrating considerable flexibility, made enormous demands on computer power, particularly if the data sets were large and response times were required which were commensurate with a conversational mode of working. These difficulties usually arose from the incomplete predictability of potential selection criteria which tended to vitiate any attempt at effective optimisation when the information was stored.

The appreciation that a conversational mode of working offered the greatest potential for effective use, provided further encouragement to many research groups to explore various ways of making available a dramatic increase in effective computer power. As the requisite electronic technology had become available (early 1970s), potential high performance could now be achieved in a practical and cost-effective way.

The various research groups directed their activities into two broad categories – text searching and relational database machines. In the former category, most of the effort was concentrated on building machines which executed boolean selection expressions involving multiple terms in a high-speed serial search. In most of these developments considerable emphasis was placed on being able to apply very flexible string matching to the individual terms. Most developments in this area were seen as special-purpose function architectures which would form part of the backing store subsystem and be under the control of a host processor. In the second category, the general approach was to build free-standing database machines, which could execute the full set of relational operators, be responsible for all aspects of database management, and offer a high-level interface to an applications processor.

This dichotomy in the research field resulted in two quite distinct classes of activity with little common ground between them. On the one hand, those concerned with text searching considered their material completely unstructured and sought the greatest flexibility at the symbolic level of individual characters. On the other hand, those who adopted the relational approach, accepted a rigid format of fixed-length fields and records and concentrated on efficient means of implementing the relational operators. In short, the former were pragmatists, who adopted a simple mechanistic approach to searching text as they found it, whilst the latter took a purist approach and were more concerned with efficiently implementing the relational operators without questioning the underlying assumptions and relevance of the relational model.

The systems now appearing on the market clearly demonstrate this background and this will be exemplified in the following sections. In general, serial text-searching machines have become heavily dependent on specialised hardware, whereas relational database machines are now tending to use arrays of loosely coupled conventional processors with each asynchronously running identical software.

There is, however, growing recognition that many applications do not fit easily into one or other of the two categories outlined above and that many have characteristics of each. Very few of the emerging database machines, however, are able to support such applications. In the operational environment of Office Information Servers, for example, the requirement is for systems that can store and manipulate a wide spectrum of data types and formats ranging from fixed-format data at one extreme, through loosely structured text (e.g. name and address files) to unstructured text at the other (Tsichritzis, 1984). Indeed, it can be argued that loosely structured text represents the most general case and that a system properly designed to handle this should be capable of supporting fixed-format data and unstructured text as subsets.

2. TEXT-SEARCHING MACHINES

2.1. General

In the field of text searching, much of the effort has gone into developing very flexible string-matching devices, most of which have been based on the concept of finite-state automata. These string-matching devices are then used as term comparison units in the actual search machines, most of which have conceptually similar architectures. The outputs of each of the term comparison units are combined by a query resolver to determine whether or not the section of examined text satisfies the overall selection criteria. There is, in addition, control logic, and usually a control processor, to handle such activities as loading search arguments and search logic, format control and retrieval of data.

Very little attention has been given to the possibility of exploiting specialised hardware to assist in the generation and manipulation of indexes as a complementary function to pure search. Some work, however, has been directed towards using search engines to scan index files containing short-form records, composed either of key words or of superimposed codes. (Roberts, 1979; Ahuja and Roberts, 1980). If interactive access to very large text databases is to be effectively implemented, efficient support of indexes is essential, particularly as to generation and maintenance.

In the following section are listed those hardware text-searching machines which are currently on the market, together with those developments that either are forming, or may form, the basis of future systems.

2.2. Commercially Exploited Systems

2.2.1. ASSOCIATIVE FILE PROCESSOR (AFP)

The Associative File Processor was originally demonstrated in prototype form by Operating Systems Inc. in 1976; it has been commercially available since 1979 and is currently marketed by Datafusion (Datafusion Corp., 1983).

The AFP uses a PDP 11 as the search controller and query resolver. The term comparator is implemented in a special hardware unit called the Associative Cross-point Processor (AXP) which provides 8Kbytes of pseudo-associative memory for storing key words. Data input from the disk sub-system is initially buffered within the AXP before being separated into individual words for comparison with the stored key words. A micro-programmed memory map, using knowledge of the current input data word, restricts the comparison process to a subset of the stored key words and permits conventional memory to be used for storing the key words.

Key words may be up to 15 characters in length and the memory is capable of holding a total of 1200 terms. The comparison process is based on an exact match algorithm which is case-sensitive. Fixed-length 'don't care' capability is available at the character level for word comparisons of equal length but stem-matching requires a separate key for each permissible length variation.

The AXP returns the word position and document identifier for all hit terms to the PDP 11 for query resolution. The AFP is capable of searching data at 1.2M-bytes per second but, in practice, the processing speed of the AXP and the query resolver (in the PDP 11) are the limiting factors and lower effective search rates may occur. This is particularly likely in short documents with many high-frequency common search terms or when parallel query processing is invoked.

2.2.2. CAFS

The CAFS machine, produced by ICL (Coulouris *et al.*, 1972; Babb, 1979; Maller, 1979, 1980, 1983), is a logical filter located in the disk channel sub-system and capable of operating at disk transfer rates. It is not a free-standing system. The hardware contains term comparator units operating in parallel and query resolution is performed in a special-purpose array processor. Disk data may be searched at rates of 3–5M-bytes/s. Several disk sub-systems can be attached to the same distributed host system.

CAFS has facilities for evaluating both nested boolean and weighted quorum selection expressions. The search arguments used in such selection expressions may be masked to 'bit' level. In addition, there are facilities for subsetting 'selected records', before they are returned to the host, and for performing aggregation functions, such as counting, totalling and averaging.

The system can handle a wide range of record formats varying from fixed-length Cobol records, through loosely structured text to unstructured text. In the most general case the record may consist of a variable number of variable-length fields. The maximum field size is 256 bytes and the maximum record length is 19K-bytes. Fields may be separately identified and up to 4096 different field types may be specified to the system. Individual field types may be repeated an arbitrary number of times within a record, subject only to the maximum record length.

2.2.3. GESCAN/2

This system was developed by General Electric in the USA and has been available commercially since 1981 (*Electronics*, 1981; General Electric, 1982).

The system uses a PDP 11 as the host processor to carry out the search controller function and special LSI circuitry for the term comparator and query resolver units. Data from the disk sub-system is 'cached' in a 128K-byte memory before being fed to a number of Text Array Processor (TAP) modules which contain the term comparator and query resolution logic. The disk-to-cache connection is via the PDP 11 system bus.

The Text Array Processors (TAP) compare stored key words with data taken from the cache memory at 2M-bytes per second. A TAP usually consists of four query processors (QP) each capable of storing key terms up to a maximum of 144 characters and carrying out the query resolution. Only one query may be assigned to a query processor. The host processor is notified of documents satisfying a query by the TAP returning the identifier of the document and the associated QP.

The term comparison process is based on the cellular character comparison technique (Haskin and Hollaar, 1983). The implementation is case-sensitive but at the character level can handle terms containing variable and fixed length 'don't cares'.

Some of the limitations, imposed by the limited connectivity of the comparators, have been overcome by providing a system that is extensible both in the number of QPs (up to 128) and in the number of characters per QP.

The system does not search disk data directly and therefore its effective search rate will be lower than the transfer rate of the associated disks. Currently, the effective data rate is 0.7M-bytes/s on disks which run at 1.2M-bytes/s.

It allows for contexts (up to 256) within a document. Each context may be searched separately. An unweighted quorum facility is available to permit documents to satisfy 'm out of n' query terms.

2.2.4. HIGH SPEED TEXT SYSTEM (HSTS)

The HSTS was developed by Operating Systems Inc. (Operating Systems Inc., 1982), under a US government contract, with the aim of improving upon the operational features of the AFP. (Logicon have since taken over the company.)

In contrast to the AFP, both the term comparator and the query resolver are implemented in hardware. A PDP 11 is used as the search controller.

The term comparator consists of a set of Finite State Automata (FSA) which carry out the basic single-word comparisons. A higher level FSA deals with the special case of phrases using outputs from the lower level FSAs.

Query resolution is carried out by another special-purpose processor. During a search, this unit will report the identifiers of a hit document, and the matching query, to a PDP 11, which acts as a search controller. Each search unit can support up to 4 disks.

The HSTS supports document zoning to the extent of sentence and paragraph marker detection. It can be programmed to support various character sets (e.g. 6-bit BCD and 8-bit ASCII). Query capacity is limited only by the search term capacity of 4,000 bytes. The use of multiple FSAs, rather than one larger one, is to provide a more efficient method of handling variable-length 'don't care' characters which can be leading, embedded or trailing.

In the multiple search unit configuration, up to 64 HSTS search units may be run, in parallel, under the control of a 'Master' PDP 11. In this configuration the PDP 11 associated with each search unit assumes the role of a simple control computer acting as a slave to the 'Master' unit.

For both configurations, the Master PDP 11 controls the search units and communicates either with the host, using a standard channel interface, or with user terminals, if it is a stand-alone system. In the latter case the 'Master' also runs the additional host software.

2.2.5. MEMEX

MEMEX is a hardware-based text-information retrieval system specifically designed to search reversibly compressed text. The product is marketed by Memex Information Engines and has been available since 1982 (*Engineering Today*, 1982; Memex Information Engines Ltd, 1982).

The system has the term comparator and query resolver implemented in hardware and the host processor (PDP 11) carries out the search controller function. The term comparator is limited to eight key words and the query resolver can only perform a simple 'AND' function of these terms over a user-defined range (up to eight) of contiguous logical units. This permits the user to define the search for up to eight key words to be within a phrase, a couple of sentences or, at the other extreme, over eight documents. The system does not support parallel query searching and has no indexing capability.

2.3. Other Developments

An important theme of virtually all the proposed string matchers is that they have an architecture compatible with VLSI implementation techniques. Two such developments, which may well be used in future systems, are the following.

2.3.1. UTAH SEARCH ENGINE

The Partitioned Finite State Automaton (Haskin and Hollaar, 1983) is an extension of the FSA design used in the HSTS machine. A machine based on this approach is being developed by UTAH State University (Hollaar, 1984).

2.3.2. PROXIMITY – PSP8000

Proximity Technology Corp. have developed a chip, the PF474 (*BYTE*, 1984), which detects the similarities between a stored search term and incoming text by statistical methods. Although slow by disk transfer-rate standards, the attraction is that systems based upon it may be made price-compatible with the PC 'add-on' market (Proximity Technology Inc., 1984).

3. MACHINES TO SUPPORT STRUCTURED DATA BASES

3.1. General

In contrast to the work on text-searching machines, which has been concentrated primarily on string matching, much of the effort in this area has been directed towards developing possible architectures for attached sub-systems to handle all aspects of the database management function. The influence, moreover, of the relational model has been almost universal and, as a result, most of the commercial systems now emerging offer a relational database with an SQL interface to the host system. Some other developments, notably ICL's CAFS, have followed the path of building specialised search hardware as an adjunct to conventional systems.

3.2. Commercially Exploited Systems

3.2.1. CAFS

A general description of CAFS was given above in section 2.2.2. CAFS is a special-purpose function architecture which can perform a high-speed search over a wide variety of data formats. These formats are parametrically described to the hardware in the search task specification and, as a consequence, successive tasks may, with equal facility, be directed to relational files, Cobol files or unstructured text.

3.2.2. DBC/1012

This machine is produced by Teradata Corporation and exploits loosely coupled micro-processors (Intel 80286 and 80386), which run the same software asynchronously in parallel. Each micro-processor has its own disk controller with up to two disk units. A relational database with an SQL interface is implemented on the system. High performance is achieved by partitioning files over many processor/disk units and running the same task concurrently against each of the partitions (Teradata Corp., 1983; Ehrensberger, 1984). Typical configurations contain 50–100 processing nodes.

Considerable emphasis is placed on the 'YNET' interconnection system which links the processors together. This is a tree-structured network with some processing power at each node. It has, for example, the capability of sorting retrieved records before returning them to the host. The 'YNET' has been described by Teradata as 'the heart of the system and the enabling technology for true parallel processing'.

3.2.3. DIRAM 32

DIRAM (Disque avec Recherche Associative et Ante-Memoire) is a disk sub-system containing a cache memory and a microprocessor (68000) that can perform associative search. It is manufactured and sold by Copernique in France and has been available since 1983 (Copernique, 1983). Copernique claim that they can interface the system to different host computers and that, to exploit the associative search functions, a special software driver only has to be added to the host system software.

3.2.4. DORSAL 32

DORSAL 32, also made by Copernique (Copernique, 1983), is a backend database machine capable of supporting both the Codasyl and relational data models, together with the appropriate data-manipulation languages (Codasyl DML and SQL). The models and the associated data are, however, completely separate.

The system has two principal modules. One is concerned with managing the disk storage units (up to 16 drives) and performing associative search, whilst the other performs logical processing on retrieved data and communicates with the host computer. Both modules may use up to seven 68000 processors and up to 16 M bytes of disk cache memory may be installed.

The system is capable of processing transactions concurrently and has facilities for deadlock detection and prevention. Before-looks and after-looks journals are maintained and automatic roll-back and recovery are supported.

DORSAL 32 has been on the market since 1983.

3.2.5. INTELLIGENT DATABASE MACHINE (IDM 500)

The IDM is an intelligent backend processor supporting a relational DBMS, which is produced by Britton-Lee and has been on the market since 1980 (Britton-Lee Inc., 1982; *System International*, 1985).

A multi-microprocessor architecture is exploited to run a relational DBMS. The system is marketed in three versions all using the same database processor. The basic system, IDM 500/0, comes with 1M-byte memory, a four-drive disk controller and an 8-host RS 232C or IEEE-488 interface which can be expanded to 24. The IDM 500/1 and 500/2 options can have up to 6M bytes of main memory, three more disk controllers (total of 16 drives) and support up to 64 hosts. The top of the range, IDM 500/2, comes with a 'database accelerator', a specialised 10 MIP processor that improves the overall performance by a factor of 2.

The system currently supports DEC (PDP 11 and VAX) and IBM PCs as host computers. Application software resides in the host.

The outline specification is as follows:

Databases/system	50
Relations/database	32,000
Tuples/relation	2,000 million
Attributes/tuple	250
Tuple width	2 K-bytes
Attribute width	250 bytes

3.2.6. iDIS/iDBP

Produced by INTEL in 1982, the iDBP (Data Base Processor) provides a set of primitive database functions. Application software is host based (and customer developed). The device is aimed at small systems and can be used for relational, network and hierarchic databases. Links to the host are via RS-232 and Ethernet interfaces.

The iDIS (Database Information System), also announced in 1982, supports a relational DBMS system but is primarily marketed as the gateway in INTEL's Data Pipeline to manage the flow of information between mainframe computers and a network of terminals and personal computers. The system is equipped with facilities for transferring files and data from hosts (including data extracts from SYSTEM 2000, a DBMS which INTEL owns) into its own relational database for access by the networked terminals. To complete the Data Pipeline connection the iPC software allows users to transfer data between the iDIS and the PC converting the data into PC data formats (e.g. DIF, SYLK and CSV). The system supports a number of hosts including the IBM 370 series, Sperry 1100 series and the IBM PC.

3.2.7. MEGA/NET

This is produced by Digital American Computers (DAC) Inc. and marketed through a dedicated outlet called Mega/Net Corp. It is a relational DBMS system and has been available since 1981.

It can operate as a backend system similar to the IDM 500 or as a complete stand-alone transaction system. Configurations may have up to 16M-bytes of memory and up to 500G-bytes of disk storage. It will support any host computer compatible with Ethernet or X25.

The database specifications are:

Databases/system	unlimited
Relations/database	unlimited
Tuples/relation	unlimited
Tuple width	64K-bytes
Attribute width	1K-bytes
Attributes/tuple	64

3.2.8. RDM 1100

This is a Relational Database Machine produced by Amperif for the Sperry 1100 Series computers (Amperif Corp., 1982). The specification is very similar to the IDM 500 product. The system can support 4 hosts with the latter containing the application and terminal-handling software. The standard configuration includes two 500M-byte disks. The maximum disk connectivity is 16 disks, i.e. 8G-bytes.

3.2.9. SYNFOBASE

Synfobase is sold by AEG Telefunken as a small backend relational database system. It is built around a Z80 micro with 64K of RAM, up to 10M bytes of disk storage, and an 8 K-byte associative store (AEG-Telefunken, 1982; *Electronics*, 1982). Data is transferred from disk in pages of thirty-two 256-byte records (tuples) and loaded into the associative store. The advantage of the system is that any 'byte compare' instruction issued by the

Z80 is carried out on all 32 records and the result is held in the 'respondent' word for subsequent interrogation. This associative compare operation is actually performed serially, but completely, within the Z80 byte compare instruction time. To benefit from this parallelism, records must be 256 bytes long or sub-multiples thereof. The disk-to-store transfer rate is only about 200K-bytes per second.

The host interface is RS232C and Synfobase provides a user query language. The system is aimed at the PC market.

The database specification includes a maximum tuple width of 255 bytes and a maximum of 60 attributes per tuple.

3.3. Other Developments

3.3.1. GRACE

GRACE is a parallel relational database machine developed at the University of Tokyo (Kitsuregawa *et al.*, 1983, 1984). It is primarily aimed at join-intensive operations, although it does exploit logical filters in the disk channels. It also uses hash-based data sort merge in its processing modules. Data from disk storage is passed, via a staging ring, to memory modules, from whence these data are passed, via a processing ring, to a set of processing modules.

3.3.2. RELATIONAL DATABASE MACHINE (RDBM)

RDBM is a prototype functionally distributed multiprocessor architecture developed at the University of Brunswick, Germany, as a successor to the SURE project (Leilich *et al.*, 1978). Logical filters are used in the disk channels, although the on-the-fly processing of SURE has been abandoned. These filters can select and project tuples, which are then transferred to the RDBM main memory. The latter is accessed from a bus and is shared by the multiprocessors, which perform join and set operations, set quantification and scalar aggregation. One of the processors is dedicated to sorting.

The system has undergone experimental evaluation.

3.3.3. MIRDM

MIRDM (Michigan Relational Database Machine) is a design proposed by Qadah and Irani of the University of Michigan (Qadah and Irani, 1985). As far as can be ascertained no actual machine has been built.

MIRDM is a back-end system with an architecture of the MIMD type. Its aim is to perform the full set of relational operators with adequate response time and throughput in an on-line multi-user environment. Data is stored on moving-arm disk storage devices and a page-indexing scheme is used to avoid lengthy searches wherever possible. The proposal requires that disk drives be modified so as to support reading or writing on more than one track in parallel.

The proposed system consists of four main units. There is a master controller, a set of mass storage devices and an interconnection network. The latter permits multiple access to a parallel buffer from both the mass storage devices and the processing clusters.

Various algorithms have been published for the implementation of the select and join relational operators but no indications of system performance have been given.

3.3.4. SCHUSS/SABRE

SCHUSS is a special-purpose hardware filter developed at the Honeywell Bull Research Centre in France (Gonzalez-Rubio *et al.*, 1984). It uses Finite State Automata techniques for search term comparisons and resolves the results in a separate boolean evaluation unit.

The SCHUSS hardware is seen as an architectural component of the SABRE database machine (Gardarin, 1981, Gardarin *et al.*, 1983). SABRE treats each disk track as an associative partition searchable by SCHUSS. As with any such filter, support for join operations can be achieved by selecting relevant subsets from target relations, which may then be joined by the standard processes of nested loops, hash-join and sort-merge.

The SABRE system, which is still in the research phase, has a functional architecture composed of virtual processors running on a bus-connected set of real processors. Some of the virtual processors may run in parallel. SABRE is a software-oriented system and is not dependent on special hardware, although functional accelerators, such as SCHUSS, may be used where appropriate.

3.3.5. SCANTRAX

The SCANTRAX project was started around 1975 at Brunel University (Bogdany *et al.*, 1984). The aim was to build an associative processor, which could act as a backend to a host machine and which would provide a powerful relational database management and text retrieval system.

The name SCANTRAX arises from the processor's primary mode of operation: namely, scanning tracks of data stored on a disk drive. The principal component in SCANTRAX is an 'associative string processor', which searches an incoming character string by content, processes it and returns the result of the operation to the host computer. The objective is that all operations can be performed 'on-the-fly' at Winchester disk data-transfer rates.

The architecture of the Associative String Processor comprises a chain of Associative Processing Elements (APEs) under the control of a microprogram sequencer. Each APE has local storage, a comparator and logic for communicating with neighbouring APEs and can execute three primitive operations, 'search', 'read' and 'write'. 'Search' matches a masked string in an input register against the contents of each word in the local memory. If a match occurs between the masked bit cells, the contents of the 'hit' word may be transferred to an output register ('read') or modified by the unmasked contents of the input register ('write').

Lea and his team (Bogdany *et al.*, 1984) showed that the functions of the conceptual APE could be effectively provided by a design of Associative Parallel Processor (APP) that was compatible with VLSI implementation techniques. During the project much effort was devoted to designing VLSI chip sets to perform these APE functions. Test chips were evaluated and the results enabled realistic predictions to be made of full-scale APP designs. Two principal variants emerged, namely, SCAPE (Single Chip Array Processing Element) and SCRIPT (Single Chip Relational Information Processing Element). The former was optimised for vector and array processing, whereas the latter was designed for performing database functions. Both could be incorporated in the SCANTRAX architecture.

One of the aims of SCANTRAX was to support the efficient implementation of relational databases and it should be noted in this context that no specific architectural provision has been made for supporting the 'join' operation.

Proposals have been made for commercial exploitation and research is continuing on Wafer Scale Integration Associative String Processor (WASP).

3.3.6. RAP-3

RAP-3 belongs to the class of Cellular Associative Systems (Ozkarahan, 1985). It is the lineal descendant of RAP-l and RAP-2. The latter were hardwired, whereas RAP-3 is software-controlled and offers much more flexibility. In particular, data formats are more general and context searching of text is now possible. Also attribute-to-attribute comparisons with arithmetic are now available.

The overall architecture is evolving in the direction of a networkable subsystem with a high-level interface. The capability of VLSI makes asynchronous parallel access to disk modules, each with its own logical filter, a practical and economic proposition. This is conceptually similar to the approach adopted by Teradata and Honeywell-Bull with SABRE.

3.3.7. DELTA

DELTA (Murakami *et al.*, 1985) is a relational database machine developed by Toshiba for the Institute for New Generation Computer Technology (ICOT). The machine is an experimental prototype having its origins in the Japanese Fifth Generation Programme and, as far as can be ascertained, there are no plans to develop it as a product.

One of the aims of ICOT has been to build a Knowledge Base Machine consisting of two main components, a sequential inference machine (SIM) and a relational database machine (DELTA). The system architecture involves a high-level interface between the SIM and DELTA, with the latter supporting a comprehensive set of database facilities.

A key component of the DELTA sub-system is a Relational Database Engine (RDBE), which has special-purpose hardware for sorting and merging. These hardware modules facilitate the join and projection operations. The designers, in a private communication, considered that these were the critical and most difficult relational database functions and, as a consequence, should be given hardware support. Hardware support for selection was given a lower priority. No studies of potential applications appear to have been carried out and, as a result, no potential usage statistics.

Quoted performance figures suggest that a sort of 16,384 8-word tuples would take 350 ms. and a join of two streams of 16,384 8-word tuples would take about 1.1 s.

Although the DELTA architecture has some interesting features, there are significant weaknesses in the approach, arising from the absence of hardware support for search, as well as the limitations inherent in the sort merge hardware for large tuple sets.

3.3.8. DIRECT

DIRECT was an experimental multiprocessor database machine designed and built by DeWitt at the University of Wisconsin (DeWitt, 1979). The machine is an MIMD device and was aimed at supporting query concurrency in a multi-user environment. The system architecture of DIRECT is that of a backend machine, having its own controller, supporting a high-level relational interface (not SQL) with a host processor.

The internal organisation of the DIRECT hardware consists of a set of query processors and mass storage devices interconnected by means of a crossbar switch to a set of cache stores (CCDs in the first implementation). A number of query processors may be assigned by the controller to a given task. The data to be searched is paged from mass storage to the cache memories (each of which can hold one page) and more than one processor may simultaneously scan a given page. No indexing is used, so each file must be exhaustively scanned. Concurrency control is based on a two-phase locking protocol and relation-level granularity.

3.3.9. GAMMA

GAMMA is another experimental multiprocessor database machine designed and built by DeWitt and his colleagues at the University of Wisconsin, in the light of experience gained from DIRECT (DeWitt *et al.*, 1986).

The performance of DIRECT was severely constrained by the limited bandwidth of its disk channels and the absence of indexing. GAMMA overcame these limitations by associating a processor (VAX 11/750) with each of the disk drives and interconnecting these to other processors and the host by an 80 megabit/second token ring. This approach is conceptually similar to that used in the Teradata machine (Teradata Corp., 1983; Ehrensberger, 1984).

As with the Teradata machine, all files are partitioned across all disk drives in the system. The records in a file, or tuples in a relation, may be distributed on a round robin, hashed or key range partitioned basis.

The GAMMA query language is based on QUEL (Stonebraker *et al.*, 1976) and conventional techniques are used for query parsing, optimisation and code generation.

The performance of the system, both for selections and joins, showed a significant improvement over DIRECT and confirmed the linear increase obtained by adding additional processors.

3.3.10. INTELLIGENT FILE STORE

The Intelligent File Store (IFS) (Lavington, 1988) was developed, under the lead of Simon Lavington, as a collaborative project between Essex and Manchester Universities and ICL.

The rationale behind this project lay in the belief that knowledge bases would eventually replace traditional databases as the core of many information systems. This belief arose from the recognition that AI techniques were being progressively incorporated in data-modelling and data-manipulation software. Knowledge manipulation tasks, such as pattern-directed searching, present formidable processing overheads for large knowledge bases and are, thus, candidates for the application of novel hardware. The phrase Knowledge Manipulation Engine is used to describe such hardware and the Intelligent File Store is an example of a KME.

The principal design objectives were a single-level memory, which can support a unified, global persistent object space with common naming conventions, together with a number of specialist processing units to operate upon results of pattern-directed searches. The first such unit to be designed was a Relational Algebraic Processor. The IFS memory consists of a flexibly organised hierarchy of storage devices with specialised hardware to support memory management functions.

The current IFS implementation consists of a SUN 3/75 CPU with the storage, management and processing units attached via a VME bus. Information is stored as 3-tuples in the Associative Predicate Store, which consists of a 300M-byte, 2.4M-byte/s disk and a 4M-byte semiconductor cache. The cache comprises 64 modules, each with its own search hardware, and provides a parallel search rate of around 250M-bytes/s for data already present. The overall search efficiency is critically dependent on the caching strategy minimising disk transfers.

Performance measurements have indicated a speed-up of 40–80 times in comparison with conventional software (Pascal, PL/1) searching in main memory. When compared with Quintus Prolog on a Sun 3/50, the retrieval rate was increased by up to 2,000 times in the best case.

4. FUTURE TRENDS IN DATABASE MACHINE ARCHITECTURE

4.1. Summary of Present Position

The previous sections show that a considerable investment has been made in database machine technology. Despite many impressive demonstrations, however, the number of different products brought to the market has been small and the impact, so far, has been surprisingly limited. In the past, many people have questioned the utility of this new technology and some still continue to do so, although to a diminishing extent.

Interest in this subject is now being focused in two complementary ways. Firstly, there are users with an appreciation of the technology, who are exploring new applications centred around ad hoc interactive working with increasingly large, complex and distributed databases. These users are seeking a competitive advantage from the better organisational control that could be achieved from a dramatic improvement in data accessibility. Secondly, there is a 'technological push' from those interested in developing parallel processing architectures, who have been liberated from the constraints of classical von Neumann processing by the advances in VLSI. Future developments, if they are to be effective and commercially successful, require a careful synthesis of these application ends and technological means.

There are, moreover, some important issues which need to be addressed if this new technology is to be widely adopted. The following are some of the most important:

a) A database machine, whatever its architecture, offers only a potential performance boost when compared with conventional software running on a standard processor. The argument then follows that improvements in software implementation, coupled with distributed processing and increased processor speeds, will do all that is required and that specialised hardware, based on non-von Neumann architectures, is unnecessary. The flaw in this argument is that it does not take into account the far-reaching implications for application system design and usage that can arise from a very large increase in relevant cost-effective processing power.
b) System integration. Many developments have been based in academia and have often lacked commercial linkage. Broadly speaking two approaches were adopted. One was to build a completely self-contained machine that performed all database functions, usually following the relational model, which would then act as a 'backend' to a host system. The other was to construct special-purpose function architectures that would be controlled as peripheral devices to a central processor by a modified general-purpose operating system. Examples of the former that have reached the marketplace are the Britton-Lee IDM and the Teradata DBC/1012; an example of the latter is ICL's CAFS.
c) Most commercially available systems, as well as many current developments, are polarised between those machines designed for text searching, which have very flexible string-matching facilities, and those designed to implement relational database systems. Few are aimed at handling more general data formats, such as Cobol records or loosely structured text.
d) In most current commercial database applications the primary requirement is to support efficiently pre-defined operational tasks. The processing demands of applications in this category, moreover, can usually be met by conventional machines, either singly or in clusters. Many users, however, are now realising that these operational databases could be of enormous value in supporting a wide

range of management functions, in which the pattern of both access and usage is intrinsically unpredictable. They are also appreciating that to provide such facilities is going to impose processing loads beyond the capability of conventional architectures, if the service is going to be effective.

e) To quantify the commercial benefits, *a priori*, that may arise from introducing an effective 'conversational mode of working' has proved extremely difficult. *Post facto* justification, on the other hand, is usually relatively easy. The situation is similar to that of justifying the investment in improving the quality of human–computer interaction. Indeed, it can be argued that database machines are essential if effective human–computer interaction is to be supported.

4.2. Future Trends

The present perception, that the set of possible applications may be conveniently partitioned into those requiring well-formatted database systems and those requiring free-text retrieval systems, is extremely naive and out of touch with the reality of many current and emerging applications.

Many applications now demand a system which seeks to combine a mixture of formatted data, loosely structured text and free text. The present work on standards for document architectures well illustrates the fact that so-called free text documents often possess a complex logical structure. The most general case is best exemplified by those applications which need to handle loosely structured text, of which a name and address file is one of the simplest and most illustrative. An entry in a commercial telephone directory, for example, can have as many as a hundred possible field descriptors of which only ten to twenty may occur in any one particular entry. Most of these fields, moreover, will be of variable length. Indeed, the study of applications such as this, suggests that a system which can efficiently support loosely structured text will also be able to handle the requirements of free text and formatted data as subsets.

In addition to the problems of loosely structured text, certain applications now need to handle records of which the logical structure may change significantly during the lifetime of the application. In some of these, such as military intelligence, the necessary changes need to be carried out extremely quickly if the overall system is to be operationally effective. This requirement not only places a major demand on the data management software but also has a significant impact on the design of any supporting special hardware.

Although early database machine research concentrated on novel hardware architectures, particularly for the task of file searching and 'filtering', the current availability of low-cost, high-performance processing chip sets has tended to steer most research towards a loosely coupled multiprocessor approach. Such architectures are provided with a high-bandwidth interconnection scheme between the processors, each of which controls a disk volume and runs the same replicated software asynchronously. Files are then physically distributed over many disk drives in order to permit concurrent access and parallel processing. This approach has greatly facilitated the join operation (Cheiney *et al.*, 1986; Demurjian *et al.*, 1986; Schneider and De Witt, 1990) and, therefore, has been most effective in building relational database machines, of which the Teradata DBC/1012 is a good example.

In the design of these machines the main objectives have been to achieve a high transaction rate for simple tasks and to exploit parallel processing to boost the performance in carrying out relational joins. No special hardware is used for file searching but a reasonable performance may be achieved by each processor executing the same search task over a limited volume. Since, in the case of the Teradata machine, there may be 60 to 100 processors operating simultaneously the performance can be fairly high. It must be emphasised, however, that this architectural approach is not used in those applications where intensive searching is required, such as text retrieval.

The task of searching text is, in general, two or more orders of magnitude computationally more intensive than searching relational tuple sets. As a result, in this application area much effort has been devoted to developing high-performance architectures capable of very flexible multi-term string matching, which are implementable in VLSI.

The pressures of those applications, which demand a mix of text retrieval and formatted database facilities, are having a significant effect on the design of 'file filter' hardware and software. Such sub-systems should, ideally, be able to scan data at disk transfer rates (5–6 M-bytes/s) and contain facilities for format control, search term comparison, query resolution and data retrieval. These functions can, of course, be performed entirely by software running on a conventional processor, but only at these anticipated scan rates if the selection criteria are modest and the record structure simple. In order to provide the requisite functionality for both formatted data and free text, as well as to maintain synchrony with present and future disk transfer rates, a careful balance is required between the various hardware and software components. Search term comparisons, in particular, must be assisted by special hardware. Such a unit should be capable of handling a large number of search arguments (possibly up to 100) simultaneously and be able to process masked symbolic or numeric data. The requirement for flexible string matching at these high data rates, particularly for 'variable-length-don't-cares', is very difficult to meet and requires advanced VLSI for a cost-effective solution. This problem is being exacerbated further by the rich character sets now being introduced to text processing.

In text searching, the effort has been put into the development of 'file filters', which are usually only concerned with selecting records from a designated file on an intra-record basis. Almost no consideration is given in text retrieval systems, to inter-record operations, which are seen as the preserve of the formatted database environment. These operations are often computationally intensive and much effort has been devoted, in relational database machine research, to developing architectural techniques to make these tasks more efficient. As the text retrieval and formatted database environments continue to converge, inter-record and record set operations will become increasingly important. They will be seen as a necessary adjunct in broadening the scope of 'file filtering' to 'database filtering'.

No matter how successful file or database filtering becomes, the problem of partitioning the search space will remain if response times compatible with a 'conversational mode of working' are to be maintained between the human and the computer. This implies using indexes, particularly secondary indexes. The argument is then raised that if the considerable overhead of generating indexes has to be borne, why bother with a filter since the whole search can be carried out by appropriately processing these indexes. The flaw here is that indexes are very primitive projections of files and cannot alone support the totality of required search functions; e.g. search arguments involving masked character strings or ranges on numeric variables.

What is required is an appropriate engineering balance between indexing and search. The literature contains several references to systems which exploit some form of variable-length page indexing (Banerjee *et al.*, 1979; Maller, 1979). In these schemes the index lists are relatively small and merely point to a page in the database, which may vary in size from a disk sector to several cylinders. Although these indexes economise in storage space and usually involve only modest processing to indicate relevant pages to be searched, the generation of them involves considerable computation, which for large databases, and text files in particular, can represent a very significant overhead. A strong case may, therefore, be made for incorporating special hardware facilities to assist both index generation and manipulation.

Two broad architectural approaches are currently being followed and are likely to continue. There will be the completely autonomous database computer, having its own operating system and being responsible for all database functions including access control, security and recovery. Such a machine will communicate with a host, via a high-level interface, such as SQL. The host, in this case, could be a conventional mainframe, or mainframe cluster, as well as a network. In other words, it could perform the function of a network server. Among current products, the Teradata DBC/1012 is a machine in this category. The other approach, likely to be adopted by computer suppliers, is to integrate functional sub-units within existing architectures. This will result in an incremental approach and, for the manufacturer, will have the advantage of building on an established operating system base.

A common feature likely to be followed in all architectures will be extensibility. This will be achieved by building the whole system from replicated sub-units, each of which will possess a disk storage unit, plus special hardware for search, join and index manipulation, together with a control processor. Such units will be linked by a high-bandwidth bus or network, which would be local to the database sub-system. The same software would, of course, be used in each unit. This architectural approach is now appearing in products such as the Teradata machine and ICL's CAFS.

An influence of great importance will be the future path taken by database technology in its conceptual formalism and methods of representation. The simple relational model has had a major impact on database machine research over the past fifteen years. The limitations of this simple model are now becoming appreciated and the move towards incorporating a higher level of abstraction in database descriptions, together with the concomitant complexity in data objects, may be expected to have a major impact on all aspects of database machine architecture in the future.

BIBLIOGRAPHY

AEG-Telefunken (1982). Synfobase, product literature.

Ahuja, S.R. and Roberts, C.S. (1980). An Associative/Parallel Processor for Partial Match Retrieval using Superimposed Codes, *7th Annual Symposium on Computer Architecture.*

Amperif Corporation (1982). RDM 1100, product literature.

Babb, E. (1979). Implementing a Relational Database by Means of Specialised Hardware, *ACM Transactions on Database Systems*, Vol. 4, 1, 1–29.

Banerjee, J., Hsiao, D.K. and Kannan, K. (1979). DBC – A Database Computer for Very Large Databases, *IEEE Transactions on Computers*, C-28, 6, 414–429.

Bansler, J. *et al.* (1984). Filing and Retrieval of Unstructured Information: Some System Considerations, ESPRIT '84 Status Report on Ongoing Work.

Batcher, K.E (1980). Architecture of a Massively Parallel Processor, *Proceedings of the 7th Annual Symposium on Computer Architecture.*

Bird, R.M. (1978). Text File Inversion: An Evaluation, 4th Workshop on Computer Architecture for Non-Numeric Processing, *ACM SIGMOD*, Vol. X, No. 1.

Bird, R.M. (1982). Database Systems: All Software versus Associative File Processor, Spring–Summer Issue of *Computer Technology Review.*

Bogdany, J., Katsaronas, S. and Lea, R.M. (1984). *The Scantrax Project*, Brunel University Report.

Boral, H. and DeWitt, D.J. (1984). A Methodology for Database System Performance Evaluation, ACM SIGMOD '84, *SIGMOD Record*, Vol. 14, No. 2.

Bray, O. and Thurber, K.J. (1979). What's Happening with Database Processors?, *Datamation.*

Britton-Lee Inc. (1982). IDM500 – Intelligent Database Machine, product literature.

BYTE (1984). The PF474 – A co-processor for string comparison.

Champine, G.A. (1978). Four Approaches to a Database Computer, *Datamation.*

Cheiney, J.P. *et al.* (1986). A Reliable Parallel Backend using Multi-attribute Clustering and Select-Join Operator, *Proceedings of the 12th International Conference on Very Large Data Bases, Kyoto, Japan.*

Contexture Inc. (1985). Utah Text Search Engine, product literature.

Copeland, G.P. (1978). String Storage and Searching for Database Applications : Implementation on the INDY Backend Kernel, *Proceedings of the 4th Workshop on Computer Architecture for Non-Numeric Processing, ACM SIGMOD*, Vol. X, No. 1.

Copernique (1983). Diram 32/Dorsal 32, product literature.

Coulouris, G.F., Evans, J.M. and Mitchell, R.W. (1972). Towards Content Addressing in Databases, *Computer Journal*, Vol. 15, No. 2.

Datafusion Corporation (1983). Associative File Processor, product literature.

Date, C.J. (1983). *An Introduction to Database Systems*, Vol. 2, Addison-Wesley.

Demurjian, S.A., Hsiao, D.K. and Menon, J. (1986). A Multi-Backend Database System for Performance Gains, Capacity Growth and Hardware Upgrade, *Proceedings of Second International Conference on Data Engineering, February, 1986.*

DeWitt, D.J. (1979). Direct – A Multiprocessor Organisation for supporting Relational Database Management Systems, *IEEE Transactions on Computers*, Vol. C-28, No. 6.

DeWitt, D.J. *et al.* (1986). GAMMA – A High Performance Dataflow Database Machine, *Proceedings of the 12th Intl Conf. on Very Large Data Bases, Kyoto, Japan.*

Ehrensberger, M.J. (1984). The DBC/1012 Data Base Computer's System

Architecture, Components and Performance, Minnowbrook Workshop on Database Machines.

Electronics (1981). GESCAN/2, 3 November.

Electronics (1982). Disk store finds text references from simple queries (Memex), 24 February.

Electronics (1982). Synfobase, 19 May.

Engineering Today (1982). Memex, 5 April.

Gardarin, G. (1981). An Introduction to SABRE: a Multi-Microprocessor Database Machine, *Proceedings of 6th Workshop on Computer Architecture for Non-Numerical Processing, Hyeres.*

Gardarin, G. *et al.* (1983). SABRE – A Relational Database System for a Multi-Microprocessor Machine, in D. K. Hsiao (ed) *Advanced Database Machine Architectures*, Prentice-Hall, Englewood Cliffs.

General Electric (1982). GESCAN/2, product literature.

Gonzalez-Rubio, R., Rohmer, J. and Terral, D. (1984). The Schuss Filter: A Processor for Non-Numerical Data Processing, *11th International Symposium on Computer Architecture, Ann Arbor.*

Haskin, R.L. and Hollaar, L.A. (1983). Operational Characteristics of a Hardware-Based Pattern Matcher, *ACM Transactions on Database Systems*, Vol. 8, No. 1.

Hawthorn, P.B. and DeWitt, D.J. (1982). Performance Analysis of Alternative Database Machine Architectures, *IEEE Transactions on Software Engineering*, Vol. SE 8, No. 1.

Hollaar, L.A. (1984). The UTAH Text Retrieval Project, *Proc. of BCS and ACM Joint Symposium on Research and Development in Information Retrieval.*

Hsiao, D.K. (1983). *Advanced Database Machine Architecture*, Prentice-Hall.

Jarke, M. and Koch, J. (1984). Query Optimization in Database Systems, *Computing Surveys*, Vol. 16, No. 2.

Kim, W., Gajski, D. and Kuck, D.J. (1984). A Parallel Pipelined Relational Query Processor, *ACM Transactions on Database Systems*, Vol. 9, No. 2, 214–242.

Kitsuregawa, M., Tanaka, H. and Moto-Oka, T. (1983). Application of Hash to Database Machine and its Architecture, *New Generation Computing*, Vol. 1, 63–74.

Kitsuregawa, M., Tanaka, H. and Moto-Oka, T. (1984). Architecture and Performance of Parallel Relational Database Machine, GRACE, *Proceedings of International Conference on Parallel Processing (1984).*

Lamb, S. (1978). An Add-In Recognition Memory for S-100 Bus Microcomputers, *Computer Design.*

Lavington, S. H. (1988). Technical Overview of the Intelligent File Store, *Knowledge Based Systems*, Vol. 1, 3, June.

Leilich, H.O., Steige, G. and Zeidler, H.C. (1978). A Search Processor for Database Management Systems, *Proceedings of the 4th International*

Conf. on Very Large Databases, 280–287.
Maller, V.A.J. (1979). The Content Addressable File Store, *Proceedings of Spring Joint Computer Conference, San Francisco, 1979.*
Maller, V.A.J. (1980). Information Retrieval using the Content Addressable File Store, *Proceedings of IFIP Congress 80, Melbourne, Australia, October, 1980.*
Maller, V.A.J. (1983). Content Addressing as an Aid to Information Management, in G. G. Scarrott (ed) *The Fifth Generation Computer Project – State of the Art Report*, Pergamon Infotech.
Maryanski, F.J. (1980). Back-end Database Systems, *ACM Computing Surveys*, Vol. 12, No. 1.
Memex Information Engines Ltd (1982). Memex, product literature.
Murakami, K. *et al.* (1983). A Relational Database Machine: First Step to a Knowledge Base Machine, *10th Annual International Symposium on Computer Architecture, ACM SIGARCH.*
Murakami, K., Kakuta, T., Onai, R. and Ito, N. (1985). Research on Parallel Architecture for Fifth Generation Computer Systems, *IEEE Computer*, Vol. 18, 6, 76–92.
Operating Systems Inc. (1982). HSTS High Speed Text Search System, product literature.
Ozkarahan, E.A. (1985). Evolution and Implementations of the RAP Database Machine, *New Generation Computing*, Vol. 3.
Pogue, C. and Willett, P. (1985). *An Evaluation of Document Retrieval from Serial Files Using the ICL DAP*, University of Sheffield.
Pramanik, S. (1982). Database Filters, *9th Annual Symposium on Computer Architecture, ACM-SIGARCH.*
Proximity Technology Inc. (1984). PSP 8000, product literature.
Qadah, G.Z. and Irani, K.B. (1985). A Database Machine for Very Large Relational Databases, *IEEE Transactions on Computers*, Vol. C34, No. 11.
Rabitti, F. and Zizka, J. (1984). Evaluation of Access Methods to Text Documents in Office Systems, *Proceedings ACM-BCS Symposium on Research and Development in Information Retrieval.*
Roberts, C.S. (1979). Partial Match Retrieval via the method of Superimposed Codes, *Proceedings of the IEEE*, Vol. 67, No. 12.
Roberts, D. (1978). A Specialized Computer Architecture for Text Retrieval, *4th Workshop on Computer Architecture for Non-Numeric Processing, ACM SIGMOD*, Vol. 10, No. 1.
Rohmar, J. (1981). Hardware Devices for Associative Processing in Database Machines, *SICOB Convention Informatique, Paris.*
Schneider, D.A. and DeWitt, D.J. (1990). Tradeoffs in Processing Complex Join Queries via Hashing in Multiprocessor Database Machines, *Proceedings of the 16th International Conference on Very Large Data Bases, Brisbane, Australia.*
Slotnik, D.L. (1970). Logic Per Track Devices, in *Advances in Computers*,

291–296, Academic Press, New York.

Stonebraker, M.R. *et al.* (1976). The Design and Implementation of INGRES, *ACM Transactions on Database Systems*, Vol. 1, 3, Sept. 1976.

Systems International (1985). IDM, product update.

Teradata Corporation (1983). DBC/1012, product literature.

Tsichritzis, D.C. *et al.* (1984). Design Issues of a File Server for Multimedia Documents, ESPRIT '84 Status report of ongoing work.

Index